NORTH AMERICAN BIG GAME HUNTING

*With
special chapters
contributed
by
Erwin A. Bauer,
Charles Elliott,
William S. Huey
and
Hal Swiggett*

NORTH AMERICAN BIG GAME HUNTING

BY BYRON W. DALRYMPLE

WINCHESTER PRESS

Copyright © 1974 by Byron W. Dalrymple
All rights reserved

Library of Congress Catalog Card Number: 74-78697
ISBN: 0-87691-142-4

Published by Winchester Press
460 Park Avenue, New York 10022

Printed in the United States of America

For Michael & Rebecca

CONTENTS

Introduction

In planning this book, two basic goals were kept constantly in my mind: to select material useful both to beginning big-game hunters and to those with some, or much, experience; and to make certain of complete authenticity. In both regards it seemed to me that contributions from several other broadly experienced hunter-writers with certain specialized knowledge might be most valuable. High on my list of possible contributors was Erwin Bauer, one of the most prolific and best-informed writers in the outdoor field. He has traveled endlessly, all over the world, has combed every wilderness corner of North America and has amassed a thorough knowledge of big-game hunting in remote areas. I felt his observations about guides and outfitters should therefore be invaluable. I knew also that he has long had an intense interest in and acquired a considerable knowledge about the bears of the continent. Bauer has covered those subjects expertly in Chapters 4 and 17.

Charles Elliott, who received another high-priority invitation, has himself written a number of books. For many years as a field editor for *Outdoor Life* magazine, he annually made pilgrimages to the far gamelands of North America. The high country of the Rockies and connected ranges—not only within the contiguous United States but also through Canada and Alaska—drew him like a magnet year after year. He has been mesmerized by wild sheep ever since he saw his first one in Montana when he was a boy, and he has also spent much time in caribou country. Charlie has for many years been a friend, and indeed often a mentor to me. When I approached him about doing something for this book, he felt that sheep and caribou would be perfect subjects for him. After reading Chapters 14 and 16 I am sure readers will agree.

When it comes to rifles for big game, there are almost as many opinions as hunters. Certainly I have mine, and in several chapters I have made brief suggestions. But I felt that a real "gun man" should conduct this specialized discussion. Hal Swiggett's name is known to everyone who has read any of the "gun magazines." He is shooting editor or guns editor for several publications, and he is a nationally recognized expert in the field of rifles. In his "Rifles for Big Game" (Chapter 5) he proves he merits the expert rating.

I felt that introduced foreign game deserved some discussion here. Horned and antlered species from other continents are common in wide variety nowadays on Texas ranches, and have long been stocked experimentally by the State Department of Game & Fish in New Mexico. I was familiar with the "exotics" in Texas, where I live. But I was well aware that William S. Huey, Chief of Game & Fish Management for New Mexico, was possibly the most knowledgeable person in the country on the subject of exotic big game. In fact, much of my own early knowledge about these animals came from Bill, who has for years been a close friend. In Chapter 18, Huey has covered admirably the story of the New Mexico experiments.

Herewith, my thanks to these several experts who by their contributions have helped make this book so much more than it would have been without them!

1.
LEARNING
TO
HUNT

Pre-season scouting is fine hunting practice.

Some people who become interested in hunting are born in country that abounds with big game such as deer and elk. Others grow up in areas where the only targets are cottontails, squirrels and birds such as quail or pheasants. Because humans seem to have a fetish for organization, for putting everything into categories, we have all come to speak of "small-game hunting," "bird hunting" and "big-game hunting" as separate entities.

It is true that each is quite different from the others. It is also true that in big-game hunting the pursuit of a bighorn sheep and of a pronghorn on the plains are just as different. Each of our rather arbitrary categories means little except as a convenient way to catalog species of game by size and by whether they run or fly. We commonly speak of a tyro "graduating" from small game to big game. However, it is not necessarily true that one who bags a mule deer, say, as his very first animal in boyhood is any more expert than the young hunter who grew up outwitting squirrels.

Becoming a consistently successful hunter—the subject to be examined in this opening chapter—requires self-training and immense discipline and concentration. The kind of game matters little. When I was a young fellow growing up in the Thumb area of Michigan, the country was certainly far less populated and much wilder than today. There were relatively few automobiles, numerous horse-and-buggy drivers. Farm wagons pulled by a team were common on the small, poor roads. Yet this was no wilderness. Earlier, before the forests had been cut, whitetail deer had been reasonably abundant here. But they had been totally gone for years although, curiously, they have re-established themselves to some extent today. In the absence of deer, I really learned to hunt big game by hunting small game.

Country scenes I saw as a boy no one would even recognize today. Rough split-rail fences zigzagged the borders of fields. There were even stump fences on my grandfather's farm. A stump fence was made by pulling—with a tall, three-legged stump puller that sunk a big auger into the big pine stumps left from lumbering days. They were pulled first to clear the land for crops. Then, with oxen or a team of horses, the stumps were hauled into a line and tipped on their sides. The big, tough roots, which would not decay for years, meshed together in line to form a formidable barrier.

Along the stump fences and rail fences, weeds and brush grew. It was not possible to plant and cultivate a crop right up to the fence. Along these natural cover lanes dwelt animals such as cottontails, skunks and woodchucks. Later, in the late 1920's and on through the '30's, ring-necked pheasants that had been transplanted from the West began to do well, and of course they utilized these swaths of cover and also the crop fields.

Every small farm had its woodlot—oak, beech, maple, occasional black walnut and butternut, and a scattering of conifers such as cedar and hemlock. Fox squirrels were abundant, and so were raccoons. A small creek meandered across our place and along it were muskrats and an occasional mink. Weasels laid out hunting routes along the stream and throughout the woodlot. No one at that time made any special effort to drain moist places. Red-willow swales were common. There was an old settlers' term for such swales, particularly those with a scattering of tall marsh grass and perhaps other tangle. They were called "cat holes." The term had been in use for a long time, and when I was a boy no one seemed sure any more whether it referred to the cattails that sometimes grew there, or whether bobcats had lurked in such places when the country was being logged and cleared. In my day rabbits and pheasants used them as regular resting and hiding places.

This is the kind of country I hunted in as a boy. I was 20 before I even saw my first deer. And though I now have hunted deer across the U.S. practically from border to border and coast to coast, I was well into my thirties before I fired my first shot at one. Yet by then I had become—if you'll forgive the seeming immodesty—a hunter. I remember quite vividly that during my early deer hunting I knew precisely what to do, how to go about it. Oh, I had to learn much about specific deer habits, and gain gradual experience in how they used their senses. But I was already a *hunter*.

This is a vital concept for anyone who reads this book. We all must start somewhere. There are old, experienced hunters who have shared practically every thrill in the book. There are those who are eager to begin big-game hunting, but never have had an opportunity, even for deer. There are young or beginning hunters who join the shooting crowd annually. And it is very important for them to realize (or in some cases to re-learn) that it makes no difference where or on what game they begin. Becoming a *hunter* really has very little to do with the game available. It is a matter of learning how to observe, how to listen, how to look, how to move, how to dress, to be ever alert for smells, attentive to conditions of light and wind. Show me a hunter who has gained enough skill to successfully still-hunt squirrels with a .22 and I'll show you a man who is already a deer hunter even though he may not know it.

As I look back on my youth, I realize now that without being especially aware of it I was learning every foot of my bailiwick. This included our own place and surrounding farms, where neighbors always allowed me to roam. I soon came to know that a certain red-willow swale always had abundant cottontails in and around it. I did not know why. Actually, it was a matter of perfect habitat. That swale was in the middle of a field always used to grow hay. Another swale, half a mile distant, was in a crop field that was plowed up part of the year, and thus partially barren. It held few rabbits.

On the east edge of a certain woodlot the farmer invariably raised corn in a field. It did not take long to learn that fox squirrels garnered a share of the corn, dragging ears from the field into the edge of the woods. I saw the evidence atop stumps and logs and even trails on the ground. By sitting immobile for hours near this edge, I could waylay squirrels moving back and forth. The west side of the woodlot edged a hay field, which held no interest for squirrels.

These rather obvious bits of information I was putting together, as a young and beginning hunter, without thinking much about what I was learning. I recall a certain corner where a rail fence butted into another, forming at the juncture a T. Here a hay field, a corn field and a brushy patch of pasture all met. This corner almost invariably held a pheasant or two. But by trial and error I learned that if I approached from corn or hay field, the birds simply slipped into the brush without flying. If, after hay and corn had been cut, I approached from the brush, they'd sit tight, trapped, and suddenly burst up noisily, giving me a chance with my scattergun.

I remember when it first began to dawn on me that the birds and small animals moved most early and late, and rested during the day. From here I progressed to the realization that a pheasant, which roosts in heavy weeds or grass at night, would be forced to feed heavily from late afternoon right up until dusk, because it could not eat again until morning. The same was true of squirrels. But cottontails moved much at night and thus were not so narrowly confined. When food was scarce and weather severe, however, the pheasants especially were forced to feed not only during the middle of the day but often in wide-open situations, such as around shocks of corn.

All of the game creatures also had quite specific travel routes. These I learned not by seeking trails, but by hunting success. A certain corner of sumac always held pheasants at a certain time of day and from here the birds followed a fence line, skulking low in grass in order to go around the edge of an open field. Then they cornered and moved along the cross fence until they came to a crop field that offered cover. One could tell quite accurately, after some experience, where they were most likely to be at any given time.

Now all of these items may seem to have little to do with big-game hunting. But every illustration I have given is precisely applicable, for example, to whitetail hunting. Certainly there are many habits and attributes that pheasants, rabbits and squirrels do *not* have in common with whitetail deer—but there are many fundamental ones that all have in common. The first long step in becoming an expert hunter is the realization that there are common denominators among all game species. The next step is gaining the perception to apply these.

At first some of the concepts may seem perplexing. For example, the area I've described as my boyhood hunting ground was by no means white-tail-deer habitat. But the basics were there: food, shelter, safe hiding places, water. These appeared in much the same order and amount and relationship as in prime deer habitat. Superimpose upon my bailiwick some jigsaw pieces of good whitetail country. The creek with its knee-high weed growth along the bank becomes a creek or river with brush and some trees. The fences with their cover lanes become strips of timber, perhaps along ridges, and the fields are more open valleys in between. The open farm woodlot becomes a heavy forest growth, the red-willow swale a dense cedar swamp.

The whitetail is an "edge" animal. It dislikes feeding or moving in the open. Whenever possible it moves through cover, and feeds along or near the edge of cover, where swift escape is possible. The pheasant is exactly the same.

When a severe storm strikes, the deer moves deep into the cedar swamp—which replaces the red-willow swale into which the pheasant retreats for safety and protection. The beginning big-game hunter who has "graduated" with honors from his courses in observing small creatures will perceive these similarities. He will be able to go into an expanse of big-game country and quickly deduce where the game *should* be, and then with some experimentation pin down where it is.

Obviously I had the opportunity—as do all sportsmen who hunt their home territory—to learn, as I've said, every foot of the area. When one moves into a strange place everything will look totally different. But the point is, the basic elements will be there. An astute observer can quickly put the pieces all in place, or exchange in his mind feature for feature, if he has carefully learned his own area and the habits of game in it.

The true hunter worthy of the name must from the beginning train himself to be wholly in tune with his surroundings. He must become a total observer. He is forever looking, listening, smelling. And he is ever so alert that by the end of a day he is likely to be tired simply from concentration. Ride sometime with a keen old hand in a vehicle through a good game area and you will see that he is incessantly looking. He points out a deer there, a grouse on a log. He spots a wild cherry heavy with fruit and can't resist stopping and getting out to look around under it.

"Been a black bear here," he says. He has seen droppings loaded with cherry pits, low branches broken, claw marks on the bark.

This kind of observer never can quit. He has trained himself to it and he gets great pleasure out of seeing the signs and understanding their meaning, regardless of whether at the moment he is actually in pursuit of game. I know the feeling. I've often been amused to have someone say as we drive along and I point out creatures large or small, or signs of them, "How do you *see* all those things?" The answer actually is double. First, because I'm forever looking, and second because I know what I'm looking for. My wife chides me gently because when we drive down to our ranch, a wild expanse on which no one lives, and I open a gate or pause anywhere to get out of the vehicle, my gaze is instantly searching the ground.

For what? Anything that's there. A deer track. If there are tracks of a doe with twin fawns in summer, I'll guess there has been a good fawn drop this season—especially if I see several more such tracks in varied locations. Or maybe I see goat tracks. That means some darned goats from a neighboring ranch have got out and are on our place, eating up browse. I'm not fond of goats. Maybe I spot a fox track, or a raccoon track. A small rock beside the ranch trail that has atop it a scat of modest dimensions, generally filled with persimmon seeds, telling me a ringtail has been there. Not that I really need to know about the ringtail. It is simply that the complete observer drinks in every sign, sound and smell, tuning in totally with the wild habitat.

Hunters constantly discuss the superb eyesight, hearing and sense of smell of big-game animals. But too few realize that their own senses and how they use them are equally as important. Hunting is basically a matter of outwitting, with *your* senses, those of animals pitted against you. Learning acute visual observation is a good way to start.

An old gentleman who taught me much about successful squirrel hunting told me years ago, "Don't look for a whole squirrel. A whole squirrel is easy to see, but a squirrel that's aware of your presence is going to try to keep you from seeing him. If any of him is exposed it'll be a small piece."

On jaunts together we looked for a part of a bushy tail through which light filtered along a limb. On one occasion we discovered just an ear sticking above a branch. Another time a fox squirrel, clinging to a tree trunk and utterly immobile, showed one forefoot with claws tightly gripping bark. Later, when I started big-game hunting I learned to look not for a whole deer, but, let's say, for sun glinting on polished antlers—just a single tine perhaps with its telltale curve and hue, amid brush. In the shadow cast by a small bush, I have found bedded mule deer because their noses, which they lick to keep moist, reflected light. Or I looked in timber or brush that was fairly open underneath for deer legs, much straighter and more symmetrical than saplings or trunks of shrubs.

One can be looking at an animal such as deer or elk in heavy cover and see no outline whatever, until perhaps the animal, bothered by insects, flicks an ear. On a rocky desert mountain, mule deer blend perfectly but their white rumps are a give-away. You glass a dozen white rocks, and suddenly find the next one is a deer. Antelope lying on a slope on the plains are

Study of tracks (above, grouse and mink) encourages habit of total observation.

easily passed over by the so-so observer. They also may appear distantly to be pale rocks. But the keen-eyed, trained observer sorts them out.

Learning how to "look" is indeed an art. The person who doesn't miss the grassy form from which a cottontail has just fled will also instantly spot depressions in grass where big-game animals have rested. He will even check to see how many there were. Two small beds and one larger one close together, in deer country, probably indicate a doe and twin fawns. One large bed surrounded by a group of smaller ones, in elk territory, well may have been imprinted by a big old bull and his harem.

As you hunt, constantly keep your eyes darting everywhere. Droppings, snipped-off twigs, tracks, bark scars, broken branches, a rotten stump torn apart, all offer information about what has been there, when, and why. I recall a pawed-out place in desert dirt in Arizona that I at first thought was sign of a desert mule-deer buck. But sifting some of the dirt through my fingers winnowed out a few javelina bristles. I've taken whitetail-deer hunters to my ranch and had them proudly show me where a buck had been pawing a scrape, when actually the spot was sign left by a dusting jack rabbit.

Thus, it is important not only to see everything, but to accurately appraise what you have seen. Granted, this requires much study and experience, but the learning is an interesting process. After all, it does little good to be able to see every sign if you are unable to correctly identify what you have seen.

There are two visual aspects of big-game hunting that differ radically from the kind of "looking" needed with small game and birds. If you have never hunted big game, but intend to, you should be aware of these, and even practice them constantly, before you begin. One is the use of a binocular. I have heard the occasional big-game hunter scoff at the binocular. "Too much bother to carry one. Just as easy to use a rifle scope for observation." Utter nonsense. No one-eyed glassing with a scope is worth much. Besides, waving a rifle around draws the attention of game, or you may just find yourself pointing at another hunter. No big-game hunter worth his salt would go out minus a good glass.

Proper use of a glass requires patience and practice. The hunter who superficially sweeps a ridge and moves on misses many an animal. One should search with a glass exactly the same way as with the naked eye. You don't necessarily have to be looking for a whole animal. Look for antlers thrusting above grass, or a rounded rump beside a tree. Even whole animals that are distant are easily overlooked if you hurry. The idea is to comb a piece of country long and patiently and with the utmost concentration. The roots of a huge blowdown with black dirt in them may be just that. On a lakeshore in moose country, the blowdown may, with painstaking observation, turn into a good bull. One time in Wyoming a guide and I sat on a high ridge glassing a majestic sweep of country for a full hour. At last we saw distant movement. Elk. Running. Obviously we had not spooked them. Meticulous glassing of the area from which the elk had run turned up two big bears, one of them dozing on a rock.

The hunter after small creatures does not need to see so far away. But as he prepares to hunt larger game, he should carry a binocular and practice with it at odd moments. Or he might even go afield not to hunt but to see what he can see with his glass. A distant woodlot may look to the unaided eye like a wall beyond which no light enters, yet it can be looked right into by the glass, with its light-gathering powers and magnification. The hunter learns what various terrains look like in different light and with light from different angles. He picks up songbirds or a woodchuck, or even cars on a distant highway. He selects a spot and decides to glass it long, to see how many items he can identify. Nothing is better practice for the prospective big-game hunter.

The other visual difference between hunting small and large creatures is range. The shotgun and small-rifle shooter seldom needs to judge range beyond 50 yards. Most of the time the shotgunner, in fact, pays little attention. He learns about how far away he can drop his targets, and anything closer is easier and makes little difference. But in big-game hunting, reasonably accurate judgment of range is acutely important. Moreover, range judgment is more difficult in some terrains than in others. On vast open mountainsides or prairies where there is nothing to compare to or mark off intervening sections that appear of a familiar distance, range judgment is often a perplexing matter. Sometimes the start of the slope, or a ridge spine, or massive rimrock makes an animal seem to be much closer than it is. Conversely, certain terrain contours make the range look much longer.

Sign tells story; antler-mangled shrub, too high for deer, was smashed by elk.

Indeed, there are hunters who never do become accurate judges. Nonetheless, practice helps. For the sake of practice a bird hunter can walk away from his vehicle, count a specified number of steps, and then look back. He should measure his average paces so that he knows about how long each pace is. He can thus determine with fair accuracy when he is 100 yards away, or 200 as the case may be. If he is starting across a field and will follow a straight line, he makes a guess at how far the opposite fence is, and counts his paces. If he keeps at this, he should soon be able to guess 100- to 200-yard ranges, and intermediate ranges, pretty well.

Depending upon the big game he will hunt, he may never need to judge ranges longer than that. But if he will eventually hunt pronghorns or sheep or elk, or even mule deer in open country, he should also do some practicing out to at least 300 yards. All of this practicing gets to be a kind of game, and is interesting, particularly as one becomes better and better at it. Then when the day comes to steady the scope on that trophy buck or bull or ram, one knows how well the time and effort have been spent.

Although the hunter's visual sense is of paramount importance, he must also learn the art of listening. The clink of a rock may indicate the passing of a deer. A rattle of shale may send a message of spooked big-game animals. A variety of sounds may tell of the presence of game, distant or nearby: the bugle of a bull elk in rut, the awesome smash as a pair of battling bighorn rams slam together, the occasional low grunt of a buck whitetail in rut. By and large, big-game animals are not very vocal creatures. But any sound in the woods, mountains or plains may have important bearing.

I would therefore suggest that the prospective big-game hunter train himself to hear everything. He will hear some sounds that have no bearing whatever on his endeavor. But the point is that in big-game hunting opportunity may be fleeting, and crucial. If the squirrel or quail hunter fails to hear a sound that may have meant a squirrel or quail in the bag, he will probably have several more chances. An elk hunter who fails to hear a bull ripping branches, or improperly interprets the sound, may have lost his single opportunity for that season.

This is really a matter of woodcraft. It is a part of total alertness. And here again I emphasize that the chance to bag the trophy of a lifetime may be fleeting. A classic example that I recall concerns not big game but a rather rare bird, the Mearn's quail. I was hunting in southeastern Arizona, the only place in the U.S. where this bird exists in huntable numbers. After a long, wearying hike over ridges at 6,000 feet, we were coming back to the car. As an old hand for many years at hunting ruffed grouse in the Great Lakes country I had learned to "hunt right up to the car door," for on several occasions I had come back to my parked vehicle, shucked out shells when within sight of it, and then seen a brace of grouse buzz off practically from under the wheels.

Three of us were within 40 yards of our vehicle, parked off the mountain trail. The two gentlemen with me, frazzled and discouraged as I

Prairie-dog hunter can pace off shots to practice range judgment for big game.

was, unloaded as they walked. I kept my gun loaded and was following my own advice of earlier years. Within mere feet of the vehicle, a beautiful covey of Mearn's burst up, and actually over my pickup. I hauled off and shot, and dropped two perfect specimens, a cock and a hen. Others we'd previously bagged weren't suitable for mounting. These were, and as I write this I can raise my head and look at them perched in my office.

A reverse experience concerns what was probably the largest whitetail I have ever had a chance at—or should have had. For a few moments I failed to keep alert as we came back toward our starting place, where we were to be picked up. Now obviously since our pickup ride had not yet arrived, I should have realized that the spot had not been disturbed since we left it hours earlier. My rifle was loaded, but instead of carrying it at the ready, I slung it over my shoulder and mumbled something aloud about what a slow day it had been. There was the slightest rustle. At least I heard it. I wheeled left and there the buck stood, broadside, immobile, head high. For three seconds. Really all I needed was three seconds—if I had been ready. But by the time I flung the rifle off my shoulder and raised it, the buck was gone forever.

Listening is important not only to be hearing what's going on around you but as a part of total concentration. When I am prowling along slowly, deer hunting, I often come in literally exhausted from listening and looking. Each time I pause, I find myself holding my breath. One hears much better with breath stopped momentarily. I choose to believe that I can hear almost as expertly as most big-game animals can. Not quite, but close. Because I have learned, so to speak, to force the quality of my hearing. Anyone can upgrade his ability to hear, given normal hearing of course, by practice. No slightest sound should go unnoticed.

If you aren't hearing full-out, you aren't seeing full-out or hunting full-out. An elk doesn't arise from its bed thinking, "I'm going to listen all day for hunters." It just naturally listens, and worries over any sound it doesn't fully understand. You, a thinking human, *can* understand each sound if you school yourself.

The hunter's sense of smell isn't by any means as important, but never sell it short. Certainly the effectiveness of the senses is an individual

Hunters learn to listen hard; this bull elk was located by its distant bugling.

matter. Long ago, at the University of Michigan, I took a psychology course in "Individual Differences." We learned that individuals differ in ability to hear, see and smell not only as related to physical disabilities, but simply as individuals. They also differ in reaction times, in degree of right- and left-handedness and ambidexterity, in color vision and color association (mine is exaggerated; to me the number four, for example, and the letter A are always red). But given a normal sense of smell, and a bent to use it and be aware of smells, any big-game hunter, regardless of individual ability, has one more ace in the hand of what might be termed total awareness.

I took a friend hunting one time for javelina in the brush country of south Texas. From previous experience, I know what a javelina smells like, close-up, and at a distance. We went into the breeze in what is called a "creek bottom" in that region. It is actually a dry wash that floods during rainy times and therefore has much vegetation. I knew that javelina commonly lie up in such draws, or follow them when feeding. Suddenly an unmistakable scent hit me, but not strongly. Unless I had known the smell, I'd not have reacted. But I knew instantly that a band of javelina was upwind, up the wash from us. We sneaked along and concluded the hunt successfully right there.

Bull elk in rut can be smelled. So can buck deer, and moose. Bear sometimes stink. I am not claiming you can blindfold yourself and home in on your trophy by sense of smell. What I am saying is that the *total* hunter tunes in with every sense he has. I personally have never had an experience in small-game or bird hunting when smell was important. But an awareness of smell is something the beginning big-game hunter must learn pretty much from scratch. I said a rutting buck deer could be scented. Not often. That's precisely the point. There might be that *one time* when you are hunting and you flare your nostrils and pick up that unmistakable musky and not very pleasant odor. Weak as it may be, it alerts your other senses, and you subsequently bag the buck.

This moves us along to a subject about which the small-game and bird hunter is required to know very little: the importance of wind direction. First let's define "wind." As used by the hunter, the term means any slightest movement of air. Most big-game animals have an exceptionally keen sense of smell, and they use it to warn them of danger. Man-scent is anathema, and is not only carried on a steady, hard blow, but wafted along on the most diminutive zephyr. Thus, hunting *into* the wind is mandatory in order to neutralize the scenting ability of the game.

In a stiff breeze, most big-game animals are nervous and jumpy, because they cannot hear keenly. The wind blots out other noises. But even on what seem to many hunters to be utterly calm days, there is usually some movement of air. It pays to keep testing. Fine dust, thistle or dandelion down, bits of dry grass sifted from your hand may reveal a minor movement of air. Unless a hunter is trying to move animals out of cover and toward a waiting companion, he must face the breeze or at least quarter into it.

In any rough country when a fitful breeze blows, air movements are whimsical. Cliffs and canyons shift air currents so that sometimes the breeze seems to be blowing from all directions at once. If you are making a stalk and feel it suddenly hit the back of your neck, there's a good chance the target has picked up your scent. In big mountains, air currents generally move upward in morning as valley air is warmed and rises. Then in late afternoon a reversal occurs as cool air settles. Learning to be an expert hunter requires incessant, virtually automatic, attention to direction of air movement.

A big-game hunter learns also to walk quietly and watch where he places his feet. This is not as important when hunting small game, but if a person hopes to go after big game he should practice every time he goes afield—walking quietly and dodging obstacles that may cause noise. Learn to avoid the stick that may crack when stepped upon. Put each boot down on solid rocks, not tippy ones that may clink or rattle and roll. The rake of a branch against some clothing fabrics is a give-away. Quiet walking is indeed an art. If there is a hardwood tree such as an oak that has shed its leaves, and it stands among conifers, the crafty walker will detour slightly to avoid walking under the oak. The dry leaves cannot be passed over silently.

It is always intriguing to hunt with a good guide who has been at it for years. He never talks aloud or coughs or clears his throat if he can possibly keep from it. He will point or motion to give instructions. He never fires his rifle at any varmint just to be shooting. He walks with eyes everywhere at once, his feet finding the quiet places. Even when mounted, he guides his horse to keep its sounds down to a minimum. He dislikes walking beside a noisy stream. He knows its sound covers his but he also knows that big-game animals cannot hear danger sounds very well when close to a noisy stream and so they are likely to avoid the location except for drinking.

Becoming a consistently successful big-game hunter is not a matter of luck. To be sure, on a particular day a stroke of luck may put the most inept hunter into position to collect a top trophy. But the man who usually brings back what he goes after is not a lucky hunter. He is an expert one, finely disciplined, totally observant, keyed in to his surroundings, constantly alert and concentrating.

2.
BASIC
BIG-GAME
HUNTING

Trip plans include check of clothes for weather.

During my early hunting days, when my quarry consisted of small animals and game birds, preparations for a hunt were extremely simple. I grabbed a cap and old jacket from a hook in our farmhouse kitchen, pulled on the only boots I owned, stuffed a few shotgun shells into my pocket, and picked up the old single-barrel shotgun.

We did also have in the family an ancient .22 single-shot. On occasion I used it for squirrels, or for rabbits and pheasants. I had even used it to kill a pheasant or two in the air, but mostly I sneaked on them and popped them from behind a corn shock. The .22 had to be utilized, regardless, when shotgun shells were gone. Money was short and there were family understandings about how often a box of shells could be bought. Believe me, a kid learned to hold his fire unless the chance was mighty good.

At any rate, having made the simple preparations, I walked out the kitchen door and started hunting. Many a time I bagged a rabbit or pheasant beside the rail fence around our big vegetable garden, not more than 50 steps from the door. Or one or the other might flush from the sassafras clump just past the garden. If such great good luck occurred, I ran back to the house and hung the kill by a string on the porch. Then I started over.

The simplicity and freedom of those boyhood pursuits had tremendous appeal. But I was to discover, when I began hunting big game, that much of the simplicity was gone. This was not wholly a matter of changing times. I realize that the pioneer hunter of large animals just walked out the door as I had done in boyhood. He wore what he had because that was all he had. He hunted with a certain kind of gun, powder and ball because nothing else was available. Today all that has changed. We have endless items of equipment, some very advantageous, some that are ridiculous. The deer hunter who must wear electric socks and carry a transistor radio with a light on top so he can find his way home ought to stay home. This type is really not a hunter but just a gadgeteer who clutters up the game country.

However, my point is that hunting big game differs from hunting smaller game chiefly in the more complicated approach. As a rule, the larger the game, the greater the preparation required to hunt it—and the greater the work and craft required. And unquestionably the greater the work (and required knowledge) after the kill has been made.

The man who starts out on a hunt for mule deer, sheep, goats or moose is not traipsing off across a farm field. There is not likely to be a hamburger stand handy for lunch. The physical aspects will be far more rugged than driving a Midwest cornfield for pheasants. Everything changes. Craft learned hunting pheasants or rabbits or squirrels may indeed be effectively utilized. But "big" means just that. When you become a big-game hunter you must work harder for fewer opportunities for shots. You may be gone a whole day or a whole week or a whole month. And I should also point out that when a deer has hit the ground, the entrails don't come out as easily as they do out of a rabbit. When you down a big bull elk or a moose, the dressing is not just a "chore," it is a major, physically demanding undertaking. Everyone should have a grasp of these basics before deciding to become a hunter of big game.

Just getting proper gear together for a hunt is extremely important, and often complicated. The rifle and scope and load must be matched meticulously to the species hunted. The hunter must be positive that his rifle is sighted correctly for the needed and most likely ranges, that his scope is focused, the mount tight, and that he has selected the best type of bullet for the game at hand. His clothing must be carefully chosen for the terrain and climate in which he'll hunt. Today's laws are many and complicated and must be checked. Some may even apply to clothing. Is blaze orange—so many square inches of it—required to be worn in the state in question? Are certain rifle calibers outlawed?

What about the terrain in relation even to the boots the hunter wears? Some soles are good on rock, some are not. Some thin boots are cool in warm-weather hunting but far from impervious to thorns and cactus spines, which are all too likely to be present in warm areas where big game is hunted. One must have a good binocular and a rifle sling, and even on pack-in trips consider gear such as mattress, sleeping bag, survival kit and first-aid materials.

To be sure, some deer hunters nowadays are able to hunt near home, to just walk off, as I used to, at dawn, try for a deer and be back in a few hours. Nonetheless, big-game hunting of any kind is far more of a "production" than is hunting a few hours at a time for smaller quarry. While I do

Black bear was taken in two-day season that would be bad gamble for non-residents.

not intend in this chapter to get into all the specifics, it is necessary for the prospective or modestly experienced big-game hunter to realize this.

It is a law of nature that the larger the animal, the smaller its population. This is a matter of range, living room. A moose requires more room than a whitetail deer, a grizzly more than black bear. Thus on a big-game trip you do not go out expecting to see scores of targets. The endeavor is more serious; it takes most hunters farther from home and for longer periods. All the preparation, in most instances, is aimed at what probably will be only a fleeting few seconds of heady action and excitement—the successful, or unsuccessful, shot.

Therefore no small bit of preparation should be overlooked. A pheasant hunter with a blister on his heel can limp back to his car and call it quits, maybe shooting a bird or two on the way. But the elk hunter may be put out of action for a crucial day, on a trip that costs much money and time and planning. Because opportunities for shots are far fewer in big-game hunting than in other hunting, all systems must be "go" or the project can end in dismal failure. This is one of the basic rules to be learned.

Where you will go is enormously important, and quite commonly places are selected too randomly, all too much like drawing straws. "Where," of course, depends on the game you will hunt. The states and provinces where sheep may be hunted are quite limited, but whitetail deer are found over a vast area, in all sorts of terrains and climates. Many deer hunters are able to hunt within their own states. However, all big-game hunters nowadays must be aware that even in their own states, or especially if they will be non-residents operating in other states, licenses and permits and quotas may be restrictive.

I am annually amazed at letters I receive, let's say in the summer or fall, from hunters in the East or Midwest asking what would be a good place for them to have an elk hunt that season. Fact is, in most elk states all permits are presently taken up shortly after the first of each year—9 or 10 months prior to season. Even antelope permits, in the better states, are usually gone by midsummer at the latest. One must plan far ahead, and bone up on the laws in the state where the hunt is to take place. Some permits—as for sheep—are so few that many who are eager to collect these trophies apply year after year, routinely, hoping for the luck of the draw sooner or later.

Obviously many hunters have special spots to which they return season after season. But the majority are always searching for new and better locations, and in today's world with transport swift and easy, thousands like to try a new spot every fall, often for a different kind of game. State game managers today keep expert checks on big-game populations. The wise hunter should do the same. A number of state game departments tabulate harvest figures by counties, or within Game Units. Certain blocks consistently show higher kills than others. In some states it is even possible to obtain figures on kill per square mile in each Unit.

In addition to these facts, which can be obtained from a game department, a hunter should learn how many hunters were in the area. And what the success ratio averages from year to year. For example, a hunting Unit that shows, let's say, a deer kill of four to each square mile may have both many deer and many hunters. An *average success percentage* for that Unit is a far more important statistic when one is checking out where to go.

My feeling long has been that average hunters do not avail themselves of masses of pertinent information that can be gleaned by watching newspaper reports, checking with local conservation officers, or making requests to information officers at state game departments. Knowing where the game is and what chances of success have averaged in the past can assist one in selecting the best-opportunity locations. It is also necessary to know something about the make-up of any harvest.

For example, with management as enlightened as it is today, deer in particular, which are not only the most popular and populous of American big game but also very prolific, repopulate swiftly. Thus it is necessary on all the better ranges to harvest antlerless deer as well as bucks to keep herds in balance with their food supply. A high consistent kill in a certain county may be composed, on the average, of 60 percent does and 40 percent bucks. Further, a breakdown of the buck kill may show that deer replenish so swiftly here that kill quotas have to hold them down—that is, they must be hunted hard each season. This generally means the large-racked older bucks get pretty well combed out. A check of kill statistics may show, if the breakdown is available, that 70 percent of the bucks taken are spikes or forkhorns. If you just want to bag a deer, this will be a fine location. But if you want a fair chance of at least seeing a few substantial racks, probably you should look elsewhere.

There also may be wide variation in size of animals, especially deer, from place to place. I'm not speaking now of trophy-antler hunting but of body size. For example, in Texas where I live, the Edwards Plateau region in the south-central part of the state unquestionably has more whitetail deer than any other part of Texas. Success is just about assured. But a hunter used to the heavy whitetails of Maine would be chagrined if he came for a sure-fire hunt without knowing what the deer are like. They are *small*. It takes a good buck, indeed, to dress out 100 pounds. Drop down into the brush country of southern Texas, however, and you will find not as many deer but large-bodied, large-racked animals.

The hunter should make a point of obtaining all such facts. And he should study the game animals, from books, to know what subspecies are like and how they may differ in size from the type species. A good example concerns the desert mule deer, which is a subspecies of the Rocky Mountain mule deer, the type species. A desert mule-deer buck weighing 150 to 175 pounds, field dressed, and with antlers 24 inches wide is a darned good deer. But to anyone used to taking Rocky Mountain mule deer of well over 200 pounds and some with, say, 30-inch antlers, a desert muley wouldn't look like much. The hunter after his first moose may be lucky enough to get a permit in Wyoming, where if he remains fortunate he'll take a specimen of the Shiras moose. It may look big to him. But it won't be as large in body or antlers as the moose far to the north, in Canada and Alaska.

Proper *identification* of all species and subspecies of big game is therefore important. There are really not very many animals to learn, and a hunter who wants to collect a few trophies or all of them should be fully and accurately informed. It's not difficult. Libraries are full of identification books. A classic instance, in my state, of common incorrect identification concerns the very small whitetail deer found in a few small mountain ranges of the Big Bend region. Locals and visitors alike keep insisting that this is the Coues deer.

It isn't. The Coues is a whitetail subspecies generally called the Arizona whitetail. It ranges over southeastern Arizona and southwestern New Mexico, and into Mexico. But its range does not reach east of the Rio Grande in New Mexico. Local hunters often refer to it as a "fantail." The little Texas deer is commonly called a "flagtail." It is actually the Carmen Mountains whitetail, a subspecies that gets its name from that mountain range across the border. The Coues is listed in the Boone & Crockett record book because its range does not bring it into contact with other whitetails in the U.S., and thus intergrades do not occur. There are some Texas whitetails, also a subspecies but larger, at lower elevations where the Carmen Mountains deer lives, and intergrades do occur. Regardless, a few Texans

Author conditions himself for high-country hunts; he dropped bear at 9,000 feet.

keep insisting this is the Coues deer and attempting to put good specimens into the book. Big-game hunters should pride themselves on knowing all such facts. These are basic to becoming a knowledgeable hunter.

When conducting a thorough check on where to go, it pays to find out the length of season plus the kill annually for several past seasons. For instance, Pennsylvania, as I recall, has had some one- or two-day seasons on black bear. The state's kill has been as high as 500 in peak years, but much lower in short seasons. A brief season would indicate a low bear population. It might be fine for a local hunter, but someone looking for a place to go on a trip would certainly be cutting it fine. In the State of Washington, on the other hand, some counties have no closed season on black bears; the state-wide kill averages 4,000 to 5,000 and has run as high as 9,000. Some 30 percent of black bears taken annually in the U.S. are bagged in Washington. A man looking for bear-hunting country would have good ammunition for decision-making just from those figures.

But now just to illustrate how carefully one should research a proposed hunt, and how easily the naive might be fooled, consider bear hunting in Texas. The game laws give a rundown on seasons in various counties, and even a special archery season in some. There are counties with no closed season, and some with no open season. There is just one little gimmick to all of this: It is doubtful that there are any bears in the state, except possibly a very few in the Guadalupe Mountains of far-western Texas. So it would be mighty important to check kill figures and success ratios.

The big-game hunter should have also a clear picture of what kind of terrain he is getting into, and what weather conditions are likely to be when he plans a distant trip. People have come from the North to visit me for a deer hunt, bringing short-sleeved shirts. Certainly I've hunted deer in Texas in short sleeves, when the temperature was 80 degrees. But in Texas and a whole lot of other states the old saw is true: "If you don't like the weather just wait a few minutes." I've hunted whitetails on my own ranch on bitter days with freezing drizzle, and I've hunted in balmy weather in the Big Bend country of western Texas only to wake up the next morning to a whistling norther, a blizzard with snow covering the mountains.

Too many hunters get to the location they've dreamed about only to

Bull elk will provide good eating and great trophy—but only after it's field dressed,

say, "I had no idea it would be like this." It's not difficult to make certain beforehand about the terrain, the vegetation, the altitude, the accommodations, the general weather to be expected. A few letters and telephone calls or a bone-up session in a library will put it all together. The man with the facts amassed beforehand is usually the most comfortable, competent, happy and successful.

Costs are also an important consideration. In the chapter on outfitters, Erwin Bauer gives some specific information and advice about expenses. But I think it will be helpful if I point out some facts right here about a subject not usually touched in hunting books—money. In today's world, hunting, and particularly big-game hunting, is no longer cheap. It never will be again. Magazines are forever running articles about "How I had an Elk Hunt for $50" or some other startlingly economical experience. But most if

butchered and packed out. This is one of many reasons guided hunts are recommended.

not all such reports are misleading. The person who wishes to hunt big game may as well make up his mind that it is a fairly costly sport.

First of all, there are license costs. These have been rising. Modern game management is expensive, and must depend upon money from license buyers. Resident licenses for various kinds of big game are not too rough as yet, but a good many non-resident permits are expensive. Big-game hunting is also becoming more and more commercialized. Guides are mandatory for non-residents in some states. Many hunters are more and more shunning public lands because these are crowded with hunters. They hunt on privately owned lands and pay a fee to the owner.

In my state, deer hunting is almost totally commercialized. Sportsmen in Texas lease hunting rights on ranch lands. Or they pay so much per day to hunt deer, or they book a so-called package hunt. The landowner fur-

Permits are scarce for species like desert sheep, so hunter must keep applying.

nishes transport on the land and a guide, and sometimes lodging and meals. The hunter pays a set price for his hunt. In some instances a deer is guaranteed, and there is no charge if the hunter doesn't get one.

Outfitters and guides who operate on public lands have to charge substantial fees. I have no quarrel with them, but I think beginners should be fully aware of what they are getting into. Today, whitetail-deer hunting is the least costly, on a national basis, simply because the whitetail ranges so widely across the continent and is the dominant big-game animal on vast expanses of public and private lands. A man can still camp out in the old-fashioned manner, hunt a whitetail on federal or state lands, and do it at reasonable cost. Even then, when all expenses are figured—license, travel, food, etc.—a whitetail hunt within modest traveling distance will average $100 to $150 at the lowest. Generally, the only hunters who can manage a whitetail hunt for little or nothing are landowners who live where the deer are.

Guide's knowledge of region enables him to find and glass most promising spots.

Hunters who live in mule-deer country can hunt this animal at low cost. But those outside mule-deer range will find the average cost higher than for whitetails. A guide, or at least a resident of the state, may be required; permits are in general a bit higher, and the smaller range of mule deer means many hunters must travel farther. An antelope hunt, when you can get a permit, is fairly reasonable, even when a guide is used. Total costs will average about as for mule deer or perhaps a bit less. A pronghorn hunt is often short—if the hunter is a good shot.

For anyone who goes after the larger animals, costs shoot up. Elk, moose, sheep, goats all come high. It's doubtful if any of these can be taken nowadays at a total cost under $400 and in many instances it is two to four times that. A black-bear hunt is apt to be cheaper; one can be booked, for example, in Ontario in spring over bait, for about $250.

This brief general discussion should give you a rough measure. Certainly a canny operator can find ways to cut costs. It's handy, for instance, to have a landowner friend who'll allow you to hunt free and even give you an assist. But the average big-game hunter will have to shell out a fair bundle of cash almost everywhere. I feel too little has been said about this, and what has been said is often not realistic. Time was when hunting of all kinds was assumed to be some sort of God-given right for one and all. No longer. You may yearn for the "good old days" (bad as they were in some respects) but there is nothing to be done about it. All leisure activities have risen in cost.

Big-game hunting is physically taxing. To be sure, in certain kinds of terrain hunting whitetail deer is no more strenuous than hunting ruffed grouse in the same location. But in general the search for large animals requires that the hunter work much harder. And if he hunts mule deer, elk, sheep and goats, he is certain to spend much time at elevations far above most whitetail habitat. Bear hunting with hounds, or stalking large bears in Alaska and northern Canada can be grueling.

A hunter should not only realize what will be required of him physically as he moves from small targets to large ones, he should also appraise accurately his own limits. Conditioning is something else. A friend of mine, preparing for a sheep hunt, had to stick at a desk job prior to his trip. But he wore diving weights much of the time on his shoes, so that each movement required toughening effort. He also walked up and down sixteen floors in his building, going to and leaving work each day.

Jogging, hiking, tennis all help to get one in shape. No hunter can expect to work at an indoor job, then leave suddenly on a trip such as an elk hunt and do well. The hunting is just too tough. Physical conditioning is a must. Even a mule-deer hunt or an antelope hunt can be strenuous. For several seasons I used to go each fall from Michigan where we then lived out to Wyoming for antelope and mule deer. The elevation change was deceptive. We hunted on the high plains, which of course didn't *look* high. Actually I was operating several thousand feet above the region where we lived. I always got along all right, but I tired more easily. Unaccustomed to the thinner air, I wasn't getting a full oxygen quota with the ease I did at home.

Nowadays I go to west Texas each fall for mule deer. The ranch house where I stay is at about 5,000 feet. We hunt from there on up to

6,000. My home, some 300 miles to the east, is at 1,600. The change is substantial. It pays to be aware of elevation, to move slowly and stop to "blow" often when you shift upward several thousand feet on a hunt. And it pays to get plenty of rest and, I repeat, to be aware of your own limitations.

Some of the best big-game hunts are on horseback. As a man who raised horses, rode with my boys daily for some years, and knocked around on quite a few mountainsides atop a horse, I know only too well that riding is hard work. Many guides don't have much sympathy because they are used to riding. Few take time to explain what the tyro should do.

First of all, it is a little bit ridiculous to expect to arrive on an airplane, let's say, and climb into a saddle a few hours later with no previous

Long horseback rides are physically taxing; practice and conditioning are vital.

riding experience. Almost anyone can find a place nowadays around any city or town where a horse can be rented for a daily ride. If you have booked a pack trip, break in your rear end as well as your new boots well beforehand. Make a point of riding. Perhaps you've never ridden horseback. Learn something about the feel of it.

Remember that when you throw a leg over a trail horse you aren't going to be doing any fancy didoes like Eastern "posting" and so on. You are going to sit your backside flat in the saddle and suffer, sticking with it hour after hour, snake-tracking up steep grades and down again. The going down is the most tiring part. Try to find some practice hills near your home.

Some riders get tired and sit back onto the cantle of the saddle to relieve the aches. This is a bad habit and very hard on the horse, pressing too much weight on its kidneys. Another bad habit is sliding over to rest one side of your rump, and then switching to the other side. This also is severe treatment for a horse, unbalancing the load. Always treat your horse with gentleness and affection. It's the best friend you have in the mountains.

There are several bits of advice that can make your horseback ordeal far easier. One is to be absolutely sure the stirrup straps are adjusted to proper length. Too short or too long will murder a rider, especially in rough terrain. Second, except when you are actually hunting don't carry your rifle in a saddle scabbard over which your leg must stay bent. If you are unused to riding, this extra bow in your leg will make you lame quickly. Third, during your first several days, while getting used to mountain riding, arrange with your packer or guide to let you stop every half hour, if only for five minutes. Get down out of the saddle and walk around. Lead your mount a few paces. Many first-timers discover that after an hour or so in the saddle their knees hurt so badly they are all but unable to stand when they get down. A few minutes of rest and walking every 30 minutes will avoid this. By the third or fourth day you won't need the respites.

I'm a firm believer in going first class, with a guide, on most big-game hunts. In some states and provinces, and for certain species, the law requires that a guide be used. Even where it's optional, except when going after whitetail deer and in some instances mule deer, any big-game hunter in *strange country* has a far better chance guided than going it alone. On an antelope hunt you may find a rancher willing to take you out on his land for a modest fee per day. He knows the land intimately. He knows the antelope bands, where they are hanging out and which ones hold the largest bucks. True, there are big-game hunters who pride themselves on going out alone for elk, sheep, goats, moose, caribou—where they may legally do so. But a good guide is worth all he charges in helping you find a good animal and raising your chances of success.

There is a very simple way to prove this. I made a study some time ago of big-game harvests in a number of Western states and in Canadian provinces. Most keep track of resident and non-resident total kills, and success percentages. On all the big-game animals where it was mandatory for non-residents to use guides or outfitters, success percentages were consistently well above those of resident hunters, who were not required to use guides. In some cases the differences were startling. For example, in one instance I recall that elk success averaged 97 percent over a three-year period for guided non-residents, but around 25 to 40 percent for residents.

This is no reflection on the ability of resident hunters. Those who live in the mountains or in small towns in elk (or other big-game) country do as well as guided non-residents. But a man who makes his living taking hunters out has a reputation to keep up. He has the game well located long before the season opens. He works hard at getting shots for his clients because his livelihood depends upon it. There's one other consideration to keep in mind when deciding whether to save money by going it alone. Picture yourself when you've left your vehicle, walked over a couple of mountains and downed a big bull elk in a remote valley. As you get out your knife and face the lone task, and think about how to get the meat out, you'll wish you'd spent your money and now had a companion in an hour of need!

3.
WHAT IS A
TROPHY AND WHAT
IS NOT

This Alaska moose is fine trophy but no record.

My dictionary defines a trophy as "a prize or memento received as a symbol of victory." That comes pretty close to what the term means to a hunter. But in common usage many of us have come to consider "trophy" and "record" nearly synonymous. "One for the record book" is a trophy. Actually that's not true.

Most hunters are not record-book hunters. Anyone, of course, hopes to collect a large set of antlers, but the trophy basically amounts to what a hunter is willing to settle for. Of the average 1,750,000 deer and 80,000 elk harvested annually in the U.S., only a minute scattering ever get into the records, and only a minor percentage can even be called "bragging heads." A substantial portion of the deer bag is of antlerless deer, and by far the majority of the bucks are forkhorns and six-pointers of modest proportions.

Yet any one of these may be a true trophy to the hunter who took it. Suppose a first-time deer hunter, operating in an area where deer are not abundant, gets a chance at a spike and takes it. He is jubilant. He has his deer. This is fine. I took a new hunter to our ranch one fall. We had some doe permits and I told him to shoot the biggest buck he saw but if he didn't get a buck or didn't want to wait he was welcome to take a doe. The first deer he saw was a doe, and he shot it and was not the least bit disappointed.

Unfortunately, little is ever said in books and magazines about making up one's mind what sort of animal one wants and then sticking with the decision. Any hunter who does that will be satisfied with his hunt. If hunting were so easy that a reasonable effort always guaranteed an outstanding trophy, the sport would be far less fun. The good hunter learns to be philosophical, enjoying himself even when he doesn't fill his tag. Too much status has long been connected with filling a tag and with bringing in a large specimen. There are many joys in hunting that have little to do with the taking of the quarry or with its size. But a decision as to what you will settle for should be made prior to any hunt, for whatever species. Then the hunt should proceed on that basis.

In deer hunting, the chance of seeing a number of animals during a hunting trip is fairly high. A hunter might hold out for a good head until the last day and then settle for a small deer, or none at all. If this was his decision beforehand, he won't be disappointed. In hunting larger game, or game that's more rare in the region, the decision becomes more critical.

Laws pertaining to sheep hunting in most instances require that only rams may be taken, and they must be sufficiently mature to have substantial horns—at least a three-quarter curl. In a case like that, a major part of the decision has already been made for the hunter. But in moose hunting, for example, or in elk hunting, situations may arise where any animal—cow or bull—is legal game. On most ranges these large animals won't be as abundant as deer. So the question arises, will you take the first one you see and be satisfied? Or will you hold out for a rack of large size? Will you turn down spike elk, let's say, but be willing to settle for branching antlers regardless of the number of points? If you decide before you go on the hunt, you avoid a dilemma when your shooting opportunity arises, and you also avoid any possibility of disappointment afterward.

As I write this it amuses me to recall a moose hunt I made a few years ago in Ontario. Things were not going too well as the week wore on. I had had no chance at all, had not so much as seen a moose. Then one day I had a perfect chance at a big cow. Any moose was legal in that region, and I decided then and there to take this animal home. The skinning and quartering took several hours, and as we were transporting the meat by canoe back to camp along toward dusk, you can guess what happened. A handsome bull stood ashore and watched as we paddled past within 75 yards. The guide was in total anguish. I wasn't. Before I went into the bush I had made up my mind to try for a good bull until time was short and then take an antlerless animal if I saw one. That cow was excellent eating and I had had a fine hunt.

Discipline is the key. As a matter of fact, the big-game hunter should practice severe discipline, even regarding the shots he will accept. That is another matter, of course, but one to ponder. Don't be so eager to collect the game that you accept a poor shot—that is, one where proper placement is not possible. There is immense pride in discipline of this sort, once a hunter has achieved it.

Besides willingly accepting a small head or an antlerless animal, there is the opposite kind of discipline. This pertains to the person who starts out determined to take nothing except an exceptional head, or one of certain

Sheep pictured are not legal game; hunter must find ram with 3/4-curl or better.

dimensions. I hunted for a number of seasons in south Texas on the 9,000-acre hunting lease of a close friend. He and I went out looking for whitetail bucks of not less than 10 points, and for racks that were heavy at the base and wide of spread. We were not actually hunting for record-book deer, even though a few have come out of the cactus and thornbrush of southern Texas. But we made the decision ahead of time not to be distracted by bucks that failed to fit our formula. We could easily take small bucks on my place farther north.

In seven seasons we each killed only two deer. I have never been especially interested in making a collection of mounted heads, and the only whitetail I've ever had mounted was one of those deer: a mahogany-hued rack of 10 points, all of them long, and with a spread of 24 inches. This is by no means a record-book deer. But it is a stunning *trophy* deer, and part of the satisfaction and enjoyment of those hunts was that we disciplined ourselves to hold our fire on anything that didn't suit us. I'll admit it is hard sometimes to back off when a shot is presented. It is even more difficult when hunting animals such as elk and moose, for many a small rack looks mighty big after you haven't seen game for several days, or if you've never hunted these animals before.

And that gets us to the crux. Horns and antlers of only fair size *do* look large and exciting at a distance, or in certain light, and also in direct proportion to the eagerness of the hunter. A running buck pronghorn that appears to have excellent horns may be extremely disappointing when you finally stand over the animal. Elk antlers are tall and even to those who have been on several elk hunts can be startling when seen in timber or skylighted on a ridge. A buck mule deer of only so-so proportions looks appealing as it bounds up a ridge. But alas, too often the size of the trophy is chiefly in the excited eye of the beholder. A guide friend used to say, "Antler size is directly proportional to the adrenalin flow the client is experiencing!"

How, then, do you judge a trophy? The best of the long-experienced guides can almost instantly spot the finest head in a group, or distinguish among "record," "exceptional," "good" and "so-so." The guided hunter should rely on his mentor. But he should also know himself what is or is not a trophy of any species he is after, and he should learn to measure them with his eye. Experience is obviously the best teacher, but there are aids to use while getting that experience.

First of all, if you are going out after a head to go into the record book, you must know what is required. This takes expertise, because record measurements today under the point system are much trickier than they used to be. You have to judge length, spread, points and their length, circumference, etc. A thorough study of an up-to-date copy of the Boone & Crockett record book is the first step. This establishes for you how the measuring is done, what is the smallest that will make the book and what is the largest recorded to date. The longer the top records have stood, the tougher they'll be to beat. Now you know what you have to shoot for.

Even a hunter who isn't interested in establising a record can glean helpful information from the record lists. The smallest heads in the book illustrate for him what it takes to make an exceptional trophy. That term can be used for a head not quite of book proportions but somewhere between the low end of the book list and on down the scale to somewhere above the so-so specimen.

Now of course any hunter, even a beginner, who sees a whitetail deer or a mule deer with obviously enormous antlers shouldn't do any studying at the moment but get his rifle into action. In other situations, two things are needed: time to study the head to make sure it can be called good or exceptional or record; a quality glass through which to do the studying. Although a spotting scope is seldom employed in whitetail hunting, it can be used to advantage in all mountain hunting and also for pronghorns. But in lieu of a spotting scope, which is used for looking over distant undisturbed animals, a quality binocular is what the average big-game hunter must have to give his eye the added reach to study details of antlers and horns.

Bear in mind that terrain may sometimes influence your attempted judgment of trophies. In a small woodlot at close range, a so-so whitetail can look big, and on a huge expanse of mountainside a distant elk may not look like much at all. The way to make judgments is by relating antlers or horns to various body features of the average animal of that species. In order to do this, it is handy to know how high an average specimen stands at the shoulder or back line, or how long its ears are, or how long it is in the body when standing broadside. Of course, specimens from various ranges differ somewhat in size. Thus the chief criteria are simply the size relationships between various parts of the animal and its headgear, as seen in any position—facing, broadside, going away, quartering.

Oddly, the most abundant and popular big game animals—deer—are in many ways among the most difficult to appraise accurately. And the whitetail is generally more difficult than the mule deer. This is because conformation of the antlers differs to some extent in the two species. Most muley antlers stand up straighter from the skull. Whitetail antlers come out of the skull rather often on a slant to the rear and slightly outward in a plane almost in line with the nose. But then they begin to curve outward and come around forward. Some continue the curve so that the ends of the main beams come clear around over the face—a "tight," basket-like rack with the ends of the beams only a few inches apart.

Seen from broadside, the whitetail is especially difficult. If the tines

Heavy-antlered elk, with six points on each side, is very respectable trophy.

Hunter who wants no wall mount may prefer doe for sake of excellent table fare.

appear extremely high and the antlers heavy, it may indeed be a very good specimen. If the deer is alert, which it usually will be, its ears will be cocked up and forward. If you have time to look closely, check how high above the skull and how high above the ear points the level of the antlers appears to be. Antlers that you judge to be a foot higher than the bridge of the nose, and seven or eight inches above the cocked ear points, are good ones, although you can't judge spread accurately from broadside. Two problems add to difficulties. First, whitetails are likely to be in dense cover, and when you jump one it bounds away too fast for accurate antler guessing.

Looking head on at a whitetail gives you a better idea of antler formation. Whitetails from place to place differ greatly in body size, but one measurement comes closest to constant. That is ear length. They are seven to eight inches, in some instances possibly eight and a half. When cocked in an alert, listening attitude the ears are of course not out straight, so from tip to tip of ears the distance is by no means the sum of the ears plus the width of the skull. Tip to tip will be roughly 12 to 14 inches, depending on deer size and how high the ears are cocked. If the antlers are well outside the ears, say from two to four inches, you are looking at a deer that probably has a spread measuring from 16 to as much as 22 inches. If the rack also appears high, you'd better shoot. Whitetails in this category are good ones.

The easiest view of the whitetail buck for quick appraisal is going straight away, and that's how a lot of them are seen. Again, bear in mind the variations among subspecies and geographic locations. But a good big buck in top health will be 14 to 16 inches thick in the body. A straightaway look gives you an opportunity to measure antler spread against body width. If the antlers thrust out past the body, don't hesitate.

Most beginning hunters and some old hands have a mental picture of deer as much larger than they actually are. If you know average sizes, you can often block off mental measurements of antlers compared to any part of the body. "Average," of course, is directly related to the locale. A Maine whitetail may be six feet long, nose to rump. One in the area where I live may be five feet at most. Shoulder height is one of the most important measurements. In small whitetails it is well under a yard, in fact about 2½ feet. It is difficult to convince hunters this is true. A large whitetail stands roughly 40 inches (or three feet four inches) at the shoulder.

Mule deer are somewhat less troublesome because a hunter often has a chance to glass the deer thoroughly, even though distantly, right in the open. As I noted earlier, the Rocky Mountain mule deer is, on the average, larger both in body and antlers than the desert mule deer. Antler formation varies greatly among individual mule deer, too. Some racks are very wide, some stand almost straight up and are narrow but extremely high. If you don't have such a specimen, a heavy, unusually high though narrow rack makes a good trophy. But most hunters will want wide, heavy antlers and these are what must be considered the most general. If you're counting points, be wary. Mule deer often vary on each antler. Also, young mule deer, even with wide antlers, may have no brow tines at all.

The ears of mule deer are 11 to 12 inches long. The skull is fairly broad. Alert mule deer do not generally cock the ears as high as whitetails do. This is true in particular of large, old bucks. They sometimes look, when aware, as if the antlers are in the way of their ears. However, the ears will seldom be held completely straight out to the sides. So, as with the whitetail, the antler width is not quite sum of ears plus skull plus any overhang.

You have to judge deer against their local background. In some places most of the muleys are extra-large. In others they're not. Overall length—not body length alone—runs from about four feet eight inches to five feet six inches. Antlers seen from broadside that appear to be tall enough to reach from nose to top of shoulder if laid horizontally, are bound to be good ones. If, seen from the front, the antlers curve well outside the ears, the deer is a good one. If the antlers are exceedingly tall but still inside the ears, you may be looking at an unusual head that you'll want for that quality.

One of the problems in judging mule deer is that almost any mature buck looks so large. Antlers are usually heavy, and points long. It is always a temptation to shoot. But it is better discipline to appraise the head first—unless, of course, you are in an area where deer are scarce and you can't afford to be selective. Mule deer are quite likely to stand and stare, even from atop a ridge after they have run off. The ear-width method is thus very handy and easy to judge by. Except for the high "freak" rack, if the antlers, regardless of how your eye and adrenalin seem to see them, are inside the ears, the buck isn't much.

At the shoulder a mule deer stands taller than a whitetail. Again depending on the particular range, shoulder height will run from a yard to about three and a half feet. Suppose now that you are looking head on at a good buck, and the antlers come well out past the ears. Given time, you can add one more measurement to clinch judgment. Let's presume you are in country where deer tend to be large, so you know the buck probably stands about 42 inches at the shoulder. If the animal has its head erect, and the measurement you guess from top of shoulder to top of antlers is well over half as high as the deer stands at the shoulder, you're onto an exceptional specimen.

Mule deer running away from you give an instant impression of antler size if you make a quick judgment. A buck's rump and body are both broad. But straight-away it will be the rump you'll see. It will be at least 17 inches wide, maybe more. If the antlers easily come out past it four inches on each side, you are looking at a 25- to 26-inch spread. If they're more than that, this is an exceptional buck. If the antlers do not thrust out past the rump in your viewing plane, it could be a nice buck but no trophy.

A rather general but handy bit of lore regarding deer measurement concerns the forelegs. They are not as long as most hunters visualize them, especially since one sees them in a plane that shows the leg from the bottom of the brisket to the ground. Seen broadside or quartering, a deer with its head erect will hold its nose so that the bottom of the lower jaw is on a horizontal plane just about even with or slightly above the withers. The withers, in case the term is puzzling, is the highest point on the back between the shoulder blades. Quite roughly (I emphasize that this is not a precise measurement) the vertical distance from top of withers to bottom of brisket will be about equal to that from brisket to ground. If you know this, you can judge antler height against both of these when given time. A mule deer measuring three and a half feet at the withers will be somewhere near 21 inches from brisket to ground or brisket to withers.

Elk antlers are judged with a somewhat different approach, at least at the first look. Unlike deer, elk seldom have nontypical antlers, that is, with numerous uneven points, or with more on one side than the other. Very old elk may exhibit freak antlers. Because elk are carefully managed nowadays, which means quota cropping of all herds, not very many bulls are seen past their prime or with freakish antler growth. In addition, although years ago some stunning bulls were killed with seven and even eight points on each side, finding such a bull today is unlikely.

Elk, incidentally, are spoken of as "five-pointers" or "six-pointers," etc. This is a Western habit and it also is because, as I've noted, elk have quite symmetrical antlers. Spike elk are males in their second year. The spikes are commonly quite long, 18 inches or more. Unlike many deer, elk do not follow with a fork-horned stage. Almost without fail, the second antlers have five points on a side. But these antlers usually are rather slender.

A five-point elk looks big to many a tyro, but is not really much of a trophy.

If the animal remains vigorous, usually the next set of antlers will have six points on a side. These first sixes may also be rather light—that is, slender, and not exceptionally long. The typical mature bull elk is a six-pointer—meaning six on a side. The six-pointers that live to be six or seven years old are the real trophy elk today. The antlers should be very heavy, very tall. The most desirable heads have ivory-tipped antlers, and the last tine rising from the main beam is invariably extra-long and heavy.

Because of the bulk of its body, a bull elk appears proportionately shorter in the legs than a whitetail or mule deer. Big bulls weighing 900 pounds or more are astonishing for any hunter to gaze upon. A good one measures at least 9½ feet in overall length. At the shoulder it is at least five feet tall. Elk antlers sweep up and back. When a bull bugles, the antlers are laid back so they can be seen from broadside against the line of the back. There are two good ways to guess at the size. If the antlers extend well past the withers, so that as the animal's neck is outstretched they are laid flat almost along the back and the tips touch or are above the dip behind the withers, the specimen is excellent. Or, if you try to visualize the antlers as detached and placed horizontally so that they stretch rearward from the front of the brisket—about where the long, rough neck mane ends—and they reach to the inside of the hind leg, you're also looking at a good bull. If they appear longer, so much the better. A reach of 50 inches is quite good, one of 60 exceptional.

But that's not quite all you should look for. Trophy measurements today (for records) count circumference of beam and tines, length of tines, and also widest spread. There is no possible way to judge the spread of elk antlers unless the animal is facing you, or going straight away. Even going away it is difficult. Recently on an elk hunt, a friend of mine searched long and with a guide's help finally decided on a tremendous old six-pointer. When we made rough field measurements of the downed bull, it would easily have made the record book except that it was a few inches too narrow in spread. It certainly was a "mounting elk." But always try to look not only for heavy, tall, six-point antlers but also for the awesomely wide rack.

Be certain, too, if you want a head to mount, that the antlers are in-

Merely average deer can look big to excited hunter, especially at close range.

tact. On two different occasions in recent seasons I have photographed elk
with a telephoto while a friend whistled them up with a call during the rut.
One big bull on which I shot a whole roll we had really closer than we
wished, hackles up and ready to do battle. Not until the film was processed
and I saw the slides without the excitement of the filming did I realize that it
had one broken antler. On another occasion three of us glassed several bulls
in a valley during rut. One was exceptional. He stood broadside in dim evening light. When he finally turned his head we were astonished to see that
he had only one antler! Normally this would immediately be evident. But in
excitement an error can be made.

When I advise nothing smaller than a six-pointer as a trophy, I must mention an exception to the rule. In some states where elk are severely cropped under present management, and particularly among specific herds that get the heaviest pressure, it may not be possible to find any six-pointers. Or they may be very scarce. Guides and local residents know quite accurately what the situation is. So do game-department biologists who survey and manage the herds. In a few instances, therefore, you might have to settle for a five and consider it a good bull for that region.

Almost without fail, moose will be hunted with a guide. Even the first-time hunter can instantly tell the difference between a small set of antlers and a large one. But judging between large and near-record can be very tricky. Antler size is also related to where you hunt—i.e., the variety of moose present in the region. There are three: the ponderous Alaskan moose; the common, or Canadian, moose; and the Shiras, or Wyoming, moose found in portions of the Rockies. The Shiras is usually smaller at maturity than either of the others.

The best and most important way to judge moose antlers is by the spread of the huge palms. Points also should be counted whenever possible and a check made of how symmetrical they are. However, the average moose hunter who is after a trophy, but not necessarily a record, will probably be best advised to concentrate only on spread. By and large it can be said that an Alaskan moose with a five-foot spread is very much worth taking. They do grow larger—over six feet. An animal with a 5½-foot spread is an exceptional specimen. As for points, 24 to 30 would be substantial.

Canadian moose have been taken almost as large of antler as the Alaskans. But here a five-foot spread would certainly be considered well worthwhile, and 24 or more points ample. Most trophies are less than five feet. It would be difficult for an average hunter who wanted one for his wall to turn down a rack of four feet or better. A Shiras moose of four feet and 20 points can be considered a good trophy.

Moose are 8½ to 10 feet long overall, and stand from 5½ to about 7½ feet at the shoulder. Trophy Shiras bulls will stand six feet, and a general average for the others is seven feet. Guides who live in moose country and have seen many should be relied upon for judging antler size. Because moose antlers flare so wide, it is difficult to compare them to any body measurement except shoulder height. Care should be exercised here, too, for moose have long legs and the bulls have a pronounced hump across the shoulder. However, if you know that from ground to withers a mature bull moose outside the U.S. Rockies will measure seven feet or close to it at the shoulder, you can make a reasonably reliable judgment.

Caribou have such a broad range across the continent, from Alaska to Newfoundland, that there are many subspecies. Even scientists are somewhat confused about them. In a later chapter given to hunting these animals, you will find more details. Suffice to say here that three main varieties are recognized: the barren ground caribou, rather small; the intermediate woodland caribou; and the large mountain caribou. These animals range in size all the way from 3½ to five feet at the shoulder, five to 7½ feet in length, and 200 to 700 pounds in weight.

All caribou have very tall antlers compared to overall animal size. This is the only member of the deer family on this continent in which both sexes bear antlers. Those of the females, however, are comparatively small and slender. The main beams of caribou antlers sweep back and up in a long, high curve. But there are also brow tines, called "shovels." Most often, the tine on only one side develops into a real, palmated shovel. The most desirable head is one with twin shovels—that is, two on each side. These double-shovel heads are not common. But a hunter after a really good head should check the shovels before looking at any other antler dimension.

The one difficult problem in judging a caribou's main beams is in guessing how long the curve would be if straightened out. A 60-inch curve will be about equal to the shoulder height of a big bull. Among the smaller varieties, of course, it will exceed shoulder height. Any five-footer is an excellent specimen. A rack measuring a foot less but with double shovels is certainly good, especially nowadays when caribou are not greatly abundant.

As I noted earlier, sheep hunters will almost invariably be guided, and restricted as to minimum curl of horn. As a rule, a ram must have at least a three-quarter curl to be legal. The massive base of the horns also counts in scoring the trophy, but this must be related to the variety. The

Dall has more slender horns than the bighorn, and generally the best specimens have flared tips. The diameter of the curl is a good indication of overall
horn size. Check it broadside if possible, against two body features. If the
curl diameter is as broad as from the animal's front hoofs up to a bit above
the knee, or as broad as from the chin (when the head is held at alert) down
to the bottom of the neck in front—though not to the brisket—it is undoubtedly a proper trophy. However, because sheep hunting is so restricted today, the lone hunter should make a point of studying good mounted heads
before a hunt, and the guided hunter should put much faith in the judgment
of his guide.

Among average big-game hunters, there has never been the competition to take record mountain goats that exists among sheep hunters. Further, there is not any extreme spread of dimensions to select from among
mature goats. Both sexes have horns. Those of the female are generally
more slender than a billy's horns. Adult billy horns measure from about nine
inches to a foot. A 10-incher is a good trophy. It's difficult to tell male from
female at a distance. Sometimes a female's horns are quite good—in fact,
nannies have been in the record book—but the shooting of females is discouraged. Here, again, the guide's judgment ought to be heeded.

Some years ago it was fairly easy to collect a pronghorn antelope
with 16- to 17-inch horns. A friend of mine hunted not long ago on a west
Texas ranch that had not been hunted in years and he had the immense good
fortune to pick up a buck of 18 inches. But because antelope are closely
cropped—tailored to the modest amount of suitable range existing today—
such exceptional bucks are few indeed. Most hunters are very happy with a
13-incher, and those of 15 are bragging size. If, in addition, a 15-incher has
massive bases—I have one with a seven-inch circumference on each horn
base—then the trophy is all the more desirable.

But make no mistake, antelope are among the most difficult of all big
game to judge with accuracy. They are generally seen at long range, and often they are running. The way a buck holds its head either standing or running, the horns always look larger than they are. The prong, thrusting ahead
instead of back, forms a puzzling picture. If the horns are heavy-based, and
the prong is broad, they look even larger. Furthermore, antelope horns (not

Three good whitetails adorn hunter's wall; note heavy, widespread antlers.

true horns; the outer shuck is annually shed) are inclined to be highly varied in form.

As I write this I can look at three sets on a shelf in my office. One set has the curve turning abruptly straight back at the tips. A second has them curving back but also inward until they nearly meet. The third has the curve clear from the prong to the tips sweeping wide and around, inward toward each other. I have also killed antelope with freak forward-curved tips, and I saw an unusual head one fall that had each horn sticking off at an acute angle. At the top they were almost 18 inches apart.

Antelope are smaller creatures than many hunters envision. A 90-pound buck is about average and one of 125 an eyepopper. Does are smaller.

Bucks measure about four to 4½ feet in overall length, but body length, from base of neck to back of rump, is seldom a full yard. At the shoulder, bucks average a yard in height, and exceptional specimens go 40 inches. If you can get a good look at the horns and judge them to be a third as long as the animal is tall, or long in the body, they are probably at least 14 inches in length, perhaps more. Remember that you are seeing their height as on a flat plane, whereas the curve of the horns will add to your trophy measurement.

There is little point in trying to set up for hunters, either beginners or old hands, any set of rules for judging bears. Most black-bear hunters consider any adult bear sighted a trophy of a lifetime. They are not overly concerned with skull size, which is what qualifies the animal as a record. And there is no way for even the expert to be certain of skull size on any bear until it is skinned and measured. Hunters after grizzlies (and browns) are few nowadays, and invariably guided. Very large bears, of course, are likely to have the largest skull measurements and therefore a chance at the book.

Guides judge bear size by what they estimate the hide will "square out." That figure is arrived at by measuring the width and length of the hide, adding the measurements and dividing by two. A black that squares out at seven feet is indeed an exceptional specimen, and an Alaskan brown at nine feet is certainly good, although there have been larger ones. Experienced bear guides who have seen many alive and then measured the hides have a pretty solid idea as to what a bear will square. The hunter in most instances must depend on his guide's judgment. Track size is a good indication of bear size. Some guides even have formulas for figuring track measurement and projecting it to squaring of the hide. But—first you must see and measure the track of the bear you are stalking.

In closing this chapter I should say a few words about javelina. The javelina is a trophy chiefly because it is unusual, not by body measurements. Hunters who've never seen one have usually at least heard wild, and mostly untrue, tales about them. I had two mounted heads on the wall of a glassed-in porch at a house we owned some years ago in northern Michigan. People who saw them guessed that the animals weighed all the way from 100 to 200 pounds each.

The fact is, the javelina is small. The heaviest I have ever weighed was 52 pounds. Average weight of several hundred (weighed alive in a Texas study some years back) was around 37 pounds, and a javelina of 40 to 50 pounds on the hoof is a good-sized specimen. When you see them in groups, one or two may appear outstanding in size, and they are the ones on which to concentrate. But there is no extensive scale of size differences. Just select one that looks the largest and have at it.

I've also heard hunters tell of going after a javelina with long "tusks"—"maybe above four inches." This is ridiculous. Javelina do not have tusks, if the term is used in the same way as for European boars. The tusks of those "Russian" boars, as they're often called, may indeed be four inches long, and they may curve out of the upper jaw and often upward, and thrust outward from the lower jaw generally in shorter length. Javelina have only a pair of tearing, or "dog," teeth on either side. Uppers and lowers mesh so the inner edges are self sharpening. They do not curl outward from the jaw. And you can measure the uppers—which are generally longest—of the next thousand you bag and not find one over two inches. Most will be less.

4.
BIG-GAME
OUTFITTERS
by
Erwin A. Bauer

Guide steadies spotting scope to judge trophy.

Fred Moore, 54, is an attorney, a city dweller of middle-America. Come autumn, he is the typical weekend sportsman. He belongs to a good duck club and frequently manages to squeeze a pheasant hunt at a nearby shooting preserve into his tight schedule. For reasons soon to be revealed, Fred Moore is not his correct name.

Because he has always been a very busy man professionally, many years passed before Moore was able to realize one lifetime ambition—to go on a big-game hunt. He simply had too many things going, had a son to send to college, plus all the other usual reasons that result from modern living. But one fall recently, all the pieces began to fall into place. Because of an emergency, one of Moore's associates had to cancel out on a hunt to British Columbia, and Fred was offered the chance to substitute. Luckily, since his schedule could be rearranged, Moore was able to accept and he plunged into the happy task of quickly getting ready.

First Fred bought the best hunting outfit he could find. That included a new eider-down sleeping bag, new boots, a .300 Magnum rifle, the works. He also gave himself a cram reading course on bighorn sheep and mountain caribou, on grizzly bears and goats. A day or so later, he boarded his jet and then sat back, double martini in hand, to anticipate *The Adventure of a Lifetime* which was about to unfold.

It is to be hoped that our hunter enjoyed the flight and the first-class service, because it was just about the last contentment he would know for a long, long time.

Even for an old hand at the game, a pack trip is not an easy undertaking, especially in the beginning. It is doubly rough on a man who is not used to the saddle and whose physique tends toward the soft and portly. That will explain why the first day's ride into the upside-down, steep hunting country was an unsettling experience. The outfitter (whom we will call Bart and who had plenty of experience with inexperienced hunters) had planned only a short ride of 11 miles as an easy starter, but even that produced one extremely sore rump on our friend. Moore went to bed exhausted after scarcely touching his dinner.

Next day's ride wasn't much better. In fact, it might be described as an ordeal. After that, things got worse. Now Fred had to walk—or climb—

on his own feet, rather than his horse's. That was bad enough, but in new boots which had not been thoroughly broken in, it was like lumbering heavily across a bed of redhot coals. After about two days Fred Moore, by his own admission later on, was nearly crippled.

There is no point in listing many other gruesome details of the hunt, except to note that the hunter had forked out over $1,800 to the outfitter, plus $550 for air fare—and for nothing at all except misery. Toward the end of the hunt, Bart somehow did manage to coax and carry Fred within easy shooting distance of a fine Stone ram. There was a chance for a happy ending. But the sheep might as well have been a mile away because Fred missed it cleanly with a rifle which (like the boots) he had never used before making the trip. Summed up, it is an understatement to say that Bart finished his own ordeal with one disgruntled, bruised and bitter customer.

Was the outfitter to blame?

On the whole, no. But in a sense he was. He might have warned his new, substitute client about the rigors of the hunt. He might have inquired about his physical condition—and also might have made suggestions. But he did none of these. Perhaps, and with some justification, he figured that any man who signs on for a big-game pack trip is himself responsible for getting ready. On the other hand, if Fred had applied the same common-sense preparation to his hunt that he always applied to his successful law practice, he would never have ended in such a painful predicament. No matter from which side you view it, here is a complicated matter and one which every serious big-game hunter must ponder some day.

In every corner of North America where there is enough big game to justify hunting, there also are guides and outfitters. Some are highly capable and skilled; some are not. Some are full-time professionals whose results guarantee that they will always be in business; others are fly-by-nighters. Most outfitters are in the profession because they genuinely love it; others are so engaged for the fast greenback, or at least a fairly fast buck. When choosing an outfitter, every outdoorsman must make the choice between the two. Often he must decide on a man he has never met and will not even see until the day he arrives to hunt. It is a difficult decision and crucial, but certainly not an impossible one to make judiciously. Let's go back to the beginning.

Outfitter has set up camp in game-rich section of British Columbia's Cassiars.

Who needs an outfitter anyway? Why? And where?

Of course, not all sportsmen do need guidance, even when venturing into strange and remote country, possibly for unfamiliar game. The most challenging hunt of all—the one with the greatest personal rewards—is that one on which a man goes out on his own, unassisted, and bags a really fine trophy. No two ways about that. But in many Western states and Canadian provinces or territories (Montana, Wyoming, Alberta, British Columbia, Alaska, Northwest Territories, Yukon), the law *requires* that a non-resident have a resident guide, and that's that. No matter how skilled and determined the sportsman is, a guide to hunt some big-game animals is mandatory.

Even where a guide is not needed, a good one can be worth his weight in solid gold ingots. And the better he knows his country and his game, the more valuable he is. Let's say you are hunting during your annual two weeks' vacation and have only that limited period to spare. You could easily spend all of it just locating game, while a local outfitter puts you into game country immediately. Depending on where you plan to hunt for big game (and the law must be checked in whatever area), a good outfitter or guide is either an absolute necessity or a valuable ally. A bad one can only be a drain on your finances and mental outlook.

Selection of an outfitter is without doubt the critical point in setting up a big-game expedition. Based on many, many seasons of big-game hunting from Mexico northward to Alaska and the Northwest Territories, it is this writer's opinion that the best—and safest—way to first make contact with an outfitter is on the recommendation of a trusted, credible, reasonable friend who has had a successful hunt—and preferably on the recommendation of *more* than one friend. Keep in mind that this is an instance where only satisfaction counts; no amount of public relations or anything else can turn a disgruntled client into a satisfied person who will supply a good reference.

There are other ways to contact professional hunters. In some states or provinces, outfitters are licensed by law and the various fish and game (or conservation, or natural resources) departments will furnish lists of these men on request. Requirements for licensing aren't very stringent in all cases, but this *is* an indication that the licensee is at least solvent and serious enough to pay his annual fee. So the odds are in his favor as being at least worth contacting to begin inquiry.

Every month the national outdoor magazines also carry numerous advertisements of outfitters everywhere. Sometimes the number of them alone is bewildering. Most of these are reliable people, but the magazines have no way to separate the bad apples from the good ones in the barrel; the reader must do that. Although it will take time and correspondence, it is possible nearly all of the time.

No matter how you make contact initially with an outfitter—and the very best advice is always to contact several for comparison—the first thing to do is to write and ask for references. Not just one reference; ask for several, and if possible get references from hunters who live near you and whom you can contact personally or by phone. Before any big-game hunt is over, a good bit of time and money, as well as hope and dreams, is going to be invested—so the expense of postage and/or long-distance calling to check details becomes very minor.

Besides the request for references, letters of inquiry to outfitters should ask for the following information: the exact hunting area, the best time to hunt in that area, the game species available, chances of success (or rather how well other hunters have fared in the past), the exact cost (noting any "extras" as well as the cost of the license), what precisely does the outfitter furnish, how many hunters are accommodated at one time, and exactly what type of hunting it is. Find out whether the outfitter or the hunter is responsible for obtaining all necessary licenses and permits.

Of course, it is possible to encounter an outfitter—some certainly exist—who is a far better letter-writer than he is a hunter, and a phony of that sort may not be easy to detect from correspondence alone. But a thorough check of references certainly should determine whether the outfitter is on the level or not. The very sad fact here is that, while the large majority of outfitters doing business in the West are entirely on the square, there are just enough others to demand that every sportsman proceed carefully.

It is vital to examine carefully any extravagant claims an outfitter may make in a letter or brochure. "Guaranteed game" or "Guaranteed trophies" certainly are suspect and, to be truthful, should be avoided. Con-

Outfitter may discuss likely weather but can't predict or avoid sudden rains.

sidering the vagaries of weather, terrain and especially of unpredictable game itself, no guide should absolutely guarantee that a hunter he has never seen before will score. The whole thing is preposterous.

There really are "guaranteed hunts," although they should more accurately be called "shoots." These are mostly for such game as mountain lions, bears or boars. What the hunter doesn't know is that after he and the guide have undergone a certain amount, but not too much, of riding or searching, usually with a pack of hounds, a captive animal is released from a hidden pen and a short chase begins until the target is brought to bay. It is a certain and expensive way to obtain a bear or lion rug, but cannot be described as sport hunting.

Not to be confused with the so-called guaranteed hunts are those on Texas ranches and other southwestern ranches where the outdoorsman goes after native whitetails and several species of exotic big game. Here the hunter depends on his own shooting skills and pays only for the animals he bags. He isn't really guaranteed anything and frequently gets nothing at all.

The hunter planning a first big-game trip is very wise to be wary of guaranteed shots or shooting, as innocent as these claims may appear. An outfitter can't honestly guarantee shooting any more than he can guarantee a trophy—even if he (illegally) shoots it himself. Also there can be no end of disagreement over what is a shot and what isn't. A bull elk standing 300 yards away may be a lead-pipe cinch for a few shooters, but for others it might as well be on another planet. Even an elk only 25 yards away is no "shot" if it is running hell-bent through heavy black timber.

The man who is trophy-hunting—looking for a good head rather than just any animal of a species—should be doubly suspicious of the "guaranteed target." In fact, trophy hunters must be particularly cautious when selecting an outfitter. Besides determining his reliability, they must be certain that he really knows a record-book head from a merely good head, an ability that normally requires immense experience. Often the difference between *very* good antlers and just a fair rack is almost imperceptible, and the greater the range, the harder it is to tell the difference. In rain or other conditions of poor visibility it could even be impossible.

Any sportsman's best bet is usually the outfitter who guarantees nothing except experience, good hunting country and to provide the best trip possible under whatever conditions are encountered. One of the very best trips this writer ever made was with an outfitter in Alberta whose spelling and grammar were not the greatest but who was a tremendously capable man in the field. His letter, in response to an inquiry, read as follows: "We live all yeer to get out with our hunters in the fall. We try to give them the gratest hunt they ever had. One way or other we see plenty game and get our share. Anyhow, all I can say is we feed our hunters good, give em good mountain horses to ride on and try like hell. The missus is sending you names of other hunters who has hunted with us the past few yeers."

The very best outfitters are almost always booked well in advance, sometimes even years ahead. It is therefore wise to plan well into the future, selecting a busy guide rather than one who has problems filling his calendar. Avoid hasty or last-minute arrangements whenever possible.

What can any hunter reasonably expect from a guide or outfitter?

Mostly—basically—it is knowledge of the game and especially of the hunting country. Depending on that country and on the arrangements made, it may also include lodging, meals and some sort of hunting transportation. Nowadays in much of the Western big-game region, the back country has been opened up by logging roads, fire access trails, or even by roads built for summertime recreation. Much of this is passable only to four-wheel-drive vehicles, and a lot of deer hunting—or at least penetrating into deer country—is done by driving these roads, then proceeding on foot or horseback. For this kind of hunting the guide, who may be a rancher guiding part-time, may provide lodging in his home or at a local motel. From there, client and guide go out on a day-to-day basis. But one fact cannot be over-emphasized: Long before the hunting begins, it should be determined in writing exactly what is furnished and what is not for whatever the cost. Is the guide to be paid by the day or by the package? When it's by the day, incentive is likely to be lost if there is a chance for the hunter to score early and depart for home, leaving the guide "unemployed." Even a perfectly honorable outfitter who feels he can find a suitable target quickly and easily may not do his best if he knows he will soon be out of work. Non-guarantee package hunts obviously are better for all concerned.

Normally an outfitter will require a deposit, sometimes for as little as 10 percent but more often for as high as 50 percent. In case a cancellation is necessary, he will return all or most of it if a replacement party can be arranged. The rest of the hunting charge is collected at the beginning of the hunt, an arrangement which may seem unorthodox to some, but that's the way it's done.

Good outfitters do not come cheap nowadays. An outfitter has problems which are unique to his profession, especially if he is active in pack-tripping sportsmen into mountain country. Specifically, he must feed a whole, sometimes large string of horses for an entire year just to operate during a short hunting season. Taking care of this livestock during the se-

Light aircraft can fly hunters to and from remote wilderness camps in many areas.

vere winters that are typical in Western hunting country is doubly expensive. Also, an outfitter must own and keep in good condition a vast array of saddles (both riding and pack), tacking, tenting, cooking gear, stoves, horseshoes and other items for constant use. Altogether, this represents a larger investment than many realize. Since the equipment gets very hard use, often in unfavorable weather, it is no easy task to keep it in perfect condition. A leaky tent on a brutal night in November cannot be risked.

A pack-trip outfitter can be expected to furnish everything except the hunter's personal gear—all but his sleeping bag, mattress (although the guide might also provide these on prior arrangement), clothing, rifle, ammo and other personal items. A rifle scabbard and saddle bags are items which the hunter may or may not bring himself. Food in a reliable outfitter's camp is nourishing, robust, normally plain and always ample. If a hunter cannot

Guide, here glassing for sheep, must be counted on to know country and quarry.

eat certain things or has unusual diet preferences, he should say so long before ever arriving in camp. Outfitters *want* to be successful in more ways than just bagging game and will go a long way toward achieving that end.

To be sure, outfitters are only human and they may unwittingly do things that irritate or even inconvenience clients. An occasional guide may be a show-off, especially of his own ability to climb into rough terrain far ahead of his hunter. That is very demoralizing. Bragging is another common bad habit and so is exaggeration. An outfitter would always be wise *never* to regale his current customer with tales of a previous hunt or with the exploits of favorite customers. This is definitely not a good way to keep the present client happy and it certainly will not result in much repeat business. Nowadays, with the number of permits and licenses being more and more limited, repeat business is critically important to most outfitters.

In many cases it is as important for an outfitter to be a good psychologist as it is to be expert with horses, camping and the habits of big game. The man who can encourage his hunter at the proper time and (if he is a neophyte) break him into the sport slowly and carefully, will be making the trip more pleasant for everyone concerned. It is very, very important to maintain a happy mood during a hunting trip, especially during trying periods of bad weather or when game seems to be scarce.

Any hunter also has his own moral responsibilities both to his outfitter and to fellow sportsmen on the adventure. The outfitter can in no way be blamed for unseasonable bad weather when all are confined to camp—although he does have an obligation to warn that the elements might be unfavorable during certain periods of the fall, with emphasis on late fall. Even the most conscientious, capable guide can make mistakes about the game. For instance, many elk hunts are planned to coincide with the rutting period so that bulls may be bugled into gun range. But unaccountably (nobody yet knows exactly why) the elk rut does *not* begin at the same time each fall, nor is the duration always the same. An outfitter, therefore, can only make his very best prediction and if he is wrong, he is not at fault.

It is too common to blame outfitters for a hunter's own shortcomings. As in the case of Fred Moore described in the beginning of this chapter far too many arrive in the West totally unfit to begin a rigorous hunt. Every outdoorsman should do his absolute best to be in good physical shape. For at least a month before beginning a mountain adventure, he should jog, bicycle, climb, exercise in every possible way. He should lose excess weight and, if possible, do at least a small amount of riding at a local stable to get his rear end toughened.

Also too often neglected is getting all hunting equipment into shape. It is astonishing that a hunter would spend so much money for a trip and then not bother to be familiar with the rifle he will use. Still, it is a common complaint of outfitters that many hunters appear with rifles they have seldom or never shot before. As strange as it may seem, hunters even arrive in camp with rifles and ammo that do not match!

Other common complaints of guides concern hunters who show up with cheap, inadequate sleeping bags and therefore cannot get the good

Successful hunt: Alberta guide-outfitter's three "dudes" took three trophy elk.

British Columbia guides lash trophies and meat aboard one of their pack horses.

night's sleep which is essential to any rugged hunt. Perhaps even a greater handicap is a pair of new boots which do not fit or are not thoroughly broken in. All these seemingly minor details may seem unimportant when planning a big-game hunt, but any one of them can prove to be the difference between success and failure.

If a man is a serious trophy hunter—looking for the rack or bear rug of a lifetime—every tiny detail of planning becomes even more important. Being able to scramble on top of a mountain just a little faster may be what is necessary to get into range of the fleeting target. Or a serene night's sleep may be all that is necessary to hunt longer, harder the next day. That makes the outfitter's job easier and he will do it better.

Big-game hunting nowadays is not inexpensive. It can be very

Camp cook jokes with hunters in New Mexico; happy, friendly mood is important.

costly—even exorbitant. In many Western states (if you can somehow obtain a license or permit) only hunting mule deer or antelope can be done on a budget. There are many outfitters who offer package three- to seven-day hunts for one or both of these at a fee ranging from $250 to, say, $600. Chances of scoring are very good and probably these hunts can be classed as fair bargains.

Generally speaking, it is necessary for a non-resident to undertake a pack trip into some remote area for the following big game: elk, moose, caribou, goat, any of the sheep, or grizzly bear. Pack-trip rates are constantly being revised—always upward.

As this is written, a week's pack trip in good elk country (with a chance at deer or black bear) in Alberta, Montana or Wyoming runs about

$450 to $500 with a good reliable outfitter. In northwestern Wyoming (which might be considered typical for elk) there is about 60 to 70 percent success on bulls, a fraction of which will truly be bragging size. Because all big-game animals are being harvested to the limit that the herd will stand, the average size of heads has slowly decreased in recent years.

The farther north a man hunts—say into the Yukon, Alaska and northern British Columbia—the more a pack trip costs, and it is unrealistic to figure at less than $200 minimum per person per day. Distance is one factor in the extra cost, and it is also harder to maintain a herd of horses in those latitudes where forage is scarce and/or very costly. On the average, the more hunters participate in a hunt, the lower will be the cost per individual, and vice versa. In most situations, two hunters go out with a single guide and that is also less expensive than for one man to one guide.

When planning a hunt, other factors than the outfitter must be considered. Air or other transportation to the hunting area is one. Add license fees, tips, and the sometimes considerable cost of shipping meat and trophies home. Normally the outfitter will handle meat and trophies as far as the nearest processing point. Beyond that it is the responsibility of the sportsman.

It wasn't too long ago that an American big-game hunter could venture northward and during a two- or three-week hunt bag four or five trophy heads. He could also be reasonably sure of having the hunting country to himself; each outfitter had a fairly large exclusive area. But those days are gradually disappearing and may be gone forever. For the approximate prices quoted above, a man who will hunt hard can figure on one, maybe two good trophies. Anything beyond is either great luck or, in some states, impossible.

Most of this has been confined to a discussion of outfitters who hunt in mountains on horses. But there are others to consider at least briefly. In Alaska, for example, many outfitters go after bears in southeastern coastal areas by boat. The client lives aboard the craft, which cruises into bays and estuaries looking for browns and grizzlies. When animals (or sign) are spotted, all hands go ashore and try to stalk the target. Success is moderate. Such package week to 10-day hunts for bears run from $1,500 to $3,500, depending on the region hunted, the duration and the number of hunters in the party.

Still other outfitters hunt by aircraft, although this is a dying practice. Planes are now outlawed for spotting or driving game or transporting a hunter directly to game. But an airplane is a perfectly legal means to deliver a sportsman into a camp located in remote game country. From there he hunts on foot. Outfitter prices for this service are so variable and even negotiable—depending on distance and location—that they cannot be adequately summarized.

In brief, then, outfitters are in business to stay as long as big-game hunting survives; most of them love the profession and want to be successful at it. To locate a good one is the means to some of the greatest adventures possible nowadays in the entire outdoor world.

5.
RIFLES FOR BIG GAME
by
Hal Swiggett

Fine pronghorn fell to .264 Winchester Magnum.

Rifles for big game, for animals ranging in weight from less than 100 pounds to three-quarters of a ton or better—that's a lot of territory. Can one rifle do it all? Normally it is said there is no such thing as an all-around rifle (meaning caliber). Undergunned on one end—overgunned on the other. This is true, without a doubt. But how serious is this undergunned, overgunned situation? I think the answer becomes clear in a discussion of the appropriate calibers and bullet weights for each kind of game.

Take bears, for instance. Is a rifle that's adequate for a two-year-old black, weighing 150 pounds more or less, completely outclassed when on an ice floe pointed at a three-quarter-ton monster white bear? The answer would have to be a resounding *yes*, wouldn't it? But a rifle that's adequate for a polar bear is obviously adequate for a black bear, so a compromise doesn't have to mean taking foolish chances.

Let's stick with these bears for a while. Blacks are the most common, and more often than not are killed incidentally by deer hunters. Most often "deer rifles" are listed as proper for this bear. I agree—but just what is a deer rifle? Here I think we are talking about calibers of .24 through .30, moving bullets weighing 100 to 150 grains at velocities ranging from 2900 through 3200 feet per second (fps). Some of the hot-rocks are even faster.

This covers a tremendous amount of country. The .24's (6mm if you prefer, as the bullets are all of this diameter) are certainly adequate for black bear if the heaviest bullets are used. This class of cartridges includes the .243 Winchester at 3070 fps, 6mm Remington at 3190 fps and .240 Weatherby at 3395 fps. To me these are minimal cartridges, but capable if good solid hits are possible.

Better by far is the popular .25-06 Remington. Heaviest bullets for this caliber weigh in at 120 grains, as opposed to 100 grains tops for 6mm factory-loaded cartridges. Add to this their velocity of 3120 fps and you get over a ton in foot-pounds of energy at 100 yards. And here lies a fairly good rule of thumb: To be a good deer cartridge the bullet should deliver a minimum of 2000 foot-pounds of energy (fpe) at the muzzle. This also qualifies it for game of similar size, including black bears. The .243 starts at 2090 fpe, the .25-06 at 2590 fpe.

Next up the ladder of calibers comes the 6.5 Remington Magnum and the .264 Winchester Magnum. These employ the same bullet diameter. Only the case size is different. Either one is an excellent black-bear caliber with the heavier factory loadings—meaning 120-grain bullets in the 6.5 Remington Magnum at 2780 fpe, and 140-grain bullets in the .264 Winchester Magnum at 3180 fpe.

Rifles chambered for the .270 Winchester cartridge have taken game all over the world. The most popular bullet weight is 130 grains, traveling at 3140 fps and developing 2840 fpe. For reasons hard to fathom, this caliber-and-bullet combination does a marvelous job on anything from varmints to moose or elk. Needless to say, it turns black bears into dead black bears rather easily.

Next we come to caliber .284—which includes the .280's, .284's and 7mm's, all having the same bullet diameter. This caliber borders on the "all-around" so far as big-game rifles are concerned. The group includes the ever-popular 7mm Remington Magnum, which has caused the downfall of many fine calibers. With factory loads featuring bullets from 125 grains to 175 grains, the 7mm Remington Magnum is truly a "flat-shooting," devastating cartridge, capable of most any task it might be asked to perform with its 3070 fps developing 3660 fpe when firing 175-grain bullets.

Caliber .30 covers everything from the miniscule .30 Carbine, which shouldn't be used on any game animal (it develops only 955 fpe directly under the front sight) to the .300 Weatherby and .308 Norma Magnum with more than two tons of muzzle energy. Most often thought of as caliber .30 is the time-honored .30-06 Springfield. Bullet weights in over-the-counter ammunition run from 110 grains (3370 fps) to 220 grains (2410 fps). Thus the .30-06 can handle all sorts of targets, from varmints up, with ease. Using 150- or 180-grain bullets, it's a top-drawer bear killer at more than 2900 foot-pounds of muzzle energy.

The venerable .30-30 also merits discussion here. Cussed by most as totally inadequate, this old lever-gun cartridge goes right on killing game— including deer and bears—year after year. Out to 150 yards it will hold its own with any of them in spite of the rock-bottom rating given it by many writers. My suggestion, for what it's worth, is to use only 170-grain bullets. This is the weight that made the cartridge famous. There is a newer 150-

grain loading, but the velocity increase isn't enough to warrant its use. The extra weight is more valuable than the minimal increase in speed.

Older calibers well qualified for use on black bears are the 7mm Mauser (7x57), .300 Savage, .30 Remington, .32 Winchester Special, .32 Remington, 8mm Mauser (8x57), .348 Winchester and .35 Remington.

Then there is that category of big-bore, low-velocity cartridges designed specifically for close-range work with big game. This group includes the .44 Remington Magnum, .444 Marlin and the revitalized .45-70. All are well suited to the taking of black bear.

Before we go on up to the bigger bears, let's talk a bit about rifles. The style of action is entirely up to the hunter. More bolt-action rifles are in use than all others combined. There are several reasons, such as accuracy, strength and ruggedness.

Be that as it may, those preferring lever-guns and choosing an adequate caliber for the game at hand will bag just as much game just as efficiently. Same goes for autoloader fans and pump-gun fanciers. It's still the man behind the gun more than the gun itself that fills freezers with wild meat. Lever, pump and autoloading guns are limited to calibers up to .308 and .30-06 except for those self loaders of Browning persuasion which are available in some of the big calibers.

Personally, I consider autoloading rifles exceptionally dangerous. I can see no need whatever for this action in a sporting rifle and make it a point never to hunt where one is being used. (This includes shying away from "paying hunters" in my capacity as a guide.) On two occasions during recent years, I've been blessed with auto-toting hunters. Each time I removed the clip and carried it in my pocket. This is strictly a personal opinion. If you like autoloaders and have friends willing to tolerate them, fine. Just don't bring one into my camp.

I'm not sure but what we would all be better off reverting back to single-shot rifles. There are some fine ones offered nowadays and it's still the single, well-placed bullet that kills game.

Rifles for big-game hunting should be relatively light in weight; not necessarily featherweight but definitely not of the heavy-barreled "varmint" type. A typical bolt-action rifle will weigh about eight pounds. Some are half

On muley hunt, Hal Swiggett's son Gerald steadies .270 mounted with 4X scope.

a pound lighter and some likewise heavier. Add to this the weight of a scope, bases and rings, and the eight-pound rifle suddenly becomes a nine-pounder plus. A sling adds more weight, the fully loaded magazine still more poundage. Every half-pound seems like five when climbing a mountain and that seems to double near the end of a long day. If the total weight of rifle, scope, mounts, sling and cartridges can be kept close to 10 pounds, you've done a good job.

On this tack, don't get carried away with the ancient "long-barrels-shoot-harder" adage. Barrels of no more than 24 inches are all that's needed and even better are 22-inch barrels in many calibers. These shorter barrels are easier to handle in brush or on horseback, and they swing faster, which means getting on target a moment sooner, and they're equally accurate.

Loss of velocity is so infinitesimal as to go unnoticed by either the shooter or the animal being shot at.

Accuracy! First, what is it? Gun magazines rave over one-inch or tighter groups, many more of which are shot with typewriters than rifles, after special loads have been worked up and barrels and actions rebedded. Any rifle shooting 1½- or two-inch groups is doing its job well so far as big-game hunting is concerned; a miss out to as far as any of us ought to be trying can't be blamed on the rifle. It's us, the men behind those rifles, who did the missing.

Black bears weigh up to 500 pounds but more often than not the bears killed will comfortably fit in the 250- to 350-pound category. Grizzly bears, adult males, will average about 500 pounds and can weigh up to twice that, though 800 pounds would be considered a big bear. Every pound is mean. Same goes for big Alaska brown bears. They will average about 800 pounds and they are definitely not noted for being mild of temper. Moreover, it's possible to run into a brown that will tip the scales at 1,500 pounds or more. This is an awful lot of mad if he is only wounded. Polar bears average still larger, with 1,500-pound males not being at all rare.

Needless to say, only rifles of a caliber speaking with great authority should be used on any of these three bears. Caliber .30-06 Springfield with 180- to 220-grain bullets, or the 7mm Remington Magnum with 175-grain bullets, should be considered minimum. The .300 Weatherby Mag, .300 Winchester Mag, .308 Norma Mag or .300 H&H Mag, using bullets of at least 180 grains, are all in the realm of reality with these animals. If there is truly a place for the .338 Winchester Mag or the .375 H&H Mag on this continent, it would be where these bears are hunted. (I didn't say there *was* a place; I only said *if.*)

These animals not only can but will fight back if given the slightest opportunity. Take no chances. Use all the rifle at your disposal. Heart and lung shots are best for most hunting, but where these maulers are concerned concentrate on breaking them down in the shoulders and getting them stopped. Killing, if more should be necessary, can be done after that. Otherwise you might end up as a bear banquet.

Sure, I know all about big bears being killed with little rifles. Specifically I know about five polar bears being killed a good many years ago with .243 factory 100-grain loads: two each by a man and his wife, on separate hunts, and one by a third party unknown to the couple. These were in the category of stunts, certainly not feats to be recommended.

I also saw a black bear being "killed" with a .22 rimfire. This, too, was a good many years ago. The bear was in a trap and the rancher had only a .22 pump-action rifle stuffed with Long Rifle hollow-points. Thinking it would be a simple matter, he pumped a couple toward the base of the ear. This had no apparent effect other than making the bear angry. The rancher knew he needed more gun but the affair was started so he pumped the remainder of the magazine into the chest at a distance of 10 feet. The bear finally gave up but it was a miserable, pitiful sight, and the rancher hasn't been out without his .30-30 since that day. He wants no repeats.

Probably the smallest animal ever included in any discussion of "big game" in North America is the collared peccary, or javelina, of the Southwest. There's nothing big about him except perhaps his novelty to hunters from other parts of the country. This little wild pig-like animal weighs up to 50 pounds but normally averages nearer 35 to 40. He appears vicious but isn't, and he doesn't take much killing. The .243 category of rifles is ideal. Shots can be from as long as you want to try, or right off the muzzle. I've seen them killed with about everything from .22 handguns and a single-shot .410 shotgun to a .300 Weatherby. The .30-30 makes a fine javelina rifle, as does any comparable caliber.

One point of minor argument here: It's often said these animals aren't fit to eat so any bullet or shot will do. This may be more or less true of old javelina boars but half-grown pigs, say up to 25 pounds, make mighty fine eating, so don't waste a lot of meat with a careless shot or an overly destructive bullet. Field dress the animal immediately, being careful to remove the musk gland located on the rump.

In terms of size the pronghorn antelope is next on the list. Mature bucks weigh around 80 pounds with an occasional one going to 100. These animals aren't hard to kill in spite of what you might have heard or read. Their eyesight is phenomenal; it is said to equal that of a man with 8X binoculars. As a result, long shots are the rule and modern, flat-shooting calibers really come into play. Though many are killed at 100 to 150 yards, I'd have to say 200 or 250 would be more average. A great many are shot at 300 yards, a few out to 500 and, yes, even an occasional one at 600 yards.

My favorite calibers are the .25-06 Remington and .270 Winchester. For the .25-06 I'll take 120-grain bullets, and for the .270 I like 130-grain bullets. The .264 Winchester Mag with 140-grain bullets is an ideal prong-horn combo. Bullets weighing 150 grains in .308 Winchester or .30-06 Springfield are also good. The big .30 Magnums are too much gun, and the .30-30 is disqualified by its rainbow trajectory beyond 150 yards. On the lower end, any of the earlier-mentioned 6mm calibers will perform adequately with 100-grain bullets. More than any other game animal, I consider the pronghorn a real test of rifle and rifleman.

Deer (and here we're going to be all-inclusive) are this continent's Number One "big-game" animal. There is one species or another in every state. Conditions and terrain vary so much that there can be no "best" deer rifle. Whitetails in the East have always been considered prime game for pump-action, or lever-action autoloading rifles. Often with open sights yet! Exactly why has never been made clear to me. I've hunted deer in thick cover throughout much of the country and have never felt at all handicapped with a scope mounted on my bolt-action rifle. I use the same rifle, by the way, for open-country deer hunting.

To each his own, but common sense will tell you scopes are easier to hit with once their use has been mastered. Therein lies the secret. Stick to either a low magnification fixed-power scope or a low to medium variable-powered glass. I'm a variable man myself, except for the scopes I mount on a few special-purpose rifles.

A scope for thick cover shouldn't exceed 2.5X and probably a better choice for the inexperienced would be 1.5X. A variable starting at 1.5X or 2X is ideal. With the scope on its lowest setting, practice throwing the rifle to your shoulder while intently looking at the target. Keep both eyes open. Soon you'll discover you are looking right through the scope at the target. Once you've become proficient in the use of telescopic sights, you will never again go afield without one. In failing light where open sights are guesswork at best, a good scope allows precise bullet placement. Try to

Hal Swiggett has used .308 on huge Idaho black bear and little Texas javelina.

Dr. Gerald Swiggett, glassing for deer, has slung .270 he likes for open country.

settle a bead into a notched rear sight at dusk, then look at the same target through a good scope. It's no contest.

But back to rifles for deer. Lever guns are popular throughout the Southwest—and some other regions, too. Many a man will tell you it was good enough for his granddad, so it's good enough for him. And for these hunters it probably is all that's needed.

Whitetails, in my opinion, are much harder to knock down and make stay down than mule deer. I'm of the firm opinion that you should use nothing smaller than the 6mm's—meaning the .243 Winchester, 6mm Remington and .240 Weatherby. And proper bullets are crucial.

In my home state of Texas, the hill-country whitetails weigh in at 75 to 100 pounds soaking wet. Deer this size are made to order for 85- or 90-grain bullets in 6mm. The 100-grain bullets are designed for heavier animals and often fail to expand on these little deer, resulting in a wounded animal all too often lost. Mule deer and big whitetails require bigger bullets to do them in properly.

Everything said about calibers for the black bear holds true here—except the heavy bullets in 7mm Remington Mag and .30-06. I feel that 150-grain bullets are better suited for even the largest mule deer in these calibers. Again, the heavier bullets are designed for still heavier game and often won't expand sufficiently on deer. None of the big .30 Magnums is needed on any deer hunt.

Open country, offering long shots, demands the use of a flat-shooting, long-range rifle which reduces the need for precise estimation of range—a feat at which many of us aren't overly competent at best. A rifle that allows point-blank holding out to 300 yards takes the "guesstimation" away and makes killing shots much more certain. This is why I recommend calibers in the 3000 fps category rather than older but slower chamberings.

Deer hunting covers more varied terrain than any other. A rifle or caliber suited to one area might be deemed totally inadequate in another. All the same, a man carrying a 22- to 24-inch-barreled bolt-action rifle chambered in .270 or .30-06 and topped with a 2.5X or 4X fixed or 2X-7X variable scope—well, if he knows how to use it, he will make a creditable showing, wherever he is.

Vernon Swiggett smiles over 11-point whitetail taken with .308; scope is 4X.

This means in the wooded East, semi-open Southwest or the wide open areas of our Western states. Mule-deer hunting can "stretch the barrel" of any rifle if the hunter allows it to happen. On the other hand, I've seen some awfully fast snap-shooting in mule-deer country. On a recent hunt in northeastern New Mexico, a friend and I were working out of the same camp. We each had a guide. His deer was killed at 40 yards with a really fast second shot after missing the first with a bolt-action .30-06. Mine, taken the same morning with the same make and caliber of rifle, was at a conservative 300 yards, according to my guide (I'm not talking). Both scopes were 3X-9X variables. Mine was set on 6X, his on 3X.

On another occasion a member of my party broke a firing pin in his bolt-action .30-06. The only extra rifle in camp was my lightweight .243 topped with a 2½X-8X variable. We were in big mule-deer country, and I suggested he hold shots to no more than 200 yards with the factory-loaded 100-grain bullets. He came in that evening with an ear-to-ear grin and a huge muley buck dropped, according to his guide, at over 350 yards with a single shot. I wouldn't have thought it was likely, but they said it happened. Which proves that anything can happen.

Shotguns are musts in some states. A good many others allow the use of smoothbores for big game, mostly deer and bear. Rifled slugs are deadly out to as far as it is practical to try for a deer in the brushy or wooded country where slugs are mostly used. The majority of single-barrel guns (single-shot, pump or autoloader) can be rigged with suitable sights, making the guns fairly practical out to maybe 75 yards. Accuracy is not outstanding, and beyond this distance it's strictly guesswork. A few companies turn out special barrels for their shotguns with regular rifle sights. These, obviously, should do a good job.

Unfortunately, far too many states (25, I believe) still allow the use of buckshot for deer and bear. In a few places it's actually required by law! Buckshot has to be the greatest crippler of all time. It also ranks as one of the most dangerous loads insofar as nearby hunters are concerned. I've never recommended buckshot for any purpose and can only sympathize with those who are forced to use it. My only suggestion is, get close, no more than 35 yards, and pray the good Lord intends for you to eat that venison.

Mountain goats and sheep in most regions weigh 200 to 300 pounds. Shots can be long but a good guide will see to it that you get close enough for a clean kill if you do what you are told. From my experience, both in hunting and talking to guides and hunters, few shots need to be more than 250 yards. There are exceptions but for every longer shot several shorter ones will be offered. The same calibers used on the bigger deer are ideal on goats and sheep—primarily the .270 with 130-grain bullets, .308 or .30-06 with 150-grain bullets or the 7mm Mag with 150-grain bullets. The .264 Winchester Mag and its 140-grain bullet fits beautifully here, too.

Caribou are a little bigger. Weight varies among the three varieties of caribou, but most bulls will be in the 300- to 600-pound category. One of the rifles for big deer is all that's needed here.

Wapiti—elk if you prefer—are big, tough animals. I've seen them killed at 40 yards and seen them dropped at nearly 600 yards. A big bull can weigh half a ton, according to many authorities, but I must confess I've never seen one I thought would go over 750 or 800 pounds. Every pound must be killed, however, as these great animals don't know the meaning of "give up." Besides, they are normally found in extremely rugged country where a wounded animal is easily lost. Still, they are flesh and blood. They die when hit properly, the same as any other animal.

I think probably more nonsense has been written regarding the calibers necessary to drop an elk than has been written concerning all other animals combined. There is one group who would have you believe that anything smaller than a .338 Winchester Magnum with 250-grain bullets is foolhardy. Then there is another group, far larger, claiming that any good 150- to 180-grain bullet through the heart or lungs is all that's needed—and it's to this group I pay my dues. Though a .270 with 130-grain bullets is light, I'd much rather see a hunter seeking his trophy with that than with a .300 Weatherby or .338 Winchester Mag that he's scared to death of. It's hard to place a bullet well when you have both eyes closed and your chin tucked down close to the chest—the typical flinch. If a man has time to learn to use the big Magnums I'm on his side. If he's fond of personal punishment he can go on up to a .375 H&H or one of the comparable Weatherby's. Otherwise he's far better off with a lighter rifle he can shoot well.

Bucks in cover like this demand low-power scope or variable turned to low setting.

The ideal elk cartridge, so far as I'm concerned, is a .270 with 150-or 160-grain bullets, a .308 or .30-06 with 180-grain bullets or a 7mm Mag with 175-grain bullets. Needless to say, any of the big .30 Mags with 180-grain bullets will be deadly, but only if they can be handled by the shooter.

Some time back I made a quick survey of old-time elk guides, six of them, in four states—men with 25 to 40 years of experience guiding elk hunters for pay. Not a single one mentioned any caliber heavier than .30-06, though one admitted to using a .300 Weatherby to anchor cripples (most of which, he said, were put in that condition by hunters trying to kill game with more gun than they could handle). Among these six experienced guides, six different calibers were used: a .30-06, .270, 7x61 Sharpe and Hart, .30-40 Krag, 6.5mm Gibbs and the aforementioned .300 Weatherby.

Far too much emphasis has been placed on sheer power. Good hits are still what counts most. The 7x61 user told me it didn't make any difference what caliber his client carried, so long as he could hit with it. One of the others said he had no objection to calibers up to and including 7mm Magnum. The remainder specifically mentioned only .270 or .30-06. The professional hunting experience of these men, some 190 years altogether, is worth thinking about.

Moose are monsters; I don't know any other way to say it. The Canadian variety stand six feet or better at the withers and weigh upward of half a ton. Alaskan animals are bigger. But, again, they are blood and flesh. A well-placed bullet designed to go deep, where the animal lives, is all that's necessary. Here again we come to the .270 Winchester with 150-grain bullets for factory-ammo shooters and 160-grain Noslers for handloaders; Remington's 7mm Magnum with 175-grain bullets, .308 or .30-06 with 180- or 220-grain bullets. Any of the .30 Mags are, of course, suitable with 180-grain, or heavier, bullets. The older .35 Remington, .35 Whelen, and the current .444 Marlin do an excellent job out to around 150 yards. Even the huge 405-grain bullet lumbering along at barely more than 1300 fps from one of the currently popular .45-70's is good moose medicine at reasonable range. This big, flat-nosed bullet hits with astounding authority, then pushes through whatever gets in the way. It kills through sheer weight; velocity not needed here, thank you.

I have a friend who has taken several moose over the years as well as elk and mule deer annually. He uses a handloaded .243 with 105-grain bullets for deer and elk, then moves on up to his "big" rifle for moose. It's an ancient 7x57 Mauser shooting handloaded 160-grain bullets. Proving once again that it's the man behind the gun that counts most.

Personally I often favor lung shots—high lung shots, to be specific— for anything except big bears or elk in really rough country. These two require stopping, and to do this takes bone-crushing shots. I can't prove it but am thoroughly convinced that animals die faster from shots high through the lungs than lower down.

Heart shots are, of course, deadly but harder to pull off. Unless the animal is standing exactly right it means going through the large leg bone, which is easy with heavy bullets but not so easy with the lighter ones.

To me head shots are the worst. Trophy hunters can't use them and meat hunters shouldn't. If hit squarely in the head, any animal of deer size, or close to it, is going to drop in its tracks. On the other hand, it's very easy to miss the head and shoot off the lower jaw. When this happens, more often than not, the shooter thinks he missed as the animal seldom shows any reaction to the hit and runs off to die a slow, miserable death from starvation. A wound such as this bleeds very little. Neck shots are almost as bad. Unless the spinal column is hit, you can have a wounded animal. The farthest I ever helped trail a deer was when a buck was improperly shot in the neck with a .270. (The caliber makes no difference, any other would have had the same effect.) The shot was low. The spinal column was not touched. The deer went over a mile.

Lungs are the biggest target on any animal. With a punctured lung, no animal can go far. Little meat—in fact, none—is destroyed. I encourage all my hunters to shoot for this spot. To me the choice location is directly over the shoulder, actually through the top of the shoulder blade. Here the bullet gets the top half of the lungs perfectly. A high shot will hit the spine, and a low shot will hit the heart. How can you do better?

To place bullets precisely in this manner requires good sights, which means a scope. Though 4X magnification is considered "all-around" I'm not really sure it's best. Being partial to variable scopes for big-game rifles, I think it is very hard to do better than one of the 1.5X-4 or 4.5X types. Seldom is more than 4X needed, and often, in heavy cover or extremely low light conditions such as at daylight or dusk, a lesser power serves far better.

My biggest black bear came right at dark. I was shooting a Model 660 Remington .308 with handloaded 180-grain bullets. The rifle was topped with Weaver's 1.5X-4.5X variable scope. As daylight disappeared I had unconsciously turned the magnification down. As you know, lower power gives greater light-gathering quality. When the shot presented itself, at 40 yards, I had the scope on 1.5X and placed the big bullet through the shoulder and heart. A 4X here would have been disastrous.

As experience increases, shooters tend to go to higher-powered glassware. My personal choice is 6X for a great deal of my hunting and my two fixed-power scopes are of this magnification. (I'm not counting a couple of 8X's and one 10X on varmint rifles.) Let me point out, though, that these 6X scopes are on special-purpose, long-range big-bore rifles.

My .375 H&H wears a 1.5-4X. One .308 and one .30-06 are similarly outfitted. The others are all either 2X-7X, which is probably the true ideal, or 3X-9X. More often than not they are set on 4X or, at the most, 6X. Never more. The reason for variables is to get the *lower* magnification when it's needed.

Reticles in scopes are the user's choice, naturally, but I firmly believe the best hunting reticle ever devised is the one known as Dual-X, Duplex, 4-Plex or Multi-X, depending on the manufacturer. This is the reticle featuring a wide crosshair on the outer edge tapering to a fine crosshair in the center. It's perfect for precise shooting at long range, yet easy to see on running shots, heaven forbid, or in failing light. The secret with this reticle is to ignore the fine center crosshairs when pinched for time or light and use the coarse edges as a "peep sight." The eye automatically centers an object, so squeeze the trigger and quit worrying. Post reticles are favored by many for early and late shooting, but I believe this new tapered crosshair far outclasses it and will eventually become the only one in use on hunting rifles.

Often someone complains of not being able to find his target in a scope. All that's necessary is a little practice. Place the rifle against your shoulder, then snuggle your head against the stock into whatever position it

Guide leads pack string bearing big elk trophy taken by .300 Weatherby Magnum.

takes to get a full scope picture. Wiggle around a bit to make sure it's not only the right position but the most comfortable. Now, memorize this position. Practice until you get it automatically. This is the important part. Know exactly where your head has to be to place your eye in line with the scope. The rest is simple. As the rifle is brought to the shoulder the head is leaned into position so that when the stock touches the shoulder the cheek is in place on the stock and you are ready to shoot instantly. You can do all this without ever taking your eyes off the target—nothing complicated about it.

A sling is a necessary piece of equipment, especially for mountain hunting. It lets the rifle hang over a shoulder, freeing both hands for climbing. It also allows that same freedom for dragging out game. A sling can also be a great aid to a steady position when no rest is available. This use is generally referred to as a "hasty sling." You place the elbow of your gun-holding arm between the sling and the rifle; by swinging the elbow out against the sling you'll tighten it against the back of the upper arm, offering a rather steady position.

A rest should be utilized whenever one is available, whether it's a stump, post, tree, rock with hat or jacket thrown over it—or whatever. Lacking any of these, I'll go to a solid sitting position unless there is too much ground cover. It's at this time the hasty sling is brought into use, and it can also be used to good advantage in the sitting position.

If I had my "druthers," no shot would ever be fired at running game. I know it's done successfully. I've done it myself, many times. I'd still prefer it not to happen. It's a last-resort sort of thing so far as I'm concerned. Same goes for rear-end shots or extreme-angle shots that make the paunch better than an even bet to be hit. Unless it's a real honest-to-goodness trophy, let the animal go. You won't be sorry. Gut-shot animals can go a long way and be awfully hard to find. Since they seldom die quickly they have time to hide. Also, they seldom leave a good trail to follow. It's best not to shoot unless a good open chest shot is offered.

Heart-shot animals often take off in what I usually describe as a dead run. The animal is dead on its feet. Normally the speed is greater than that of a scared but missed animal. On occasion a lung-shot animal will react about the same way. In either case the animal won't be far away—usually from 40 to 100 yards.

I think it's best to give wounded game time to lie down before starting after it. The only exception would be an animal shot at dusk. Move slowly. Search every hiding place ahead for any possible movement—the flick of an ear or an eye. Be ready to shoot instantly. This is the only time I'll agree to rear-end or extreme-angle shots. Get another bullet into the animal any way you can.

Assume every animal shot at is hit until you have thoroughly checked the area. This is particularly important in cover so thick the animal can't be seen after the shot, and it also applies to deer topping ridges. It's easy to lose sight of the target in a scope during recoil and not know for sure whether a hit was made or not. The assumption has to be that the shot was good until you know for sure it wasn't.

Many times there will be no indication of a hit where the animal was standing, as it takes a few seconds for blood to start draining. If there's no blood in 50 yards or so, chances are no hit. Sometimes a bit of hair or shattered bone will be found. This demands a thorough search for a blood trail. If none is located in 100 yards, chances are the animal was only nicked. If an animal is worth shooting at it is worth a diligent effort to prove the shot was either good or a miss. A real hunter accepts this obligation every time he fires the shot.

To get maximum performance out of your rifle, sight it in about three inches high at 100 yards. This will provide the optimum trajectory for hits at the longest possible range with no hold-over. After assuring yourself the sights are set properly at 100 yards, shoot groups at 200 and 300 yards to confirm the point of impact at those distances. Your bullets should not hit over four inches high, 4½ at most, at 200 yards. This should place them only slightly low at 300 yards. This is a generality but it will serve well with most rifles having a velocity of 3000 to 3200 fps. Since each rifle is a law unto itself, make sure where yours is hitting.

A sight setting such as this allows point-blank holding on game out to 300 yards. Hold low on the chest if the target is close, high on the chest if it is near the limit. A 400-yard shot is possible by placing the horizontal cross-hair directly on top of the back in most cases. Few of us are good enough to try beyond this range, so unless you are competent and have proved it by lots of practice, be fair to the animal and yourself by letting it walk off.

Way back at the beginning I said there was no such thing as a "perfect all-around" caliber. Technically, I think I was right. But if one were to buy a good bolt-action rifle chambered for the .270 Winchester, .30-06 Springfield or 7mm Remington Magnum, then firmly plant a good-quality 2X-7X variable scope on top, he could go through a lifetime of big-game hunting without ever finding out that he didn't own "the perfect all-around" rifle.

6.
ADDITIONAL
EQUIPMENT

Author's favorite scabbard is shown in position.

A few years ago I made a hunt with friends in desert terrain, and we met another pair of hunters on the trail. They were coming out. One of them was in extreme discomfort. He had slipped and fallen against a big prickly-pear cactus. Occasionally a cartoon shows this as a comic episode. It isn't the least bit funny. The big spines can be pulled out easily, but the thousands of hair-fine ones require special technique, and they are agonizing.

Every movement caused the injured man such pain in hip, leg and arm that he'd finally suggested calling a halt to the hunt so that he could get to a doctor. His friend had tried to pull the spines with a knife blade but had only succeeded in breaking off many of them. I noticed that both of these hunters had beautiful, hand-crafted, well-scoped rifles, but neither had packed a couple of valuable little items that were in my own duffle—a small magnifying glass and a pair of tweezers. The moral, of course, is that any big-game hunter should select *all* of his gear with great care, and with special consideration for the kind of country he will be hunting.

Almost as important as the rifle and scope is the binocular. I know some hunters who do not use a binocular, but I try to avoid hunting with them. A few claim they are so sharp-eyed they have little use for a glass, which is preposterous. Others, worse yet, use their rifle scope as a stand-in for a binocular. This means they wave the rifle around, a good way to spook game and also a good way to find yourself aiming at another hunter. There might be a few hunters who'd highly resent being glassed through a scope, and who, if they noticed someone aiming at them, might do something uncivilized about it. But the best argument against using a scope to look for game is that you cannot see as well with one eye as with two.

At least 90 percent of the hunting endeavor consists of looking. A binocular extends the range of your vision, and it gathers light to allow you to see into dark places, such as the edge of a woods, that would otherwise appear blank. Particularly when hunting game such as sheep, which blend well with their surroundings, glassing with a binocular is the biggest part of the hunt. It should never be done standing up on a ridge, regardless of species hunted. Every animal within two long rifle ranges would see a hunter who was so incautious. The best way in mountain country is to get up high and glass across and also down. All big-game animals see much better down-slope than up. This reminds me that where I live and in many other areas, tree blinds are common for deer hunting. Deer seldom look up, and the same applies to all big game.

Using a glass doesn't mean a single quick sweep of ridge or valley. It means long, meticulous study. I've stared long at distant pale rocks lying on a gentle slope on the plains and had them finally turn into antelope. And I have studied black upturned roots and dirt from a large tree blown down on a lakeshore and confirmed it from across the lake as just that, then picked up another blow-down that suddenly came through as a moose.

There are all sorts of binoculars on the market, and quite a few varying opinions about them. A friend of mine amuses me because he carries a tiny tricked-up binocular that fits in his shirt pocket. He says he just doesn't want to be bothered with a full-sized glass dangling from his neck. He never can see anything through his miniature binocular, and whenever I get looking at an animal he wants to borrow mine. Cheap glasses and miniatures, in my opinion, are just good for one thing—throwing away. A quality glass costs a substantial amount of money. But it is a lifetime piece of equipment.

The size of the binocular is important, and is related to what you will hunt. But some compromises have to be made to keep down weight and bulk. A 6x30 glass is a bit too small for most use. A standard glass probably carried by more hunters than any other is the 7x35. In a lightweight model this glass serves very well for almost all hunting, and it is compact enough and not tiring to wear. Today a number of wide-angle binoculars are available. I used an 8x35 wide-angle one season and found it excellent, although a bit bulky. Forget about the huge, heavy, high-powered models such as the Navy uses. They're just too much glass for a hunter to carry and to use.

A good many sheep, goat and antelope hunters like a 9x35 glass. This gives higher magnification, which is very useful in studying or searching for distant animals. This glass is generally longer than the 7x35 but in lightweight models does not weigh much more. It is something of a special-purpose binocular, however, and I would not recommend it for all-round hunting use.

I would suggest that anyone who has never owned a binocular should get one with individual focus on each eyepiece. Center-focus glasses are operated by focusing at the center for one eye and then focusing the other eye separately at the eyepiece. This has always seemed to me an awkward idea. Further, individual-focus eyepieces are marked in plus and minus (-1, $+1$, $+2$ etc.). When you find the proper focus for each of your eyes, you simply memorize the combination. Then if someone else picks up your glass and changes focus, or when you take it out of the case to begin hunting, you can instantly make the eyepiece setting.

If you wear eyeglasses, it is possible to purchase binoculars with eyepiece rims that quickly screw in and out. These are especially designed for wearers of eyeglasses. When the rims are screwed in, you can get as close to the eyepiece lenses with your glasses on as you need to in order to see a full field. Instead of these threaded rims, some models have rubber eyepiece rims that fold back for use with eyeglasses. Both designs work.

All binoculars come with the strap about twice as long as it should be. For some reason many hunters seem to believe they have to leave them that way. Consequently, they walk along with the glass hanging at belly level, bouncing and swinging. Your strap should be just long enough so the glass rests against your chest. It is easy to reach there. It can be zipped or buttoned partly under a jacket, and it won't flop around much. It will when you bend over, but you can buy a leather holder that straps around low on the chest and into which the glass can be set.

Years ago I hatched a simple and more economical idea for holding glasses in place. It is a length of ordinary half-inch (or less) black elastic, a little longer than enough to go around your chest when you wear a light shirt. Hooks and eyes are sewn to the ends. One of these is set at proper fit, not really snug, with the lightweight shirt, and another is set to fit when you wear a heavy wool shirt. The elastic is run around the center spoke of the binocular, then pulled around the chest and hooked. The glass rides snugly against your chest, yet the stretch allows you to lift it and look through it.

In addition to a quality binocular, any trophy hunter should have a spotting scope. Not many deer hunters ever use them, although hunters after exceptional mule-deer heads might well do so. For elk, caribou and moose in terrain where they can be seen distantly, a spotting scope can save

Good binocular is almost as important as rifle and scope; most popular is 7x35.

a lot of effort that might otherwise be wasted in stalking closer to an animal that isn't good enough but looks as if it might be through the lower-powered binocular. For goat and sheep hunters, a spotting scope is practically mandatory, and for antelope hunters after a really good head it is invaluable.

The purpose of a spotting scope is not to glass an expanse of country, but to study distant animals at close range after they have been located with a binocular. Modern spotting scopes are light in weight and of excellent optical quality. A few hunters try to use a spotting scope by steadying it over a log or rock. Because of the scope's high powers of magnification, this is not steady enough. The scope should be equipped with a small folding tripod. Scope and tripod are carried as a rule in a backpack or rucksack.

There are several types of spotting scopes. Magnification runs from 15X all the way up to 60X. Some have interchangeable eyepieces for changes of magnification. Some use a turret-type eyepiece to give several magnifications. There are also zoom types on which you turn a knob and zoom over a variable magnification, as from 15X to 60X. Some of these work well, but at high magnifications the field of view is exceedingly small. It's difficult even to find the animal in the scope. Absolute steadiness is required and cannot always be achieved. Haze and mirage sometimes wipe out the view. The best compromise is a spotting scope of from 20X to 25X. It will allow you to accurately appraise heads at least a mile away.

There are many items of equipment about which individuals may legitimately have differing opinions. For example, cases. I carry my binocular in the leather case that came with it. En route, regardless of means of travel, this goes into my canvas duffle bag. Of course, air travel has changed views on how to transport gear. A good idea for cushioning a spotting scope during any kind of rough travel, and especially by air, is the tough plastic or metal case, foam-padded, which is too bulky to go into your personal duffle. I even carry my cameras everywhere in one. On most trips I carry three cameras in a tough plastic foam-lined case, the foam cut to fit each camera and lens, and with a place for a supply of film for an average day.

Foam-lined plastic or aluminum gun cases are standard nowadays when rifles must be shipped. Personally, I dislike using them when I go by car, but they give top protection for gun and scope, regardless of transport. Some very excellent pliable gun cases of more traditional design are available. Some have rugged material to surround the scope, and most have soft protective lining. I would advise buying a quality case. Cheap ones are not much account, and protecting a rifle in travel is extremely important. Remember, however, not to leave your gun in a zipped-up case that has a thick, soft lining and a plastic exterior. The slightest dampness that seeps in or is on the gun when it is put away can rust it.

One of my favorite gun cases is of quality leather, and it is unlined. Actually it was designed both as a carrying case and as a zip-up saddle scabbard. Straps are attached so it can be used either way. The leather is thick and firm and a gun can take quite a lot of banging around without any harm. When it's used as a scabbard, with the top zipped closed, the gun is fully protected.

If you will hunt on horseback for elk, sheep, moose, goats or caribou, you should think about acquiring a quality scabbard. Some moves are being made in the industry to fashion formed hard-plastic scabbards that are shaped

On some trophy hunts, spotting scope is vital; best magnification is 20 to 25X.

to take a rifle and scope. One I've seen recently has a top half that fits on as a kind of cap. Certainly a gun can be safely transported in such a boot, and it can be fitted onto a four-wheel-drive vehicle or a motorbike (if anyone *must* hunt from a bike, which in my estimation is an abominable practice). The same boot can be secured to a saddle by slinging it in front of one knee. To cock a leg around it, as is done with most scabbards that are slipped on a slant through a stirrup strap, would cripple a rider in jig time.

What a beginner should realize about a scabbard is that its use is solely to transport the gun via horse. Not long ago a young man was showing me how he had fixed his open-top scabbard in such a manner that he could hit the ground, whip out the rifle and fire in a matter of seconds. He had been reading too many old-timey Westerns. A fellow who shoots that fast has to be mighty hungry, and probably will get hungrier because of a miss, and he just might also become instantly afoot. Not many horses will stand still for shooting within inches of them.

The best scabbard I have, at least the one I like most, was tailored for me by an excellent saddle maker. He designed it so that the gunstock is exposed. A carefully cut flap comes around snugly over the comb. There is a small hole that slips precisely over the bolt handle (I use mostly bolt-action rifles) and it has a sturdy turn-lock. A rifle can be removed from this scabbard quickly and easily.

Some hunters who favor ultra-fancy stocks might not like the idea of exposing the wood. But there are a lot of things more important than a few scratches. I take pride in a couple of banged-up stocks on rifles that have seen a good many miles.

I think every big-game hunter, even the man who just goes into the woods for a day of whitetail hunting near home, should have some sort of compact rucksack. Some hunters may need to go all out, with pack frame and the works for backpack camping, but what I'm talking about is a small canvas bag in which to carry extra ammo, a lunch, a few survival items. It should not be carried on the belt or over the shoulder. There are scores of small bags with straps for carrying on one's back. The size depends on what sort of hunting you'll be doing.

In any strange country, you see, it is all too easy to have your camp "get lost," even during what was supposed to be just an afternoon prowl. A few items stowed in a small pack can be mighty consoling, and can fix you up in reasonable comfort (or what I like to call "graceful suffering") for an unintended overnight stay, or even longer. If you ride a horse, you can use a pair of saddle bags instead.

I don't mean that you have to carry anything to hunt in your own back woodlot, but I can tell you from experience that when you're off your own reservation it pays not to be smart-alecky about what a great woodsman you are and to scoff at carrying along a few pounds of survival. When I lived in northern Michigan some years ago, the fall never passed that I was not called upon to go help hunt a grouse hunter or a deer hunter. There was an ample amount of forest. It didn't take any real trying for a fellow strange to it to lose himself, and in fact, even after I got so I thought I knew it pretty well, a few places changed direction on me, too.

Here are a few odds and ends you might consider when making up a pack, basing your own selection on the kind of country you'll be in, how remote, and for how long. I'd assume any hunter would have a compass and, equally important, a knowledge of how to use it. A map of the area is mandatory, even where there are roads. A Forest Service map or a detailed county map is usually all you need. For long, remote treks, U.S. Geological Survey maps are invaluable. But again, they are worthless without knowledge of how to read them.

A first-aid kit is a must. How elaborate it is depends on the type of hunting trip. Kits are available all made up, in varying sizes, and with a first-aid booklet, which is important. In snake country, a snakebite kit and instructions should be stowed. Where and when insects may be bad, a small squeeze bottle of potent repellent is needed. Tweezers, small magnifying glass (you can light a fire with it), whistle, signal mirror all may be useful in emergencies, and they taie little room. A tightly rolled-down underwear jacket (for a pillow if need be in warm weather), a blaze-orange nylon-shell windbreaker and light nylon rain suit all fold very compactly and weigh very little.

Consider also the following: gloves or mittens, spare socks, inflatable Res-Q-Pak, small flashlight, extra batteries, paper salt packets in plastic bags, tea, spare folding knife, leather thongs, length of small nylon rope, spool of heavy fishing line, hooks, roll of copper wire, nylon tarp, large plastic sheet, hatchet, large matches in waterproof container, a dozen fire-starter cubes, a couple of short, fat candles, heavy foil folded flat, a few packets of freeze-dried foods, raisins, nuts, cocoa. A simple mess kit can be made up containing two nesting containers and a spoon. A bottle or container of Halazone tablets for purifying water should always be carried, and of course in arid country you'll want a water canteen.

In most instances the average hunter has no need for all of these items. But the hunter who has it all with him can live quite well for some days in an emergency.

Anyone who hunts in snake country during a month when they are likely to be out should by all means wear snake leggings. As a very general rule (and don't trust it!) rattlesnakes or other vipers are not likely to be active when the temperature is below 50 degrees. I've seen exceptions.

One of the worst snakebite cases of my knowledge occurred in Wyoming during an antelope hunt. The man very nearly died, and was hospitalized for months. I mention it because it is so easy to forget such dangers. It may be frosty at dawn, but by afternoon warm enough for snakes to crawl. So if there is any chance of snake action, don't feel silly about putting on your leggings. There are three general types: double canvas with a layer of fine copper screen sandwiched; aluminum, designed to fit the leg and over the instep; and plastic. The plastic leggings I've worn are hard but springy. When off, they curl up. You grasp the curled edges, open them, snap the leggings on, and they stay snug. There are also knee-high snake boots made of extremely heavy leather. They are expensive and hot, but they certainly do the job.

There is such a welter of excellent apparel for sportsmen nowadays that any hunter can select practically anything he wants, to fit any climate and terrain. Choices are not difficult to make. However, a few suggestions may be helpful. In numerous states hunters are required by law to wear a certain amount of blaze orange or another bright color. It is unfortunate that crowded conditions, and therefore danger of accident due to misidentification, occur so broadly.

It is not the color that may spook game but the shine—the blaze quality. Big-game animals see colors poorly or are totally color blind. What they notice is a shiny block, or a shading from white to black through the varied grays, that looks unnatural in the surroundings. If you hunt where blaze orange is not required, and in uncrowded country, reds in soft hues do nicely, and are easily seen by your hunting partners. Yellow, in fall in aspen country, blends in with the leaves and may not always be readily visible to your distant partners.

Camouflage clothing is, of course, fine for hunting. In instances where you need to stalk close to game, even a camouflage headnet and

Huge "drag" in Mexican road is reminder about value of snake leggings or boots.

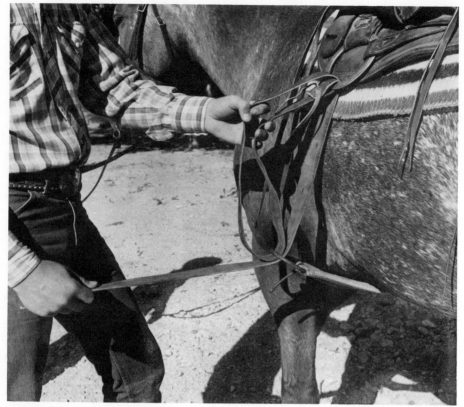

You may want your own comfortable saddle; check condition of cinch before trip.

gloves are helpful. Some deer hunters wear red camouflage, which can be spotted by other hunters but to a deer looks much the same as the standard dark green pattern. A number of hunters dote on green camouflage clothing even when in country where there is much dead grass and pale rock. Actually they are not well-camouflaged at all, but in high contrast to their surroundings. Tan camouflage is available for such situations, and even some reversible clothing can be purchased.

On any hunt where you will be prowling and wish to keep very quiet, it is best to wear wool or soft cottons. Any hard material such as poplin is noisy when you move through brush. Obviously, if the stalk is only to long-shot distance, as for sheep, for example, it makes little difference what outer material you wear as long as you are comfortable.

Light and efficient down garments have decidedly altered hunting apparel over past years. A good-quality wool shirt with a light down jacket over it will keep you warm in quite severe weather. Down jackets with a nylon or poplin windbreaker exterior are excellent for riding, or for hunting when chill winds blow. However, there is something of a revolution going on with regard to filling for garments and sleeping bags. Hunters should consider some of the modern synthetic fillings. Down is lighter but when it gets wet it bunches and loses its "loft," or fluffiness. Loft is what makes down a great insulator.

The most talked-about modern insulation is Fiberfill II, a Du Pont synthetic. It is a bit heavier than down, and compresses about 90 percent as compactly. A jacket utilizing it as insulator will weigh not quite half as much again as a down jacket, if the covering is equal, and it will be a slightly larger roll in a packsack. The advantage of this silicone-coated spun Dacron is that, whereas down is extremely absorbent, the absorbency of Fiberfill II is below 1 percent. Therefore, in rain or damp conditions, a jacket or sleeping bag using it might conceivably be somewhat clammy, but its loft, and therefore its insulating effect, will remain almost normal.

Boots for the big-game hunter are of infinite variety. The tremendous upsurge of interest in backpacking over recent years has brought many climbing or hiking boots onto the market that may be fine for mountain climbing or family hikes but should not be confused with proper hunting boots. Most hiking boots are ankle-high, with various types of lug soles.

In the saddle or walking, any big-game hunter needs boots at least nine inches high. Insulated boots, even in rather warm weather, are a good idea. And glove-leather linings offer more comfort than raw leather. Some of my favorite boots are the waterproof leather kind. I've had several pairs that really were waterproof and extremely comfortable.

Soles should be selected for the terrain you'll be in. Lug or deeply cleated soles can be an abomination when walking a slope that has grass on it and mud underneath. A good, tough nonskid sole—nonskid on wet going as well as on dry rocks—serves well. Having hunted much in country abounding with thorns such as scrub mesquite and spines of low-growing prickly pear or tasajilla, I'd advise the gent who thinks he wants a real lightweight leather in his boots to think again. Jumping cholla and the large spines of prickly pear, and especially low mesquite, can go through such leather as if it were butter. The ultra-tough "hummock mesquite" of parts of the Southwest can also puncture a thin sole easily if your entire weight comes down on an upturned thorn. Thus, thin soles are out. They're hard on your feet, anyway.

There are scads of items a hunter can add and probably will add to his gear—scope cover, knives, belt cartridge carriers, maybe a hand winch to be carried in a hunting vehicle for hanging up a buck, and so on. The stores are full of gadgets, many useful, many just clutter. At least the suggestions in this chapter should help steer the tyro on the right track, and may be helpful to experienced hunters as well.

Certainly any hunter who travels to remote areas must have a comfortable, quality sleeping bag. Never depend on an outfitter or guide to furnish such gear. They may do so, but their idea of comfort and yours may differ. I've watched guides and packers bed down with no mattress or pillow in a skimpy little bag and freeze and groan and turn all night. A good night's rest is immensely important. Use a roomy bag with adequate fill for the temperature you'll be in. Mummy bags may be compact for go-light backpackers but you can spend a lifetime learning to sleep comfortably in one.

In addition, a good mattress is a must. I used an air mattress for the last time a good many years ago. A fabric-covered light foam mattress is far better. It is even lighter than a good air mattress. It is bulkier to transport, but as I told one guide, when it's rolled snugly and stuffed into a canvas drawstring bag, "the mule doesn't spend much time thinking about it." I even roll up a down pillow in my sleeping bag and zipper the whole works into its case. If you have ever spent much time trying to sleep with your head on an air pillow you'll know why.

The serious big-game hunter who goes on numerous horseback trips, collecting one species after another, is well advised to have his own saddle. Good saddles, especially wholly handmade, are expensive, and there's no such thing as a cheap saddle that's worth putting on a horse. But if you can afford the trips, you can afford the comfort of a saddle that fits you, one you are used to, and if you don't ride much, perhaps a padded one. Some outfitters have good saddles and some do not. An outfitter's saddles all get grueling use, and certainly won't be as comfortable for a two-week trek as your own, if you're willing to put some money into a quality one.

I have mentioned saddle bags. Horseback hunters should have their own. They should also have a poncho. Many outfitters furnish these, but not always without leaks. A good poncho will keep you and your rifle and bags dry in a mighty hard rain. A few hunters also like to own their own panniers, so that they can stow all their gear for a long pack and have it ready to load. These should be of high quality, and made by a professional who is experienced in their design. The casual hunter doesn't need such gear, and most outfitters are adequately equipped with them anyway. It's just a matter of personal preference.

The best rule to apply when putting together hunting gear for any trip is to try your best not to overload or underload. You don't need a mountain of equipment. But be sure you have the basics for comfort and safety and game finding in the terrain where you'll be operating. After dark if you find your flashlight batteries dead, it's a long jaunt to the store!

7.
HOW
TO JUDGE
GAME
COUNTRY

Weathered antlers are abundant in winter range.

t is obvious that unless you can judge which hunting locations are likely to be poor, which fair and which excellent, the hunt becomes a blind, bumbling affair. There are, of course, many sportsmen who hunt close to their homes and know their bailiwicks intimately, but most of us make annual trips to unfamiliar places, and unless we can size up the potential we are apt to do a lot of aimless roaming. Even the hunter with a guide should be able to judge for himself the quality of the range.

As noted in an earlier chapter, a good hunt does not always depend on getting into country that has the greatest number of the species sought. Trophy hunts in particular often depend on combing range where the game is not abundant. Still, the man in new territory must ask himself two important questions: Is this range capable of sustaining a population of the species in question. And are the animals here? Thus, you appraise the range first to see if the basic needs of the game are present. These are proper forage, water and cover. If the basics are evident, then you check for the signs of animal presence.

"Abundance," applied to the various big-game species, is a relative matter. Certain animals are by natural design more numerous than others. Deer may be present on a given range in a ratio of a dozen per square mile. Moose, on a range of comparable quality for their needs, would probably be present only on an average of one per square mile or maybe one for every 10 square miles. It is a general law of nature that the larger the animal, the greater its requirement of living room, and thus the fewer there are of the large species.

Quality of range will always make a decided difference in abundance, but you have to define "quality," too. Where I live, the whitetail deer are extremely abundant, but small. Water and cover are no problem, and most years there is a more than adequate food supply. To the south a hundred miles or so, in the Texas brush country, there are by no means as many whitetails, but they are much larger. They are vigorous, healthy deer. Thus the range quality, for them, certainly must be prime. But it is either not capable of sustaining as many deer as the oak and juniper country where I live, or there are other factors such as higher fawn mortality that hold the herd to lesser numbers.

There are ranges that are just plain inadequate, and these one should be able to spot quickly. I rode a hard-gaited horse all one day a few years ago in a hunk of northern Arizona mule-deer range, and with a guide at that, when I would have bet before the horses were unloaded from the truck that the country couldn't produce a deer in 10 square miles. Water was scarce, cover was sparse, and the deer foods that should have been present were only meagerly evident. During the whole hard ride I never saw a deer, and only one old track. The guide should have known the deer weren't there. He was a cowhand, and any poke who knows cattle range surely should be able to judge deer range, too.

In their normal day-to-day routines, deer are generally distributed with some evenness over any given range. The same is true of moose, which are solitary or in very small groups. And it would also be true of bears, which travel alone as a rule except for a sow with cubs.

But all animals do not follow the rule of even distribution. Elk are almost always in bands. To be sure, there are always old solitary bulls. But the major share of any elk population is gathered here and there in groups—groups of cows and calves, of young bulls, or even several mature bulls. And during the rut the bands are harem groups, a bull with his cows, sometimes as many as 40 with lesser bulls tagging the fringes. Their range may be broad, but their distribution over it at any given moment would hardly ever be as even as that of deer.

The same applies to antelope. They run in bands, large or small. When undisturbed, the actual range of any single band may not be especially large. But a hunter might cover a lot of territory before seeing a target for the simple reason of their gregariousness. Caribou are notoriously herd animals. Here again, lone bulls are often seen, but caribou distribution over a vast expanse of tundra is at any given time spotty. Goats and sheep consort in small bands, and among sheep in particular groups of rams live together congenially much of the year. Therefore, the fact that you don't quickly see game of a certain type may not mean that the game is scarce or absent from the area. It is the hunter's job to assess the quality of the range, and then note the probable abundance of the game using it by the sign they have left.

To a large extent, elk eat much the same foods and utilize the same cover types in all the states where they are found. The same applies in general to most other game animals. Each species has colonized a region of the continent, and has to some extent been restricted from further colonization because it cannot cope with conditions beyond those arbitrary boundaries.

But deer, especially whitetails but mule deer also, have been able to push their numbers into every conceivable combination of climate, terrain and vegetation. I have hunted whitetails in the dense forest of northern Maine, in Southern swamps, along brushy stream courses of the Northern plains, in the cactus and thornbrush of Mexico, and at 6,000 feet among the piñon and madrona of the desert mountains in the Big Bend country. One of the mule-deer relatives, the Sitka blacktail of coastal Alaska, can be found eating seaweed in winter along the beaches. In Wyoming I've hunted mule deer in gullied plains without a tree in sight for miles, and in Utah among aspens and spruce high in the mountains. In southern Arizona I've jumped big bucks in the cactus and brush on the desert flats.

To a whitetail deer hunter whose entire experience has been in Pennsylvania, the thornbrush and cactus country of southern Texas is apt to be confusing. At home the deer would be found eating maple and poplar, or munching acorns from below a big oak, browsing on witch hazel or wild grape and any number of familiar shrubs and plants. In Pennsylvania there are creeks and ponds galore. Water is no problem for deer. And unlimited cover is available in the brushy woodlots, and the larger forests in the north-central part of the state, as well as the timbered draws of the mountains.

Southern Texas has no mountains. The brush country is gently rolling, with no sizable trees. It is a seemingly endless, arid expanse of highly varied thornbrush and prickly-pear cactus. None of the common food plants of deer back in Pennsylvania are here. There are no streams, just dry washes eroded during infrequent but often severe rains. So how do you size up this new country? It doesn't look as if a deer could live in it. And there seem to be no distinct divisions, as there are in the North, between cover types or forage and cover.

But an animal's preferences and basic requirements remain the same everywhere: food, water, cover. The water is not difficult to discover. It is almost entirely in stock tanks (dug ponds that hold run-off from rains) scattered over the ranches. A quick check around a few of these will show, by the number of deer tracks, which are being most used. You know that whitetails like to hide in dense cover. Here the heaviest cover is in the so-called "creek bottoms," the dry washes along which vegetation grows thicker than elsewhere because when water is present most of it winds up along these. As to what the deer feed upon here, you simply have to find out locally by asking questions or by making inquiry ahead of time from game-department sources. And then you have to be able to identify the plant species. Huajilla, a shrub with feathery leaves and very small thorns, is one example of classic deer food here, and it is not difficult to recognize once you know it.

If you hunt mule deer in a Southwestern desert you may find the animals foraging heavily upon the lower portion of lechuguilla leaves. This viciously sharp-leaved, low-growing plant appears densely on many slopes and the deer paw up the more tender buried lower leaves and eat them. An

This is poor deer habitat; despite scrub vegetation, water and browse are scarce.

Tracks like these black-bear prints tell about game's abundance and movements.

abundant growth of the plant, plus sign of deer working on it, would help you judge the quality of this hunting ground. But far up the Rockies you might have to look for abundant mountain mahogany as a favored forage, or for a good crop of piñon nuts.

I cannot emphasize too strongly that a hunter should know his quarry's chief forage plants in any given location, and he should be able to translate cover and water and food conditions, in a strange region, from what he knows at home. The animals do not change from place to place. They simply adapt by satisfying their fundamental requirements with the available food, cover and water.

Of course, game animals find small amounts of water in all sorts of places unknown to the visiting hunter. However, if water is genuinely

Elk or deer rubs help hunter judge abundance and haunts of mature males.

scarce around the year, the game will be, too. If it is only seasonally adequate in a given location this can work either for or against the hunter. He must ascertain which.

Along with being able to identify preferred forage, it is important to know to some extent what plants are *not* useful to the game. A couple of examples come to mind. A great amount of high, dead grass in meadows surrounded by forest or woodlot may look like an amply furnished larder for whitetails, but it's not. Green shoots buried in the dead clumps would be avidly eaten but the dry, dead grass that might sustain a horse would probably not be touched by deer. Or in some mule-deer country there may be flats heavy with creosote brush in arid mountain valleys. Although it may look green all winter, it is of no use whatever as food for mule deer. Nothing will eat it.

Such odds and ends of knowledge are important in judging game country. The successful hunter is the one who will constantly ask questions of landowners or guides or local hunters who know the area's trees and plants, water sources and cover especially favored by any given animal. One can never collect too much local lore; every fact pertinent to any place is sooner or later useful.

Game-department biologists assigned to specific studies are a marvelous source of information if you can get a chance to visit with them, or read their official reports which may be available free or at small charge. All big game is so carefully managed nowadays that in any given state the biologists working on deer, elk or sheep, or whatever, know precisely where the best ranges are, and *why* these are the best ranges. The range supporting the greatest number of animals may have to be cropped hard, and may contain a herd of deer or elk made up chiefly of antlerless and young male animals. In any event, it's a great idea to try to obtain from a game department reports of game studies or, if opportunity affords, to make an appointment for a chat with the biologist in charge of a species you're after. He'll know the chief foods of given herds in any part of the state. These differ sometimes even from county to county. He'll know where the best chances are for trophies, and the best for simple tag-filling. Incidentally, you should keep in mind that forage changes seasonally. You need to know which of the animal's preferred foods are abundant during fall and winter, when hunting the seasons are open.

Among certain animals—mule deer in high-mountain country, moose in some places, elk, sheep, caribou—there are seasonal migrations from summer ranges to winter ranges. Most of these are from high elevations to lower foothills. The migrations are forced by weather, which either snuffs out the food supply or covers it with deep snow. It is very important to know if there are seasonal migrations in the area where you will hunt. For one thing, in certain places where the movements follow definite routes, animals can be waylaid during migration.

Also, because food is always more scarce in winter even at lower altitudes than in summer, groups of game animals are likely to be concentrated on winter range. If the season is open at that time, and you know where a winter range is located, you may be able to pick a trophy you want. One year I hunted mule deer late in the season, after a migration to the foothills on one prime Colorado winter range, and in four days I looked over 45 excellent bucks.

There are other reasons for knowing about winter ranges, and their whereabouts. Droppings of deer or elk, when moist from frost or rain or snow, sometimes look fresh to a less-than-expert eye even though left from the winter before. You can tell by the way browse is cut, or if many weathered antlers are present, that the range is used in winter. Early in season it will be empty. The deer or elk or moose will be up higher.

Here's a rule to remember if you hunt the mountains where big game must migrate in winter to lower country: The vigor and size of the herd on the summer and early-fall range are directly proportional to the quality and size of the winter range. In other words, a stable herd can only be as large as the *winter* range can support. If the winter range is small or its forage meager, you can bet the herd up above will be small. If winter range is severely overbrowsed (and you can see the evidence of this even in summer or fall) it indicates that a herd has outgrown it and is either headed for disaster—winter starvation and poor reproduction—or else the debacle may already have occurred. If you have the opportunity, a check of the foothill wintering ground prior to a fall hunt will help you make some judgments

Aspens show barking line gnawed by elk; fresh scars haven't yet turned black.

about what you're likely to find higher up. If the winter range looks vigorous and not over-used, undoubtedly the herd up high is well tailored to it and just as vigorous.

In the final analysis of an expanse of game country it is, of course, the signs left by the animals that tell most about it. The sharp hunter should be well informed about what to look for, and must be able to interpret correctly what he sees. Beginners sometimes misread sign, and even some old hands overlook important sign.

Tracks are the most obvious kind of sign. The expert hunter is always looking for tracks. He can tell by meticulous study of tracks how abundant any species is in his hunting territory. He can get a fair idea of the size of some of the animals, and he can learn much about their movement

Texture and type of droppings can indicate browse that game is concentrating on.

habits on this range. The freshness of tracks is of great importance. Under some conditions it is not possible to tell—for instance, in dry dust in a protected place away from wind. On a strange expanse of range it is a good idea to find out when the last rain occurred and how heavy it was. Starting fresh, after a hard rain has washed out most of the old tracks, gives you an edge.

Tracks look different in different soils. In soft mud they tend to appear larger than normal and can fool an inexperienced hunter. In certain sandy loams and clay soils in arid country, tracks made after a modest rain a month or so ago may at first glance look fresh, especially if there is any dew or drizzle on them. Feeling the earth and finding it hard tells the story. They were made when the ground was soft from moisture and then baked later by the hot sun. In a wet place, a track that has water still trickling into or out of it is obviously one made only a few moments before. Tracks in deep, soft snow are difficult to appraise because size is exaggerated. But of course you can tell instantly what the animal was doing. If it was running flat out, probably you spooked it. If it was wandering at a walk, probably it has been feeding.

I should mention here that deer hunters often claim to be able to tell a buck track from a doe track. The fact is, it's guesswork. You certainly can make educated guesses. A very large deer track made by a lone animal and deeply imprinted because of weight may well have been left by a buck. It also may be the track of a big old doe. A set of three tracks, one large, the others small, undoubtedly was made by a doe and twin fawns. It is generally a waste of time to follow a "buck" track, because it may not be. Among the larger animals such as elk and moose there is a substantial difference in size between cow and bull and the tracks confirm this. But if you have nothing to compare to, telling one from another is not easy.

The type of terrain makes a difference in the tracks. For example, if you're used to seeing tracks in soft soil, and you go on a trip to an area where the same species lives in rocky, hard country, tracks may puzzle you. Mule deer living in high meadows where ground is soft will leave tracks showing the hoofs quite pointed. Mule deer living on slopes of shale and rock, as in much of the desert mule-deer range, will commonly have the hoofs worn down to rounded tips. The larger, older and heavier the deer, the more rounded are the tracks.

Small water holes, lake shores and stream courses are among the best places to study tracks. At a small watering hole in country where water is not plentiful, keep in mind that a few animals can leave a lot of tracks. But such a spot is tailor-made for finding out whether the game is abundant or not, and for sizing up the large and small tracks. Most watering places have enough soft soil around them to accept prints plainly. You can even tell if more than one species—such as elk and mule deer—are using the place. A water hole with no tracks states plainly that game is not plentiful here, and several trackless watering spots in the same general area tell you to move on and forget this region.

Over most of the continent, there is not likely to be confusion as to what animal made any given tracks. But there are a few exceptions you should be aware of if you're going to travel widely. In all of the whitetail country east of the Mississippi, there is rarely any confusion, for no other hoofed big game is present. Local exceptions might be in the northern Lower Peninsula of Michigan where there are a few elk, and in northern Minnesota where there are a fair number of moose. Elk and moose tracks are so much larger that no one could puzzle over them. In North Carolina or Tennessee you might find the tracks of a large wild boar, but the prints are rounder than a deer's, quite splayed, with the widely spaced dewclaws of the forefeet usually printing in soft earth. They don't really look much like deer tracks.

West of the Mississippi there are some places—like Wyoming and parts of Montana, the Dakotas, western Texas—where whitetails and mule deer may be present on the same range. Distinguishing between the tracks of the two is not easy. Adult male mule deer tracks are somewhat larger than those of whitetails, but in a welter of tracks of varying sizes that becomes meaningless. If you spot tracks left by a running—bounding or galloping—deer, close scrutiny will tell you which species left them. The whitetail swings the hind feet past the forefeet at each bound; the mule deer brings all four feet down almost together and with hind feet behind the forefeet. In most deer hunting, however, telling species tracks apart has little if any importance. If your license calls for one or the other, or if both are legal, you have to wait until you see the deer to decide.

There are a few places, as in western Wyoming, where elk and moose may be using the same territory. The elk will invariably be more abundant, and the tracks do differ under careful scrutiny. Moose tracks are larger—over five inches for adults as compared to four or maybe four and a half for elk—and they are more pointed. If tracks confuse a hunter in this case, then he must seek other sign, about which more in a moment.

The most common misinterpretation of tracks occurs on cattle range where elk are present. This brings to mind a photo I took several years ago up in the high country in northern New Mexico. There are several bull elk in it, bugling and challenging each other in a meadow, and up near the aspens are a couple of big Herefords. Old, heavy cattle leave tracks that are much more rounded and blocky than those of large elk. But tracks of younger cattle are difficult to tell from elk tracks. Again, one must look for other sign.

I've never felt that checking up on antelope tracks is very important. In open plains country where these animals live it's easier to find the pronghorns themselves than to bother looking for tracks. Certainly the tracks can't be confused with cattle tracks. It is handy to check waterholes sometimes, to see if bands of pronghorns are using them. The only possible confusion here is if deer happen to be using the same place. But pronghorn tracks, when plainly imprinted without distortion, look chopped off or slightly squared at the rear, whereas those of deer are more rounded.

Mountain sheep and mountain goat tracks are somewhat similar. Both are rather elongate with straight outer edges and often with toes spreading. However, in hunting these animals so much glassing is done, and each so commonly selects different types of feeding and bedding spots, that distinction between the tracks is not especially important. Further, almost all of this hunting is done with guides, who are invariably familiar with the tracks.

In most caribou country there are few other tracks to cause difficulty. In some instances moose are present. But caribou tracks are unmistakable. Each half of the hoof is excessively rounded, and almost hooked at the toe. The two halves also are spread wide apart. Down in the Southwest, javelina tracks occasionally are confused with the tracks of small deer. They shouldn't be. The tracks are not only small but very blunt.

A bear track greatly excites the average hunter, and most black bear are taken as incidentals by "lucky" deer hunters. In much bear range there are not enough animals in any given locality to let you judge the quality of the hunting ground by the number of tracks. Nonetheless, tracks, old logs torn apart, a wild cherry tree with branches ripped down in fall, claw marks on logs or tree trunks, piles of dung—all tell of bear presence. A place where much fresh dung is found is a more important discovery than any number of aimless tracks. However, trophy bear hunters must obviously be able to judge by size of track the size of the bear that made it. Guides use various formulas that seem to work quite accurately. Suffice here to say that if you find a clear front foot imprint of a black bear that measures six inches across, or a grizzly front print measuring seven, or an Alaskan brown measuring nine, a mighty big bear is at the end of the trail.

Later on, in the chapters dealing with hunting individual species, we will cover their signs in more detail. But here, in discussing how to size up a piece of game country, a few should be touched, to illustrate some short cuts in appraising range quality. In connection with the vertical migrations of some animals, such as elk, I mentioned that the presence of numerous weather-whitened shed antlers almost always means that you're on winter range. The elk have moved down as deep snows drove them and the bulls have dropped their antlers during the winter. But you must use a little caution in drawing conclusions.

There is, for example, a certain vast expanse of prime elk country I have hunted in the Rockies where I have found numerous shed antlers while actually hunting for a bull and listening to many of them make the mountains ring with their bugling, during the rut in late September or early October. Such an area can be a fooler. A cursory look early in fall, before bugling started, might lead one to believe this was winter range, and that the animals were up higher. The fact is, this particular area serves as both summer and winter range. In most years there is little or no migration.

There is in this same country a phenomenon that all elk—and moose—hunters should always look for. It is especially relevant for elk hunters because elk, running in bands, generally leave much more of the sign than other animals. This is what might be called a "barking line" on trees such as aspen. Everyone who has hunted the high country in the Western mountains has seen mountain meadows surrounded by aspen. The division between the crowded aspens and the open meadows is invariably abrupt. Many a hunter has gazed at such an aspen stand and seen, even at long distance, hundreds of black scars on the bark at about five feet or so from the ground. These are often so distinct and so numerous on every tree in the line across a ridge, that there appears to be a dark horizontal swath running across the entire edge of the aspen stand.

Close examination will show that these old bark scars were made by elk biting out hunks of bark. The presence of such barking lines is a dead

Hunter is fascinated by "hot" sign like this. It's large, recent and well-used elk

giveaway that this range has had a substantial number of elk on it over a period of some years. The dark or black scars are the healed ones. Again, a
close look will usually show many fresh, tan-colored gouges. That's a better
sign yet. In some places most barking is done in winter, but in others it occurs in fall as well. Any elk range with prominent barking lines all over the
ridges has numerous elk in residence either during fall or winter or both.

Game trails give a clear indication of animal presence or lack of it. If
you glass a ridge or a narrow valley and plainly see a trail or trails, have a
close look. In cattle country some may have been made by cattle, but game

wallow, signifying that rutting bull has been here and may still lurk in vicinity.

animals follow such trails as well as those they have made. In checking out trails be sure to ascertain if they are active—that is, being regularly used. Some, particularly whitetail-deer trails, may have been made in summer and not be in use in fall. Regardless, an abundance of game trails, added to an abundance of recently made tracks here and there, will tell you you're on a well-stocked game range.

I constantly look for more specialized signs, too. These, which we'll discuss much more in connection with the individual animals, include places where buck deer or bull elk have been rubbing their antlers. A large number of rubs throughout a large expanse of country means plenty of bucks or bulls. Bull elk rip up grass and dirt with their antlers. This is good sign, too. Bull moose decimate bushes and small trees by "fighting" them with their heavy antlers. The presence of elk wallows—which they use chiefly during the rut—indicates that bulls are here or have been here. Feeding signs, such as close-cropped willows or places where mule deer have torn up lechuguilla, tell how abundant or few the animals are on any expanse of hunting territory.

Possibly next to tracks, droppings are the most useful sign, or perhaps they're even the most useful of all for judging a range. Game biologists get quite accurate counts of game animals on a specified area by dropping-count studies. It's done by marking all existing piles of droppings found in the study plot with spray paint. Then counts are made of new ones over a certain time period. The biologists know the average number of dropping piles left per animal per day, and a herd count can thus be ascertained.

In appraising a hunting territory, note the abundance and age of droppings. If they are simply everywhere, and fresh, the game is plentiful. If all are old, they state that the game has moved or declined or, in early fall, that you are on winter range. I recall a mule-deer hunt I made one time on an Indian reservation. During the entire first day of walking, I saw only three piles of droppings. It was not terrain where tracks would show well anyway. I would have bet deer were scarce, and they were. In five days I saw a single doe. Later I learned that resident Indians, hunting at any time, had really pared the deer down to near zero.

A great deal can be learned from droppings. For example, if you aren't quite sure whether the tracks you see are from elk or cattle, look around for cow chips and elk pellets. If only one is there in abundance you know where you stand. If both are copiously present, you know that you're on cattle range where elk are also abundant. You can also get an idea of what foods the game animals are eating. This sometimes may lead to confusion for a tyro if he scouts a piece of game country in summer or early fall, well before the season. Deer droppings, when the animals are eating soft foods during summer or early fall, are not rounded, firm pellets, but a conglomerate, adhesive scat. A hunter who is unaware of this fact might not recognize them. The same holds true for elk, moose and other animals.

The many facets of judging game country may seem complicated, but the fundamentals are really quite simple. Any hunter who constantly practices alertness, keen observation and concentration will find himself rather intuitively sensing whether or not an unfamiliar area is worthwhile. Are the basic requirements of food, water, cover present in proper balance? If so, and the signs of the animals themselves are abundant and fresh, you are in good hunting country.

8.
GAME
SENSES AND
HUNTING
METHODS

Unavoidable riding noise is bound to warn game.

T he senses of animals are keen, but they are no supernatural phenomenon. Some big-game species see better than others, some use their noses more adeptly. Man also has well-developed senses, but in our modern civilization these senses are not used, or constantly honed, to the same purpose as those of animals. A hunter who will practice completely concentrated hearing and looking can develop abilities that rate with those of many game animals. Of course, by crediting game with uncanny powers, man consoles himself for his hunting failures and builds his ego where his successes are concerned.

The most marvelous ability with which man is endowed is *reasoning*. It may well be that some animals have minor reasoning powers, but most of their reactions are instinctive. This is not to underrate their abilities. But I get weary of the nonsense so often presented as fact regarding the ability of game to outwit man by use of its senses. If that were really true, the Indians would have starved.

I have sat upright in grass on a Wyoming plain and had antelope walk almost up to me to see what on earth that thing with the big hat was. I have camouflaged myself totally and talked very quietly to deer only a few yards away. They were nervous only from lack of understanding. I have photographed javelina from so close that I had to back up to get them in focus. The lens I was using could be focused at 13 feet.

What the hunter should get firmly in mind is that the one immense advantage he has is that he can accurately appraise the meaning of sounds, sights, and to a small extent smells: He can *think*. An elk far back in a remote area does not run from a hunter walking toward it because it knows this is a hunter. It runs because the man is not a familiar creature in its domain. Unless an animal has been hit by a bullet, or had gravel bit its belly from a near miss, it has no way to relate danger to the sound of a gun. It doesn't run from a sharp clap of thunder. And it doesn't run from the sound of a rifle if the sound is at a comfortable distance and no hunter is seen.

A correct appraisal of the sensing abilities of each big-game variety is most valuable. A hunter should know, for example, that he has in some respects far better eyesight than most big game. This is particularly true when he is looking straight ahead. His eyes are set for seeing in a fairly broad arc ahead of him (as are the eyes of most predators). The eyes of game animals are set to the side and can pick up movement more adeptly when it is to right or left, but their forward vision, although very good, is less efficient.

Further, although big-game animals see more in a horizontal plane than a hunter can, objects above their straight-ahead line of vision are obscure to them, and usually go unnoticed. As I mentioned in discussing the glassing of game country, whenever possible a hunter should be above his quarry. The animal can see down by dropping its head, and it can see straight ahead and to the sides, but it does not look up very much, and only then with some physical difficulty.

What is it that big game animals *need* to see? Food, obviously, and their own kind, and their general surroundings—and *danger.* Danger may be anything strange in the habitat. But danger for all practical purposes is equated by animals with *motion:* possible attack. Of course, when a possible danger is spotted, all the senses are brought to bear. Information is gathered by ears and nose, and the decision to flee or not to flee is made instinctively from the assembled information.

However, if the hunter is immobile and the wind is in his face, the animal must rely on sight alone to make the decision. It may retreat if the hunter is too close simply because it suspects the presence of something unidentified. I've watched in amusement many times when mule deer walked away from me, nervously lifting each foot high, bobbing the head and neck, almost as if in puzzled embarrassment. It was as if the deer were saying, "I'm not sure what you are, if anything, but maybe I ought to tiptoe away just because I can't dope this out." A hunter skylighted on a ridge will undoubtedly spook game across from him, sometimes at great distance. But in almost all instances a hunter who hunches or stands absolutely still, against a backdrop of cover or even spang in the middle of an open meadow, will not be accurately identified by a big-game animal—if the hunter's form was immobile when first spotted.

There is one exception to that rule, and it concerns contrast. Horned and antlered animals, being color-blind, see everything as white, black and various shades of gray. An immobile hunter dressed in white coveralls in country where snow is everywhere means nothing to an animal that doesn't

Hunter's binocular gives him vision to equal that of any game—if he's alert.

smell or hear him. The same hunter standing in snowless terrain will be spotted immediately—not necessarily as an enemy, but as something wholly strange and out of place in the animal's domain. Although I've never tried it, I'm sure game animals would run from such a sight, even while the man remained immobile. A hunter dressed in red, however, looks to the animal like a gray blob against other grays in the background.

Thus, a basic rule is to dress as much as possible to match the terrain, but in terms of grays—translating the shades of clothing in terms of intensities and contrasts. The greater the contrast of your apparel with the surroundings, the more easily and quickly you'll be noticed by the quarry and, more important, the easier it is for the animal to see the slightest motion. A hunter moving very slowly along the edging of spruces on a high mountain meadow may—if dressed to match—get only a cursory glance from elk across the meadow unless they scent him. But a man in a bright yellow hunting coat moving in the same place and manner is just too much. He is such an unusual phenomenon that the animals might first show startled curiosity and then, if not put to wild flight, will at least retire into the timber.

Animals do not purposely remember danger and dwell on it, as humans do. If unduly harassed they become very wild, but this is a conditioned reaction. Also bear in mind that the flight from a possible danger differs in length among various big-game species. An elk might run miles; a mule deer is more likely to stop on the far side of the ridge. But as a general rule, in wild country where animals are not incessantly disturbed, it is "out of sight, out of mind."

An odd fact, of which most hunters are unaware, is that animals see motion with heightened definition because they are color blind. The world of color which we see may be beautiful but it is also infinitely confusing. When everything is brought down to an utterly simple level, a world of gray, it is obvious that contrast and the slightest movement are the only fundamental features needed to distinguish one object from another.

Knowing these facts should indicate to any hunter that all of his motions should be slow, and against backgrounds of matching intensity. If you are sitting on a stand and need to turn your head or raise a hand, do it in slow, even motion. Any jerky movement is easily picked up, but a very slow, steady one may be ignored. If you sit to watch a valley, sit with your back against a tree, not out beside it. If you want to study animals, lie down. At ground level you are not as easily detected, nor as easily identified, as at sitting or standing height. If you move up behind a tree, for example, keeping its trunk between you and an animal within range, and you want to have a last look, get down on the ground behind the trunk and peek around at ground level. A hunter who darts his head around a trunk at standing height is just asking to be seen, and he'll scare the daylights out of any animal near enough to have a look.

It is interesting to note that visual abilities are in some cases directly related to the terrain in which animals live, and there is a wide difference in the strength of eyesight among various species. Deer and elk are fundamentally cover animals. In open terrain they can see a long way, but they do not depend as much on distance for safety as they do on brief flight and concealment. Pronghorns, which evolved on the wide-open plains, have always "looked far." Even the way in which their skull is fashioned, with the eyes set far out at the sides, indicates that vision is extremely important to them. They have exceptional eyesight, and they are capable of long swift flight, faster than any other big game. They have no cover in which to hide. Spotting danger at great distance and fleeing from it is their best, or only, protection.

Mountain sheep and goats live in an environment where vistas are long. Their eyesight, too, is exceptional, and they are constantly alert for distant danger, just as pronghorns are. But they do not require swift flight. Their habitat limits the speed of the pursued and pursuer. Moose are animals of the willows, and the birch and spruce of the North. Only a few, as in Wyoming, Utah and Montana, are mountain animals, and even there they are animals of heavily forested habitat. Their need to be alert to danger at long distances is not great. In the lake country of Canada a moose pays little attention to a canoe across a small lake from it; one reason (probably the major one) is that danger to them means wolves, which cannot come from the water.

In this instance, there is also a personality difference not altogether tied up with quality of eyesight. Moose are rather dull-witted creatures, neither very curious, nor nervous, nor unduly alert. The caribou falls into more or less the same category. Caribou and their relatives, the reindeer, are the livestock of the far North. Around the world their only important enemies—except man—have always been wolves. There seems sometimes to be a kind of resignation among these gregarious animals. They have been characterized by numerous hunters as "beautiful but dumb." Whether they are actually stupid or simply naive is open to argument. At any rate, their eyesight is generally regarded as by no means exceptional.

It should be noted that caribou and pronghorns have one common trait that relates to the sense of sight. This is curiosity. Unidentified objects, even moving ones, excite their curiosity and sometimes will bring them toward potential danger instead of putting them to flight. Caribou at times act as if they aren't ready to believe anything they see that they do not immediately recognize, and so they trot toward rather than away from a hunter—even a mounted hunter—as they get into position to make identification by scent, occasionally at astonishingly close range.

Large animals built close to the ground, such as the bears, do not display evidence of keen vision. Bears are notorious for staring at distant (and sometimes close) hunters and acting as if they have no idea what they're seeing. The javelina is another example of unusually poor eyesight. It's too low-slung to see over typical thornbrush or cactus cover, anyway, so it has little need to see far. It probably has poorer eyesight than any other species included in this book.

The sense of hearing is well developed among all big-game animals. But in most instances the eyes will attempt to confirm what the ears may have heard. This doesn't mean that hunters should not operate with extreme stealth and silence. Any animal on its home grounds is surrounded by sights and sounds with which it is intimately familiar. A suddenly interjected, strange, out-of-place sound will disturb it. So will the sound that might be called the "noise of stealth." The slight, continuous rustle or whisper of footfalls as one stalks a deer at close range will spook it simply because, regardless of whether or not it has ever been stalked by a predator, it knows instinctively that a prowling sound equals possible danger from a predator.

Game animals also have a truly amazing ability to pick out sounds from among those that would be natural to the habitat, and identify certain ones as possibly dangerous. A deer or elk walking over loose rock and making an occasional clink is usually properly read by other deer or elk that hear the sound. I've watched them raise their heads to look in the direction, then go back to feeding. Yet a mounted rider whose horse rattles rocks, or a walking hunter who clinks one rock against another, will almost invariably put these animals to flight.

The crack of a breaking twig is mentioned more often than any other game-spooking sound, and there is a reason. The wind rustles leaves or branches and that is natural; a falling tree may startle nearby animals but this, too, is a natural wilderness sound. Now think of a feeding animal on a calm, still day. Suddenly a stick snaps close by. That is totally unnatural. If it

Rimrock stand is high enough to lessen chance that muley will scent or see hunter.

cracked near you as you were still hunting, you'd jump, too. The game doesn't pause to wonder what caused the sound. It leaves in high gear.

Acuteness of hearing is less important to animals that depend chiefly on their eyes. Antelope and sheep certainly hear well, but they are not as concerned with sound as with seeing. One of the most difficult accomplishments on earth is to get close enough to a pronghorn or a bighorn so that it hears you walking before it sees you. Forest animals, on the other hand, use hearing and sight in conjunction because in cover it becomes more important to gather several varieties of information. Animals with poor eyesight, such as the bears and javelina, depend on hearing quite heavily, but oddly they are sometimes not overly concerned about what they hear.

A hunter who diligently practices alertness can get so he sees and hears almost as sharply as many of the animals he hunts. But when it comes to sense of smell, he can never begin to compete with his quarry. All big-game creatures have a remarkably developed scenting ability. Generally speaking, it's the most important of their senses and the one that poses the most difficulties and exasperations for the hunter. Antelope don't need to use scenting ability to any great extent. Neither do sheep and goats. But all big game is equipped with a superbly keen sense of smell.

Bears are gone in a flash when a human is scented, often at long distance. All antlered game constantly uses smell to warn it. The smallest air movement will waft telltale scent and it is picked up occasionally at unbelievable ranges. On damp, still days when smoke—and scent—drop to the ground, a hunter in a tree may be scented by an animal that comes within range. The man-scent drifts down to ground level and oozes out in a circle. A man on stand in flat country, hiding in a brush clump on an utterly still afternoon, will in an hour become the hub of a circle of scent that has spread slowly outward from him. It may be an infinitesimal amount, but deer or elk will pick it up instantly. There are times when stalking game close is anguishing or impossible. That's what keeps hunting ever a new challenge. But the rules are simple: Move quietly and slowly, staying out of sight, and if possible don't ever let the slightest movement of air touch the back of your neck!

The various methods of hunting big game take into account the ways the game uses its senses. In chapters dealing with individual species we will cover in detail methods especially applicable to each. But here we can review in general the methods practiced by modern sportsmen. One of the most common and popular is *stand hunting*. The "stand," as it's called, is simply a spot selected by the hunter where he will sit, or stand, and wait for game to pass within range in an area he is watching. The popularity of stand hunting has increased as our population has become more and more urban. A vast number of hunters just don't want the hard work of other methods, and they argue, with logic hard to deny, that a stand properly chosen offers just as great a chance of success as any more difficult method.

However, stand hunting is not very successful with certain species.

For example, the wait for a bear to cross a mountain meadow might be a long wait indeed. Sitting on a ridge above timberline, waiting for a band of bighorns to come through a saddle, would be a long gamble and a waste of hunting time. Antelope are not normally hunted from a stand, either, because it's much more productive to cover ground, scouting for them.

A stand is chiefly used for forest game, deer and elk. It is also occasionally used for moose. The hunter takes a stand on a small lake where moose are known to feed. Deer stands in trees have become common in states where they are legal. And as I mentioned earlier, in some places such as my area of Texas, deer blinds on stilts, with sliding windows and comfortable chairs, are common.

The stand hunter must select his spot with craft and judgment. Of prime importance is that it allow him to watch a fair amount of open area or at least an area where trees are not dense. And he must be sure the wind is either quartering or full from the front. The watch area is selected by what sign is present. For example, it may be a deer or elk trail that appears to be well used—as revealed by tracks, droppings, buck rubs, and so on. Many natural runways can be found where sign shows that game moves from one place to another, such as from bedding ground to feeding ground.

A stand hunter must keep himself well hidden, and he should remain quiet and move as little as possible. If he will do this, he has only to overcome the game's sense of smell, and with the wind toward him or quartering from his left or right, that will be taken care of. He should also arrange himself so that he won't have to make any great flurry of motion to take a shot. The best plan is to have a rest, over a limb perhaps, and to have the rifle up and ready so it can be swung instantly toward any aiming point within view.

For productive stand hunting, you should know the best times of day for the area you watch. A winter oat patch in farm country will have deer feeding on its edges at dawn and late afternoon, but usually is not worth watching through midday. A stand in a cedar break where deer are known to bed down might be a good spot to sit during the day. You should also consider comfort. Even on mildly chilly days, more clothing is needed than for physically active hunting. And be sure you fix up a comfortable place to sit. Otherwise you'll be hitching around and moving constantly and may give

Tree blind is good for deer, as they seldom look up or expect danger from above.

your location away. Many deer hunters carry a stool along when they plan to go on stand.

Regardless of comfort, the mandatory attribute of the stand hunter is infinite patience. Personally, I can sit for 15 minutes, but after that time hangs heavy. Thus, I'm not a very good stand hunter. However, for the rifleman who can sit for several hours and enjoy it, the method is certainly effective if he scouts the territory thoroughly beforehand and selects a good stand.

Still hunting, which means walking slowly and quietly in search of game, is a much more challenging method. In this endeavor you must outwit all the senses of the game. Still hunting is, of course, done into or across the wind so your scent doesn't precede you and spook your quarry. You must walk noiselessly, avoiding wherever possible dry leaves, or sticks that may crack, or rocks that may rattle. And you must remain out of sight or at least as obscure as the terrain will allow.

What the still hunter hopes for is to sight game within range before it sees, hears or scents him. I was prowling around my own ranch last year and peered out from a dense group of cedars to see a fair buck at less than 50 yards and totally unaware of me. I collected it. On the other hand, what often happens is that the still hunter jumps his game at close range—which usually means he has to accept a running shot, although an expert may occasionally surprise game bedded down in rim rocks or in a forest.

One of the advantages of still hunting is that time of day means little. You can prowl feeding areas and bedding areas, and thus put in a full day of hunting with expectations high at any hour. A good many hunters combine stand and still hunting. They take a stand at dawn and stay on it until mid-morning. Then they prowl until mid-afternoon, and at that time go back to a stand again until shooting light fails. One rule the prowling hunter should obey above all others: He, too, must be patient. That is, he should walk very slowly, keeping always to edges and cover. Some expert prowlers spend an hour traveling a quarter of a mile.

This method, too, is chiefly applicable to game of the brush and woodlots and forests, although it also works well on javelina. Still hunting is hardly feasible for antelope or for sheep, goats, caribou. It can be used in

Author still hunts muley . . .

. . . uses log and cedar for "hide" . . .

. . . rests on ridge stand . . .

. . . and tries to avoid cracking twigs.

Author checks for both deer and javelina—and he may smell any nearby peccaries.

some kinds of bear hunting—for example, black-bear hunting in spring when they first come out of hibernation. I've walked grassy logging trails in the bush in Ontario at such a time, when black bears were stuffing themselves on new grass. But ordinarily, unless you are in bear country that has an unusual population, still hunting is likely to be a long walk.

Actually, the moose hunter who operates from a canoe is a still hunter, and it is grand sport, quietly paddling in shoreside shadows as much as possible around or along a Northern lake, through a channel to the next, and so on, utterly still, watching for moose. In some places it is legal to float quietly on a stream for deer, with boat or canoe. This, too, can be considered still hunting.

Stalking is a third hunting method, though still hunting and stalking are often intermingled. Stalking game means first sighting it at a distance too

Southwestern trick of rattling up bucks is now proving effective in many regions.

long for shooting, and then making a sneak into rifle range. Quite commonly a still hunter will spot a deer or elk far off. At this point his still hunt becomes a stalk.

Usually, however, a stalk is preceded by scanning a likely area with a binocular and perhaps using a spotting scope. Whether traveling afoot or by horse or vehicle, the hunter pauses to glass a sweep of big country. When he spots what he is looking for the stalk begins, and it must be carefully planned so that the shooter keeps to cover and keeps the wind in his favor. In most instances, at least during the initial phase of a stalk, slight noises are not as important to avoid as in still hunting. The stalker is too far from his game to be heard. Nonetheless, he should take no chances. Sliding shale may echo and make an alarming racket in the mountains.

Stalking does not always start from a point where a hunter sits down to glass the slopes. Commonly in antelope country, hunters cruise ranch trails in a pickup or other hunting vehicle, spot a distant band and glass it quickly to determine if a good buck is present. Then they drive on around a knoll—out of sight—and from there the stalk begins, sometimes partly by vehicle if the road leads properly. Hunters on horseback can ride the mountains or open country on the lookout for distant game. Here again, they dismount and glass the animals, and if one looks good the horses are hidden and a stalk made.

Stalking is occasionally used on all big game, but it is the basic method for hunting sheep, goats, caribou, antelope, elk and the large bears. In fairly open country, mule deer are commonly stalked, and so are moose, particularly in Alaska and western Canada.

Three hunting methods are based upon bringing the game to the hunter. The most common of these is the drive. It is a technique best utilized with deer and elk. For best results a drive requires several hunters, though on occasion a drive can succeed with only two. Certain hunters take stands while the others try to push the animals toward the waiting rifles. Drives can be dangerous if many hunters are involved, or if they're too eager. But safe drives can be arranged by sensible, cautious hunters.

As an illustration, we have a high ridge on our ranch with a stand of large Texas cedar. There is little undergrowth. The place is always shady and cool and it is a favorite bedding spot for our whitetails. A ranch road runs parallel to the south side of the ridge. At the east the ridge ends in a cliff overlooking a creek. But just back a bit to the west and on the south side there is a little basin, an open field of about two acres. Every deer season my boys and I pick off a couple of deer with a quick drive here. We come in from the west and two of us drop off just west of the cedar stand atop the ridge. The third hunter drives the vehicle on along the south edge and parks it at the top of the hill above the small field. When deer are jumped atop the ridge, they may slip off the south side, but the parked car often discourages this. Most of them, as two of us move in from the west, run east along the ridge, come down the slope and cross the small field into the creek bottom.

We agree that only the man hiding at the edge of the field is to do any shooting. And he is to shoot only at animals on the flat of the field, never

Stalking desert muley, Dalrymple goes slowly, into wind, using any possible cover.

Bear has keen sense of smell but its poor eyesight may not detect hunter.

up toward the ridge. Thus the two of us who drive are in no danger and the deer every now and then do just what we want them to.

Driving requires a careful study of the terrain. Some drives are made by the drivers really whooping it up as they march through the cover. However, animals that are thoroughly frightened by this noise are likely to double back or scatter in any direction. A drive made by several hunters who simply walk along quietly, usually downwind so their scent precedes them, will move animals out without unduly spooking them. Deer or elk moved thus will generally take the easy way, following a trail they are used to traveling, going through a saddle that is handy, or along the base of a mountain that is a habitual travel route. They are not actually *driven*, but simply *moved*. The shooter or shooters farther downwind, or on points overlooking trails or valleys, are not presented with wildly fleeing targets, but often with animals that walk or trot, or even pause now and then, if the drivers work very slowly.

Among the most interesting and dramatic of all hunting methods is calling animals to you. Elk can be whistled up during the rut with an elk call. Moose in rut also are called, by an imitation of the bawl of a lovesick cow. Buck deer can be "rattled up" during rut by banging antlers together. Antelope can sometimes be tolled in by appealing to their curiosity. In chapters about individual species you will find detailed coverage of these techniques.

Another method of bringing animals to the hunter is by putting out a bait. There is not a great deal of legal baiting in North America today, and most of it is for bears. Check the regulations before you do any baiting; it's illegal for bear or anything else in a majority of states. To attract bears, a horse or cow that is about done in may be driven to a suitable spot and shot. When bears begin feeding on it (in spring as a rule) a hunter takes a stand nearby. In Ontario I hunted one season over a couple of bushels of suckers we had dip-netted from a stream when they were making their spring spawning run.

There are also natural baits. Logging camps in Canada that employ numerous men in winter but shut down in spring often attract bears fresh out of hibernation to their garbage dumps, or to the green grass shooting up in the clearings. In Wyoming one spring I hunted over the carcass of an elk that had succumbed during winter, and collected a nice black bear. In western Canada and Alaska when big game kills such as moose are made by hunters, the entrails often serve as an attraction for bears. It's perfectly legal to wait near the spot where you field dressed a big-game kill—or where you've come upon a winter-killed carcass—in the hope that a bear arrives, even though purposeful baiting is outlawed across most of the continent's big-game regions.

The only other method of big-game hunting commonly practiced is running animals with dogs. In a few places deer are still hunted legally with dogs. Hunters take stands and hope that deer jumped by the dogs will run past them. But that method, once a prime sport in the South, has been declining for years. Dogs are used very occasionally for javelina, but it's rough on the dogs. The big exotic boars of Tennessee and a few other spots (there are a good many in parts of Texas also) and feral swine, are run by dogs. The mountain lion is hunted thus. And in a number of states black bears are hunted with packs of tough hounds.

In closing this chapter I cannot resist telling of a highly specialized and rather amusing bear-dog operation I once ran into in Arizona. More than 30 years ago I was driving the highway that runs up through Globe, Show-Low, Snowflake and on up to Holbrook. It was not much of a highway then, and I had to contend with snow to boot. Somewhere up in the mountains there was a small house sitting among pines beside the road, and I happened to see an enormous black bear hanging in the yard. I couldn't resist stopping to have a look and to ask about it.

As I drove into the yard in the snow, a tiny and very feisty fox terrier came yapping out at me. A man came out of the house, grinning, and I told him I just wanted to look over his bear. As we visited he told me about his hunting method.

"I like to track an animal down," he said. "And I've killed several bears with this little dog right here."

That seemed ridiculous, but it was true. What he did was to take his rifle, put the tiny terrier in his hunting-coat pocket, and strike off on a bear track in fresh snow. When the track got smoking hot, he'd put the dog down. It would take off yapping on the track. The bear, instead of running, would pause to swipe and snarl at the tiny dog.

"That fool dog," he said, "doesn't have enough sense to quit, and the bear gets real annoyed because the dog is too little and quick to hit. While the bear is busy with the dog, I slip around with the wind favorable and finish the critter!"

There are, indeed, a few rugged hunters who enjoy tracking animals down. Over the years there have been magazine stories, quite well authenticated, about hunters getting on the track of a jumped whitetail buck in snow country and hanging with it until the deer, circling and getting as weary as the hunter, finally makes a slip. Tracking has brought a few hunters up with bears, too, and very occasionally with elk. Nonetheless, tracking down a big-game animal is a bit too much hunt for most modern-day sportsmen, and most of us who accomplished a kill this way would be so worn-out we'd have to sit beside the critter until we ate it up, just to get back enough strength to go home!

9.
WHITETAIL
DEER

Prime buck tests wind for sound or scent.

Of all North American big-game animals the whitetail deer is the most plentiful and is taken in the greatest numbers. It is also the most adaptable of all horned and antlered game. The species ranges over all of the contiguous U.S. except small portions of the Far West, over much of southern Canada, most of Mexico and even down into Central America.

No other big game requires as much craft of the hunter, though some species vie with it in certain respects. The mountain sheep, for example, is awesomely wary and intelligent. But sheep terrain actually challenges the hunter more than the quarry itself. Whitetails often live on the very edges of dense settlement, yet they are masters at keeping their private lives private.

The whitetail was the first big-game animal hunted by the Colonists. It was called the Virginia deer, and thus the Virginia whitetail became the "type" species, which means the physical type from which all other subspecies are differentiated. As settlement spread and very similar deer were found elsewhere, scientists decided none of the whitetail tribe was different enough physiologically to be termed a separate species. But a number of geographical races showed differences enough to place them as subspecies of the Virginia deer. Over many years of deer study and identification, at least 30 were named—16 in the U.S. and Canada, and almost as many south of the U.S. border.

As deer management began to take form, numerous transplants of whitetails were made from one region to another. The identifying characteristics of a number of subspecies were diluted, and in some instances the race disappeared or at least was no longer recognizable. In most parts of the country, hunters do not need to be overly concerned with whitetail subspecies. Official trophy records group all the related subspecies except one with the type subspecies, Virginia whitetail *(Odocoileus virginianus virginianus)*. The exception is the Arizona whitetail, or Coues deer *(Odocoileus virginianus couesi)*. On its home grounds the Arizona whitetail is also commonly known as a "fantail" because the erect flag appears extremely wide on this diminutive deer.

The Coues is granted separate recognition because it is isolated from other subspecies. Its range is below the Mogollon Rim in Arizona, west of the Rio Grande Valley in New Mexico, east of the Colorado River, and on down into Mexico. The Coues is a highly rated trophy, the rack very snug, the beams often almost meeting in front. It is small, grayish, with rather long ears. The prime range of this sprightly and extremely shy whitetail is in the mountain ranges of southeastern Arizona and southwestern New Mexico. In New Mexico, the Animas and Peloncillo Mountains in Hidalgo County are considered the best locations, and in Arizona the Galiuros, Santa Ritas, Tumacacoris, Catalinas, Grahams and Santa Teresas. This is a deer of intermediate altitude, usually found well above the floor of the desert, in the zone where grass, oak and juniper combine, and a little below where the pines begin.

One other subspecies is of special interest to at least a few hunters who may have an opportunity to try for it. This is the very small Carmen Mountains whitetail of a few small and isolated mountain ranges in the Big Bend country in western Texas, and across the border in similar Mexican terrain—particularly in the Carmen Mountains. This little deer is in some respects quite similar to the Arizona whitetail. It is not a candidate for official records because its extremely limited range is an island within the southern portion of the range of the Texas whitetail.

I have taken several specimens of this deer, locally called a "flagtail." It lives almost exclusively in the higher part of the mountain ranges, where it is often only a flash of waving white flag to a hunter prowling the piñon and juniper up above 5,000 feet. There are a good many within Big Bend National Park, up in the pine zone, but of course no hunting there. All of those available for hunting in the U.S. are on private lands in Texas.

For those whitetail enthusiasts who like to try different places and different subspecies, the big Northwest whitetail offers good hunting on the west slope of the Rockies—for example, in eastern Washington, northwestern Montana, portions of western Wyoming and northern Idaho. This deer also ranges into portions of Alberta and British Columbia. And the big Northern woodland whitetail, particularly far up in Maine or other remote areas of its northeastern range, is a grand trophy. Some of these deer top 300 pounds. A few astonishingly large specimens have been killed farther west, in Wisconsin and Minnesota.

Whitetail buck will travel edges but usually avoids crossing wide openings.

When the first settlers arrived, whitetails were fairly abundant even though the dense and uncut forests were not the best habitat for them. As the country was settled, farming and lumbering actually made better deer habitat. But market hunting, plus changes in agriculture and other habitat-reducing factors, eventually decimated the whitetail population. It is estimated by some researchers that fewer than a quarter-million were left at the turn of this century. The growth of the conservation movement may well have saved the species. First, laws ended the slaughter for meat and hides. Then whitetails became the targets of sport hunters, and deer management grew to a meticulous science. Meanwhile, transplants were made to deer-barren areas and the whitetails came back in great numbers, swiftly adapting to man's civilization. Today every state where the deer are present—and every Canadian Province and Mexican state—has a hunting season on whitetails. That is a remarkable record.

It is difficult to say where the best whitetail hunting is, for "best" means various things to various hunters. A man who owns a square mile of woodlot with a modest number of deer in it may have superb hunting right at home year after year, simply because he knows where his deer hang out. Another hunter may equate "best" with where the most deer are. Although a state with large numbers of whitetails may also have tremendous competition for them by an over-abundance of hunters, one can get a good idea of whitetail distribution by looking at average harvest for the various states, listed below. Bear in mind that these are conservative averages over a number of years, rather than precise figures for a single season.

Maine . . . *30,000 or more*	Iowa . . . *10,000 up*
New Hampshire . . . *10,000 or more*	Missouri . . . *22,000–28,000*
Vermont . . . *18,000 or more*	Arkansas . . . *20,000*
Massachusetts . . . *2,000 or more*	North Dakota . . . *25,000 (whitetails &*
Rhode Island . . . *a few*	*mule deer aggregate)*
Connecticut . . . *25 or less*	South Dakota . . . *25,000 (whitetails &*
New York . . . *65,000 up*	*mule deer,*
New Jersey . . . *5,000 up*	*whitetails dominant)*
Delaware . . . *500*	Nebraska . . . *15,000 (40% whitetails)*
Maryland . . . *8,000–12,000*	Kansas . . . *3,000*
Virginia . . . *25,000 or more*	Oklahoma . . . *5,000 up*
North Carolina . . . *35,000 or more*	Florida . . . *15,000 or more*
South Carolina . . . *25,000–40,000*	Alabama . . . *25,000 or more*
Georgia . . . *30,000*	Mississippi . . . *25,000 or more*
Pennsylvania . . . *100,000 up*	Louisiana . . . *30,000 up*
West Virginia . . . *10,000 or more*	Texas . . . *350,000*
Kentucky . . . *8,000*	New Mexico . . . *a few (Coues mostly)*
Tennessee . . . *7,000 or more*	Arizona . . . *3,000 (Coues)*
Michigan . . . *60,000, variable*	Colorado . . . *a few*
Wisconsin . . . *100,000, variable*	Wyoming . . . *12,000 up*
Minnesota . . . *50,000 or more*	Idaho . . . *10,000 up*
Ohio . . . *1,500 up*	Montana . . . *20,000–25,000*
Indiana . . . *4,000 or more*	Oregon . . . *a few*
Illinois . . . *6,000 or more*	Washington . . . *5,000 up*

Because of the vast range of the whitetail, it is impossible to pinpoint in every state where the best opportunities are. And because of the number of hunters today, kill statistics by counties or portions of states do not always reflect where the highest *success* percentages are. However, it is possible—

and may be helpful—to note a few of the continent's prime whitetail areas.

Across Canada, beginning in the east, Nova Scotia's Cape Breton Island (whitetails were not native here but imported) is excellent, with high success; in New Brunswick, Kings, Queens, Victoria and Restigouche counties average success for one out of four hunters; in Manitoba, the southeast and southwest have excellent populations, and the same is true of southeastern Saskatchewan.

In New England, Maine rates high, with the northwest, southwest, southeast and coastal counties best. All of New Hampshire has a good success ratio, and in Vermont the east-central portion produces highest, followed by the south and central. New York is a high-harvest state, with the Catskill and Adirondack areas and the central and western counties best.

Along the East Coast, Virginia is considered a quality whitetail state, with the west-central counties, and parts of the southeast getting the highest rating. The Carolinas get a good harvest, but hunting except in the National Forests and on state lands is predominantly on private and club lands. In recent years there has been a sharp rise in success among Maryland hunters. In Georgia the highest deer population presently is in the central portion of the state, and in Florida, although deer are well distributed, the north and northwest offer the most opportunities.

Pennsylvania is a phenomenal whitetail state. Excellent hunting is found over most of the state, but the north-central counties have a decided edge. In the Great Lakes region human encroachment has presented problems. Michigan still has a high deer population but a tremendous number of hunters. The northern Lower Peninsula, and the western part of the Upper Peninsula have the most deer. In Wisconsin the hunter picture is similar. Northwestern and northeastern counties get the high-production nod. Northeastern and north-central Minnesota have the most deer in that state.

North Dakota is something of a "sleeper" state, with better whitetail hunting than many suppose, and high success, especially along stream courses anywhere. In South Dakota, the Black Hills offer the prime hunting for visitors. Although mule deer are predominant in Nebraska, this state also is a sleeper for traveling hunters seeking new locations. The eastern half has the most whitetails. In the Ozarks region, the country south of the Missouri

River in Missouri rates high, and in Arkansas the southern and southeastern counties are best. Outstanding trophy bucks have been taken in Missouri in recent seasons.

In the Deep South, excellent hunting is found in Mississippi—in counties that border the Mississippi River. In Alabama the National Forests draw the average hunter because most hunting in this state is on private club lands. The most Louisiana deer are presently in the north, with northeastern counties rating a bit above north-central and northwest. Much club hunting here, too, complicates life for visitors, but National Forest and state lands offer opportunity.

Texas rates all by itself in the national whitetail picture. It is truly a phenomenon. As this is written, the last tabulated season shows over 350,000 whitetails harvested! It is estimated that at least one-fifth of the nation's total deer herd is in Texas, all but a small percentage of them whitetails. Because of the peculiar hunting situation here, the rising interest of non-residents in this state, and the extremely high success percentage (for visitors nearly 100 percent on a consistent basis) a few details are in order:

Compared to the size of the state there is only a picayune amount of public land. Deer hunting is almost entirely by fee on ranches. This is done by groups leasing hunting rights by season or several years at a time; or by day hunting, which means you pay so much per day to hunt; or by package hunts. The package hunt is booked ahead with a rancher, at a fixed price. Some offer lodging, some furnish lodging and meals at stipulated extra fees, some allow camping. The best of the package hunts are those where guide and transport are furnished. A few ranches with exceptionally abundant deer furnish guide and transport on a no-kill, no-pay guarantee.

The most abundant whitetails in Texas are in the so-called Hill Country of the Edwards Plateau. The largest ones are in the brush country south of San Antonio and fanning out from Laredo and running on to Del Rio. The Devil's River region, north of Del Rio, is also excellent. As I've mentioned, the small Carmen Mountains whitetail is in the mountains of the Big Bend country of western Texas. There is good hunting for Texas whitetails in the Panhandle, chiefly along stream courses.

We have already covered the hunting spots for Coues deer in New

Mexico and Arizona, and for the Northwest whitetail in Washington, Idaho, Wyoming, Montana. However, it's worth adding that in eastern Montana there is fine whitetail hunting in virtually all of the river bottoms. The subspecies is the big Dakota whitetail. In Wyoming this deer is extremely abundant in the northeast, the Black Hills area of the state. The counties here usually furnish all but a small percentage of the entire state's whitetail kill. Crook County is the hottest spot.

Undoubtedly the wariness of the whitetail—plus the fact that it is an animal of dense cover and the edges—is what makes hunting it such a challenge. It is forever jittery and tense. If you watch a feeding whitetail you will hardly ever see one keep its head to the ground, or to browse, more than a few seconds at a time. It jerks its head up to look, listen and sniff the air. For no understandable reason it may suddenly dart away a few yards, raise its tail part way, stare and snort, then resume feeding again. But only for seconds.

Indeed, the whitetail never seems to feel safe or relaxed. The first-time whitetail hunter, even though he may have taken many mule deer, must understand that this deer runs first and perhaps wonders later what frightened it. A doe may occasionally stand momentarily to stare, but mature bucks seldom do. At the slightest unusual sight, sound or scent, they are away. A whitetail doesn't often pause to look back, and when it goes over a ridge it doesn't usually stop there but keeps on running, over several ridges, or at least to put substantial distance between it and the danger.

Whitetails invariably run into and through cover. They are inordinately wary of wide-open places. Where I live, it is fairly common at dusk or dawn to see a number of deer feeding on a patch of green winter oats. But this is definitely unusual. And even then they usually have cover close enough to get into in a hurry. When a whitetail flees, unless hard-pressed it is reluctant to cross open fields. It may bound across a small opening, but usually it keeps to the edge of cover, taking the long way to avoid exposing itself.

I have emphasized in earlier chapters that any hunter must familiarize himself with what animals feed on in any given location, what kind of cover they prefer, and where their water sources are. The whitetail can be

Colorblind and with poor frontal vision, buck has come almost up to stand.

Snowshoes can be very helpful. In some states shotgun is mandatory for deer.

perplexing to a hunter who travels far from his home state, because it has adapted to so many widely differing habitats. Watering places are not a problem for whitetails in most of the range, but may be in the case of Southwestern deer. In such instances it is mandatory that the hunter scout the watering places. It is also a good idea even where water is not scarce to look for places where the deer habitually cross streams.

Cover, of course, is always present where whitetails abound. Regardless of the type of country you hunt, remember that mature bucks especially will seek truly secluded spots to bed down. This means dense cover. In some places the cover may be on the ridges; in others it may be down low, where heavy brush fringes a dry wash. When the deer travel undisturbed, they will go from bedding ground to water or forage along the edges of cover. A small saddle in a low ridge, where brush grows below taller trees, makes a safe, hidden crossing and may be a great place to watch. I have collected whitetails on several occasions in just such a spot, and within mere feet, by checking out sign first and then watching.

The whitetail's food is extremely varied, and will of course differ widely from state to state, depending on what is available. The main observation for the hunter to make is of *seasonal* foods that may be especially abundant, and thus draw whitetails almost like a bait. Slashings left from pulpwood cutting, where poplar shoots abound, draw deer. I've watched them come day after day to a certain big oak that was dropping a bonanza acorn crop. I've also seen them come eagerly to a lush crop of wild black cherries or choke cherries. A big beech with abundant fallen mast may be a hot spot to watch. An old abandoned apple orchard bearing fruit is a deer magnet. Farm crops also draw many whitetails to the field edges near their cover.

Wherever whitetails are found in a region of woodlots and farms, perhaps with creeks flowing here and there with cover along them, they are easier to hunt than in broad expanses of wild cover. They will be awesomely wary, but a hunter can read the cover more easily and predict almost without fail where the deer must move. An important scouting operation in any agricultural area is to walk the fences before season. This is also very worthwhile in ranch country.

There will invariably be certain places where the undisturbed deer, moving from cover to food or water, and vice versa, jump a fence. Maybe there's a low place where a top wire is down or the fence sags. A perfect setup is such a spot with a feeding area on one side and a woods immediately on the other. The deer can come out to the edge, look the situation over, and if they feel safe, hop across into the field. A hunter who takes a proper stand inside the woods is very likely to connect.

There is another interesting little fence-watching trick. Until I came to Texas to live I had never seen a deer try to go *under* a fence. But they do, most often in open country without a lot of tall cover—such as the brush and cactus range of southern Texas. Here, in small gullies there may be a modest opening under the low wire. I've seen big bucks come barreling up to a fence and drop down to crawl under. I've also seen them race straight toward a spot on a cross-pasture fence where a middle strand is broken. They were obviously used to going through here. I learned to hold fire until the running deer got to the fence. It would pause to scramble through, and thus offer almost a still shot. Why they fail to jump over, which they easily can, I'm uncertain, unless it is to keep from prominently showing themselves.

Numerous Eastern and Southern hunters use the drive as a productive method of deer hunting. (In that category I include the use of dogs, where legal.) Driving is not nearly as popular in the Great Lakes area and westward. Sitting on a stand watching for deer is the method favored today by most hunters, or else, for more restless ones, prowling around—still hunting. In Chapter 8, these various methods are covered in some detail. But we can add a bit here that pertains specifically to the whitetail.

As noted, edges of crop fields near cover are good places to set up a watch, a stand. In hunting whitetails in large forest tracts, the ridge saddles, the stream crossings, the deer trails, the concentrations of abundant seasonal foods all make good watching spots. Old logging roads in forests are excellent. Look for a place where deer have been crossing. The opening offers a shot. Try to find a sitting spot at the trail edge where you can see both ways for a fair rifle range. This same type of stand is used extensively in parts of the South and in the Southwest on large ranches.

I used to hunt old logging roads in the Great Lakes region. When I moved to Texas I discovered the challenging whitetail hunting for burly old bucks down in the cactus and thornbrush. On these ranches seismograph crews have bulldozed many trails, checking for oil-well sites. And ranchers also build such roads in order to get around on large expanses. They're just bulldozed tracks through the brush. In this cover deer are difficult to spot, because they do not stand as high as most of the brush. Thus it is common practice to take a stand beside a ranch road, or *sendero*.

Regardless of where you try this, North or South, you must realize that quite often does and fawns wander into the trail and along it for short distances. But bucks have an exasperating habit of coming to the very edge, peeking out, then bounding across. Watch the edges very carefully. Keep glassing them constantly. Often you'll pick up the head and neck of a peering buck. That's the time to make your try.

In hilly whitetail country, take your stand when possible on a slope so that you can look down and into the valley and onto another slope. Deer will not spot you as readily as if you are lower. But keep in mind that when shooting at any angle, up or down, you will tend to shoot high. Depending on how steep the slope is, you may need to compensate. Tree stands over deer trails or crossings are unusually successful, because the animals don't look up, and your scent is above ground except where wind may blow it toward a flat or ridge, or on days when it is down-drafted. Also, try to select stands for whitetails in any wooded country with small openings so you are watching an opening that has at least some cover growth in it. Whitetails always feel safer in such places than in wide-open forest meadows.

Still hunting for whitetails requires true craft and is a classic method, with success an infinitely satisfying experience. The hunter who becomes adept at it must be as patient as the stand hunter, and he must also practice restraint and severe self-discipline. "One slow step at a time" is the rule, watching where each boot is placed, to avoid any sounds. Still hunters soon learn that certain trees are to be avoided. For example, in climes where both live oaks and Spanish or other deciduous oaks grow, the ground beneath the latter will be littered with dry, fallen leaves during deer season. But you can walk quietly under live oaks, which drop their leaves in spring. Walking on gravel and small rocks is noisy, but sand or short grass or clay is quiet. In cedar swamps or breaks, or among conifers, there are seldom dry leaves to contend with, but brittle twigs and sticks must be avoided.

Some hunters incorrectly believe that prowling the course of a noisy stream is effective because the sounds of the stream cover the sounds of the hunter. By and large, whitetails shy away from noisy streams except to cross them. They cannot hear keenly near a loud stream, and thus instinctively avoid it. The still hunter should always be alert and listening for sounds deer may make. Deer break sticks and clink rocks when they walk, too. I once collected a nice buck in northern Michigan because I heard it cross a stream and instantly dropped down to wait for it.

Whitetails are not vocal animals, but occasionally a fawn may bleat, and quite commonly a buck in rut makes a low, guttural grunting sound, in series, as it follows a doe at a brief distance. The whistling breath of a deer

His outline broken by fence, hunter has good rest and wide view of deer country.

signals that it is alerted but probably has not yet fled. Occasionally one can also hear a whitetail so alerted stamp its foot. A quick, loud snort means high alarm. A loud one followed by several short ones of lesser intensity invariably means the deer is running away.

Still hunters should always carry their rifles at the ready. Shots at close range may need to be swift. The whitetail deer is such an alert and wary creature that it seldom allows danger to get extremely close. A still hunter who moves in slow-motion, noiselessly, in cover and shadow, and with the wind in his face, now and then completely hoodwinks a deer and suddenly sees it in its bed within a few yards, or standing quietly. At such times whitetails may seem utterly chagrined and disbelieving that this could happen. A buck in its bed may lie immobile for a few moments, hoping it has not been seen, and a buck on its feet may simply stare.

On a hunt several years ago on my ranch I shot a big buck that rose from its bed over the lip of a cedar-shaded canyon and stood utterly still in shadow. It had heard something it didn't like and had arisen. But I heard it, too, and saw it, and froze. It was not certain what, or exactly where, I was, and the air was very still. The animal's dilemma obviously was whether to run and give itself away, or to stand like a statue in shadow. I very slowly raised my rifle and collected the buck at a mere 15 feet. On another occasion, still hunting, I was walking on flat rocks, noiselessly, among cedars. Up the slope there was tall grass beneath Spanish oaks. As I paused after a few steps, listening and looking, I heard grass and leaves rustle. I moved not a muscle. Finally I saw a good buck walking straight at me. I waited until it was only a few paces distant. Then I quickly raised the gun. The deer jerked to a halt and stared for a couple of seconds. It was just gathering muscles for a bound when I let it down.

Because you hunt the edges after whitetails, it's a good idea to keep your own shadow in mind. Under certain conditions, a man moving late or early along the edge of an opening may be in shadow but bright sun filtering through trees may throw his long, exaggerated shadow intermittently out into the open. As he moves, his shadow moves, and it may spook a deer feeding or standing along the edge some distance away. Also, whenever you are hunting whitetails by the still method early or late in the day, never hunt into the sun. It will blind you and make using a scope difficult, and it will also highlight you at any unexpected moment, making you easier for deer to spot. Conversely, hunting with the sun behind you places the deer at a disadvantage. With the sun in its eyes, it, too, has difficulty seeing. All of the above applies to still hunting for any game.

Quite commonly, still hunting changes to a stalk. You see a deer too far off for a shot, and have to get closer. Sometimes you may have to move in quite close because of brush or trees interfering. Thus you need to know what reactions to watch for in the deer. If it throws its head up and stares, stop and freeze. It may move its head from side to side. This is an attempt to see you better but it doesn't necessarily mean the deer will run. Foot-stamping says the deer is curious and uncertain. If after a bit it lowers its head or changes the direction of its gaze, you can probably move again. It has decided no harm is near.

Author carefully approaches young buck he has downed from stand on deer run.

One way you can tell is to watch its tail. Typically, the whitetail that stares will have its tail down, and as its mind is made up that all is well, it gives the tail a switch from side to side. When you see this, you know it will go back to feeding. If the tail raises, more or less straightening out, the deer is really alarmed. If, after that, the tail moves over to one side, it is about to run. As the tail goes straight up, that's the flight signal.

Whitetail bucks leave special signs that assist a hunter. One of these is the rub. The bucks utilize small saplings for polishing their antlers, and for practice battles. In most instances the selected tree will not be more than an inch or so in diameter, and it will have the bark scraped off and small branches broken, in an area perhaps a couple of feet vertically, and at about the shoulder height of the deer as it holds its head forward. A rub, if it is fresh, means that a buck is probably in the vicinity. Several rubs in a small space usually mean that a buck is definitely in residence.

Bucks each have their own bailiwick and as the rut nears, and during it, they patrol the area. Several fresh rubs throughout any given expanse are a hot sign and sometimes a stand can be selected to watch much of it. Bucks in any given geographical area will generally select certain varieties of saplings for rubbing. This is not infallible but the tendency is emphatic enough so you should always look, after one rub is found, for rubs on similar trees in the sector. They like small spruces or balsams in the North because these and their branches are stiff enough to rub against and to battle. In lower Texas I have noticed that the retamas, green-barked small trees with vicious thorns, have a special attraction for rubbing bucks. All such lore is vital for the whitetail hunter.

Without question, the buck scrape is the most important and surefire whitetail sign. If you can locate and watch scrapes that are in use each season, assuming the rut occurs during the season, you're close to filling your tag. The scrape is a spot pawed out by a buck. The animal urinates in it as a sign to does on his home ground. Sometimes, does visit the spot and they urinate in the scrape as a sign to the buck that they have been there and are ready to be bred. A scrape is almost always located near a tree from which a branch overhangs it at a height the buck can reach. The buck, standing over his scrape, will reach up with his nose and nuzzle and pick at the branch, and brush or rip at it with his antlers. No one seems to know just why this is done, but it is a part of the ritual and it assists in locating scrapes. The buck may have several scrapes marking his domain, and he will visit them again and again. The hunter who first hunts scrapes when the rut is in progress, and then watches one hour after hour, especially early in the morning, has indeed learned his whitetail lessons well.

This brings us to calling. Whitetail bucks fight often during rut, if two happen to come in contact and particularly if one is trespassing on another's breeding ground. Mouth-blown deer calls have been used in some states. Bucks do occasionally respond to them, but after trying them here and there I am convinced that such calls, which are supposed to imitate the bleat of fawn or doe, work best in summer when does will run to them. Nonetheless, some bucks are killed every year because they came to a mouth-blown deer call. Some callers even whack a stick on the ground to imitate the stamped foot of a deer. However, success is limited with this kind of calling. In passing it should be mentioned that whitetails can be spooked out of brush pockets by squalling loudly on a coyote or fox call.

The most effective kind of calling is the technique known as rattling—and, for me, successful rattling is the supreme thrill in whitetail hunting. Its use is not yet as common in the upper part of the whitetail range as in the Southwest, but the idea is spreading as hunters hear or read about its attraction for bucks.

When I moved to Texas, it was said that the rattling of antlers would not work anywhere but down in the brush country. Then it was tried in the Texas hill country and worked like a charm, and it has now been successful in varied locations all over whitetail range. To be successful, it must be used during the rut. The rattling antlers are made by cutting a pair from a skull. Usually the burl next to the skull is sawed off each antler. A hole is drilled through each base and a thong slipped through both and tied, so the pair is easily carried over the shoulder. Brow tines are sawed off, and the sharp ends of other tines, to avoid hurting your hands. The rough sawed places are smoothed with a file. An eight- or 10-point set works best.

When bucks fight, their antlers slam together, rattle and crack. Their hoofs rake gravel or rocks and they smash into brush. Thus, a good rattling technique is about as follows: At dawn the hunter stakes a stand where he can see for at least a fair distance. He conceals himself. A good stand might have a stiff and leafy bush nearby, and a rough-barked tree and a patch of gravel.

The hunter, with his gun leaned close and handy, smartly brings the antlers together, tines intermeshed, with a sharp crack. This is followed by a rattling of the tines. Then comes an animated raking of gravel with the tines, smacking of the bush, raking tines against bark, and even sometimes turning an antler over and pounding the ground with it—followed by more rattling. After this spasm there is quiet, and then the fight begins again.

I've had big bucks come racing right at me, sliding to a stop within a few feet, hair up, eyes wild. Others come sneaking, unsure, or else bent on running off with a doe while two other bucks fight. Spike bucks act downright silly. If one looks behind or all around, the hunter should, too. A big buck may be coming to run the spike off. If a buck comes into sight but is wary, just a quiet tickling of antler tips sometimes convinces him, or a simple raking of gravel and bush beating. Rattling up a whitetail is always a dramatic experience, no matter how many times you've done it. Be assured it can be successful anywhere.

Deer scents are used, too. Some of these are simply a mask to cover the smell of the hunter. I have read about apple scents for whitetails; a New York State whitetail may be attracted by apple scents, but a deer in southern Texas or northeastern Wyoming might not even want to investigate the strange smell. Other attractor scents are based on the scent of the deer. During rut the metatarsal glands on the hind legs are wet with a pungent excretion. Scents of this sort may well attract whitetails, but my use of them has been as a mask for human scent while in the process of rattling antlers.

10.
MULE
DEER

Middle-sized muleys like these are gregarious.

S econd in importance only to the whitetail is the mule deer of the West. Thousands of hunters have grown up hardly realizing there was any other kind of deer. In one form or another, mule deer range from far down in Mexico all the way north to southeastern Alaska, and from the Dakotas to western Texas and all the way to the Pacific.

Taxonomists have split the mule deer tribe into 11 races, or subspecies. The type species, or more properly subspecies, from which all the others derive, is the Rocky Mountain mule deer. No big-game animal on the continent has as wide a range as this particular mule-deer type. Nor has any ever been known to show such amazing tolerance for varying latitudes and climates. Rocky Mountain mule deer have been found living slightly above the 60th parallel in the Far North, and they are abundant as far south as the 35th parallel, which runs roughly across the middle of Arizona and New Mexico. The western boundary of the range is marked by the crown of the Cascades and the Sierra, and the eastward boundary is about at the Missouri River in the Dakotas and the Panhandle in Oklahoma.

It is the Rocky Mountain mule deer that most hunters pursue. No big-game animal is held in higher esteem by sportsmen who live in or visit its range. Some Eastern hunters, and perhaps properly, consider the big, blocky mule deer "dumb" by comparison with the whitetail. But vast numbers of hunters from various parts of the continent have for some years eagerly migrated to "muley" country each fall for the excitement of hunting this animal.

All of the mule-deer tribe are deer of the slopes. Looking at the entire range among all subspecies, one is instantly struck by the fact that they have been able to colonize over a vast area, all of it either mountainous or at least hilly. But they have been unable to permanently spread eastward to any extent across the flat plains. Mule deer may be considered forest animals, but not in the same way as whitetails. Typically they are deer of far more open country. In the heavily timbered Rockies they may be found in timber, but most subspecies quite commonly consort on open slopes, in foothills and on mountain meadows, where only a scattering of cover may be present. With one exception (the Columbian blacktail) muleys are seldom found in dense brush.

The mule deer is wary, but not by any means as wary as the white-tail, and never jittery and nervous. It gives the impression at times of being a rather trusting creature, extremely gregarious and congenial with its own kind. Whitetail does are always bickering, mule deer almost never. Mule deer are irrevocably tied to the wilderness. They have in a few cases been able to sustain themselves properly on the fringes of civilization, as whitetails quickly learned to. In fact, the encroachments of civilization are causing serious difficulties for mule deer in several states. They simply seem unable to adapt.

It is not necessary for hunters to be able to identify all of the mule-deer subspecies. The Rocky Mountain mule-deer range encompasses roughly 70 percent of the entire domain. However, at least three subspecies are of importance. One is the desert mule deer, found in Texas west of the Pecos River, in a few counties of southern New Mexico, in southeastern Arizona—and south of all these states, well down into central Mexico. It is a deer of the desert and of desert mountains. On the average it is smaller than the Rocky Mountain mule deer; large bucks field dressed weigh from about 125 to 190 at most. The antlers are well formed but generally not as large as those of the type species. A desert mule deer with a 25- to 27-inch spread is a good trophy, indeed. This deer is extremely important to its numerous fans in Texas. It is supremely abundant over its modest range there, but almost entirely hunted on private lands whose owners accept only a limited number of hunters and carefully manage their deer as a crop. Thus, the total annual kill averages only 10 to 12 thousand. In New Mexico it is not purposely sought to any great extent, but is avidly hunted in Arizona, with an average kill of three to four thousand.

Apart from the Rocky Mountain mule deer, the subspecies of greatest importance is the Columbian blacktail. The range of this deer is on the western slope of the Coast Ranges in British Columbia and southward. In Washington and Oregon, the crest of the Cascades is the boundary, and the deer are plentiful all along the west slope to the Pacific. Farther south, the range extends along the coastal slope about to the middle of California.

The blacktail has for many years caused confusion among both sportsmen and scientists. Hunters even in west Texas and up in the Rockies

Small, fat buck tops ridge; cautious hunter may find it feeding just beyond crest.

often erroneously speak of their mule deer as "blacktails." And for many years the Columbian blacktail was considered a species by itself. Later scientists determined that it is simply a race of mule deer. But it has so many distinctly different physical characteristics that it may be well along in the evolutionary process toward becoming a true species.

The blacktail is darker in winter coat than the Rocky Mountain deer, and it is smaller. The antlers are usually smaller, too, and quite often with fewer branches. The shape of the tail is reminiscent of the whitetail's, only shorter. It is black on the top, with a bit of white showing at the edges. The tail of other mule deer is slender and in the Rocky Mountain and desert varieties it's white with a black tip. When a whitetail deer runs, it raises its tail erect so the white underside shows and it waves the tail back and forth. The Rocky Mountain and desert mule deer and other subspecies—except the Columbian blacktail—run with the tail down. Only very occasionally does one raise its tail, and then not even to straight-out height. But the blacktail sometimes runs off with flag raised, though not waved from side to side in whitetail style.

The Columbian blacktail lives in a very different world from that of its relatives. It is a denizen of the dense coastal brush and rain forests with heavy undergrowth. This makes hunting it astonishingly similar to whitetail hunting, and indeed the blacktail has learned many of the tricks of hiding and flight in heavy cover that characterize the whitetail. It is an extremely important game animal throughout its range. For instance, in Washington, where the deer herd is estimated around half a million animals, blacktails make up at least half of that number. In many seasons as much as three-fifths of the total kill consists of blacktails. In Oregon more Rocky Mountain deer are taken, but still the blacktail is extremely important. In one fairly recent season the Oregon harvest was about 87,000 mule deer and about 54,000 blacktails.

In California, which has six subspecies of mule deer, the blacktail is the most abundant. The Rocky Mountain deer is of some importance, and so is the California mule deer. Other less consequential subspecies in California are the southern mule deer, Inyo mule deer and burro deer. Several other minor subspecies are found in Baja and coastal Mexico. There is, incidentally, a substantial amount of interbreeding between the blacktail and the Rocky Mountain mule deer all along the boundary where their ranges overlap.

A third subspecies of importance—it should receive much more attention than it presently does—is a close relative of the Columbian blacktail. This is the Sitka deer, found in southeastern Alaska, northern coastal British Columbia and some coastal islands there. It has severe ups and downs of population because of difficult winters, but it is often extremely abundant and with high bag limits—in some past seasons as many as four. It has received small attention from hunters simply because visitors are after bigger game. Some natives hunt it for meat but many prefer larger animals, such as moose or caribou.

As this is written, a number of Western states are disturbed over declines in mule-deer herds. Colorado, which at one time allowed as many as four deer per license in some hunt units, has cut back severely; Arizona and Oregon are both conducting studies to try to pin down unexplained reasons for instability of mule-deer herds. Certainly at this point mule deer are not in any danger. But in view of spotty declines, the fact that they do not adapt well to man's inroads, makes prediction of the long future for this hunting uncertain.

However, a lot of mule deer are still harvested each season. A look at average seasonal harvests over recent years in the mule deer states and provinces will serve as a guide to show the general density of distribution.

North Dakota . . . *5,000 up*	Wyoming . . . *60,000 to 80,000*
South Dakota . . . *5,000 or less*	Idaho . . . *60,000*
Nebraska . . . *9,000*	Montana . . . *75,000*
Kansas . . . *500 or less*	California . . . *40,000 to 75,000 (all subspecies)*
Oklahoma . . . *a few*	Oregon . . . *100,000 to 145,000 (all subspecies)*
Texas . . . *10,000 up*	Washington . . . *60,000 to 90,000 (all subspecies)*
New Mexico . . . *30,000*	Alaska . . . *10,000 to 20,000*
Arizona . . . *14,000*	British Columbia . . . *70,000*
Utah . . . *100,000*	Alberta . . . *modest kill*
Nevada . . . *15,000 to 45,000*	Saskatchewan . . . *2,000 to 4,000*
Colorado . . . *50,000 to 80,000*	Manitoba . . . *near extinction*

Although it is not possible to pinpoint all the best hunting locations, it will be helpful to list general portions of states where mule-deer populations are highest. For example, in North Dakota the southwestern counties are the mule-deer range, and in South Dakota virtually all mule deer are west of the Missouri River. There is intermingling in both instances with whitetails, which are predominant. The same is true in Nebraska, where most of the mule deer are in the western half of the state. Kansas has a few in the northwest, and in Oklahoma there are a few in the extreme western part of the Panhandle.

In Texas, desert mule deer are abundant in the few counties west of the Pecos River, with Brewster County probably the one with the largest population. There are also a few Rocky Mountain mule deer in the Texas Panhandle, chiefly in the Palo Duro Canyon region. New Mexico mule deer range over most of the state. Some of the best opportunities are in the Sangre de Cristo Range in the north, in the Gila National Forest of the southwest and (for abundant deer but modest racks) the Lincoln National

Forest in the central southern area. Arizona has Rocky Mountain mule deer over much of the state, desert mule deer in the southeast, the latter making up perhaps 20 percent of the total mule-deer harvest. The North Kaibab furnishes the major share of the Rocky Mountain deer kill, but there is excellent remote hunting for trophy deer in the extreme northwest, and fair to good opportunities in most of the National Forests. Desert mule deer range the foothills of the small ranges in the southeast.

Utah, a high-kill state, offers good chances almost everywhere. The Kanab region and the Dixie National Forest to the north, the Book Cliffs in the eastern part of the state, the rough country around Price, the Manti-La-Sal National Forest are a few prime locations. In Nevada the top location is in the northeast, in the forests, foothills and mountains of Elko County. However, there is good hunting in all of the National Forests. This state is generally overlooked by non-resident hunters. It shouldn't be. Colorado is a welter of opportunity, with deer ranging over all of the 13 million acres of National Forests, as well as other lands. Almost anywhere in the western two-thirds of the state you have a better than average chance of success.

Wyoming also has mule deer almost everywhere. The largest one I've ever taken came out of virtually treeless country of rough canyons and gullies west of Gillette. Such terrain makes an interesting and different hunt. The most highly productive areas of the state are as follows: the Black Hills in the northeast, in Crook County; the several blocks of the Medicine Bow National Forest in the southeast; the foothills and higher country in the region of the Big Horn National Forest in the north-central counties. Like Wyoming, Idaho offers good chances over much of the state. The best harvests are generally in the counties across the middle of the state. Montana is one of the best mule-deer states, with deer distributed from border to border. The southwestern region is a prime one; another is along the east slope of the Continental Divide. But there is so much excellent hunting that choice of location is a toss-up.

In California you have a selection of subspecies. Up in the northeast, the Modoc National Forest and parts of the Lassen furnish Rocky Mountain mule deer. The forests to the south offer California mule deer. The western slopes of the Cascades and the Sierra, and all of the coastal forest and foothill country from the Oregon border south into Santa Barbara County swarm with Columbian blacktails. Overall, the northern counties furnish the bulk of the kill.

The blacktail picture in Oregon is bright, with abundant deer all the way from the crown of the Cascades west to the Pacific. The blocks of the Suislaw National Forest near the coast, and the southwestern counties, are prime locations. Rocky Mountain mule deer blanket much of the state from the east Cascade slope to the border with Idaho, but the highest success is generally in the counties of the northeast. Washington blacktails are extremely abundant, ranging as in Oregon from the west slope of the Cascades to the Pacific. The counties of Puget Sound—San Juan, Island, Kitsap— swarm with these deer. But almost all the western counties offer excellent chances of success. All of the east slope furnishes fine Rocky Mountain mule deer hunting. So does Stevens County up in the northeast, and the Blue Mountains region of the southeast.

There is excellent hunting for the Sitka deer in the Alaskan Panhandle and surrounding islands. This deer is also abundant along coastal northern British Columbia. The southern coast and Vancouver furnish quality hunting for Columbian blacktails, and inland the Rocky Mountain mule deer is prominent, with the best populations in the south. Alberta mule deer—what remains of them—are in the foothills of the southwestern part of the province. The same is true in Saskatchewan, but the population is not at all large.

There are many facets of mule-deer personality that make this animal tremendously appealing to hunters. But those who have launched their hunting experience on whitetails will find the new endeavor quite different. Also, the tyro hunter who gains his first hunting experience with mule deer may be lulled into believing this is an easy animal to bag. Some are, especially young deer. But the collecting of an old buck, at the peak of his prime or just past it, requires all the craft any hunter can muster.

The mule deer is a far more placid animal than the whitetail. It is a heavily built, rough-hewn animal that always seems to me much more like a kind of wild range stock than a highly suspicious game animal. Without doubt, the habitat of the mule deer lends some of this calm quality. Vistas

Hunters are seeking big bucks that lie close during day but may be jumped from beds.

In years when juniper berries are abundant, scout them for browsing mule deer.

are long, and in most instances the deer can see much farther than whitetails can. Muleys are also curious. I've watched big mule deer on scores of occasions standing on distant slopes and staring at me as I walked or drove or rode a horse. A whitetail would seldom get caught that far out in the open, and if it did it would run first and never look back to see what frightened it.

Another attribute that makes these deer sometimes seem like livestock is their gregariousness. Bucks of certain age groups seem to thoroughly enjoy hanging around together. I recall one fall photographing seven big eight- and 10-point bucks together. Each day when I drove out along a ranch trail where they lived I'd see them. On another occasion I counted a dozen bucks together. Not always, but generally, groups of mature bucks will be together without does, except of course during rut. Spikes and fork-

Piñon is plentiful in some parts of muley range, and deer love piñon nuts.

horns commonly tag along with groups of does. Only the very old and out-size trophy bucks are likely to be loners, secluded and far back in remote hiding places. One fall I spotted with my binocular a group of antlerless mule deer on an open slope and was able to get close enough to count them. There were 32! This kind of grouping is seldom observed among whitetails.

In an earlier chapter in discussing tracks I mentioned the difference between the way mule deer and whitetails run. The hunter who closely observes mule deer can tell from their actions, as with whitetails but in a different manner, what they are likely to do. A mule deer that is surprised by a hunter may stand and stare. Then, if not panicked, it may start to walk away in a very odd routine. It takes somewhat exaggerated steps, and as one front foot is placed the head is drawn back, then as the other foot is brought forward the head is, too. This is a comical display, the deer seeming to tiptoe away with head bobbing. A deer that does this is not spooked but uncertain.

If suddenly startled, mule deer may hop away a short distance, stiff-legged. No other American game animal has this gait. It bounces into the air by slightly bending the knees and then straightening them. It hits the ground stiff-legged on all fours and bounces again. Each bounce takes it only a short hop, like a youngster on a pogo stick. A deer reacting in this manner will almost certainly pause, a short distance away, and look back, long mule ears cocked in puzzlement. It is well startled and not much liking what it sees, but it isn't all-out spooked.

However, after this display, if the deer decides to run, make no mistake it can really go. Mule deer are extremely powerful, vigorous and fast. Long leaps eat up the distance. A galloping mule deer bounds so that all four feet come down together, the front ones striking a split second before the hind. But the hind feet do not pass the forefeet, the way a whitetail runs. They strike in position and all four feet push back for the next bound. Mule deer also have a trotting gait which is quite different—a pacing movement, one forefoot at a time, and hind foot likewise. A deer using this gait is only mildly disturbed.

Curiosity has killed many a mule deer. Scores of times I've watched a buck take off across a flat as if the Devil were after it, bound up a slope, and then at the crest suddenly stop, turn broadside, and look back down at me. You cannot always predict that a deer will do this, but so many do that it pays to know the trait. A hunter who holds his fire and gets a good rest may well get a standing shot. Further, mule deer do not seem to stay frightened long. Very often one will race over a ridge, even after being shot at, and then if the hunter climbs the ridge the deer won't be far down the other side, and may even be feeding. A whitetail would put three ridges behind it before stopping. I have also watched an unsettling sight occasionally when a buck from a group of bucks was shot: The others would race off a short distance, then come trailing back to look at their fallen companion.

However, the perplexing side of mule-deer hunting is that the species is definitely unpredictable. A deer may do any of the things I've just described, yet the next one will run right out of the country. Of course, much depends on how hard deer are hunted in a given territory. When mule deer are pushed hard, they are uncanny but quirky at hiding. I've seen one that had spotted me make a quick sneak into a small thicket and lie down, head flat out. And I've walked within yards of a big buck hiding among rocks and it would not move a muscle. If I'd not seen sunlight glint from an antler tip I'd never have known it was there. Sometimes these deer defeat themselves by their ways of hiding. You may jump one from a bed among a few piñons on a grassy slope, shoot at close range and miss it. The deer, instead of barreling over the ridge, may run behind a clump of bushes and whirl into them, to stand there immobile.

When hunted hard, mule deer will move far greater distances than whitetails. The whitetail learns to keep out of sight on its home grounds but if you disturb mule deer unduly, especially mature bucks, they will drift back into wilder country. This is natural. They live in "big country." Moving over a mountain is no problem for them. Any secluded canyon that is plenty tough for a walking hunter to get into may well contain a real old buster of a buck, and perhaps several.

In order to be successful consistently, a hunter must learn that these deer commonly bed down in places that would horrify a whitetail. A single bush on an open slope may be the spot. A scattering of small junipers or low piñon on a hillside may have a dozen deer under them. Rocky points in forest country that overlook a valley are typical of mule-deer resting places. So, too, now and then are totally barren shale buttes thrusting up from a flat almost as barren.

Because of the vast expanses in which they live, the drive is a method not much used in hunting these deer, but in certain situations it can be used. Deer in foothill country will move up a mountain when disturbed by keeping to draws that lead to the top. In Utah one time I helped push deer up such a draw in the Dixie Forest. No attempt was made to frighten them. I simply rode a horse a couple of miles through foothill cover and into the lower mouth of the draw, hoping for a chance shot as I went. Another hunter was waiting far up on top. Several bucks moved on up, where of course the draw narrowed. When they topped out, the waiting hunter picked off the largest one.

Mule deer migrate from summer to winter range. Dalrymple photographed these in high

Drives are sometimes used when hunting coastal blacktails. The cover is invariably dense, and there are numerous narrow canyons. A couple of hunters stake out on the rim while one or two move deer out of the draw and upward. However, Rocky Mountain mule deer live in much more open terrain. Glassing (from a ridge where a large sweep of country can be seen, or while cruising trails in a vehicle or riding a horse) is one of the important methods of mule-deer hunting. A good many hunters nowadays use four-wheel-drive vehicles, and the fact is, when they're properly used and kept on the trails they disturb deer less than a horse. Make no mistake, back-country mule deer are easily spooked by the sound of a horse plodding

pine country near Williams, Ariz. Later in season he'd have hunted lower elevations.

along. In open terrain in particular I've heard groups of mule deer racing away over a shale slope long before I saw them.

On one occasion, I vividly recall pulling up my horse to glass a canyon and hearing deer clattering off around the point from me. They had not seen me but had heard my horse as I moved over the flintrock shale.

The routine of mule deer very generally is to bed down fairly early in the day. Given good weather, they may be down feeding in foothills or on the low ridges during the night, but at first light they will go to water and then begin to move up. Mule deer in good health are always much fatter than whitetails because they are such calm creatures. It doesn't take much heat to make them uncomfortable. A day that a hunter might think chilly would be warm for a larded-up old buck.

In country where there are numerous rimrocks up high, the deer will move from the ridge bases up toward them sometimes as early as eight a.m. and almost certainly by mid-morning. In country where the animals are not disturbed, they often will follow well-worn trails, just like cattle. A hunter who scouts such trails, which he can sometimes find by glassing, can place himself in a good position to have deer pass him on their way up. Other good stands may be found. The Burnham Brothers, famous for their animal calls, showed me a spot in remote back country in Colorado one time where many mule deer moved along a small draw and they had to come around and under a narrow overhang of rock. It was a place where anyone could collect a deer almost any day.

However, stand hunting is not as much used as for whitetails, simply because the country is so immense. Except in special situations such as that noted above, deer are not likely to simply wander past. Still hunting, stalking and glassing are the common methods utilized. Vehicles and horseback hunting may be considered forms of still hunting even though they are relatively noisy. They do cover a lot of country, which is advantageous.

After the deer have moved up to their bedding places—at least most of them move up—some excellent opportunities await the gent who is physically fit and can take climbing that may be rugged. This is prowling the high rimrock areas. Almost without fail the deer will be on the shady side. A high rim may look from below as if there is no place to hide. But once you get up there it's a totally different world. Huge chunks of rock are a jumble, and there are innumerable pockets among them where a deer can lie in cool shade and survey the entire slope and valley below. The animals will lie tight, too. A hunter should move slowly and quietly. Sometimes a buck will bound out practically underfoot. At other times one will be seen to sneak off silently around a corner of the rock pile.

On one hunt I combined glassing and rim hunting. I was out a bit late in the morning and, glassing a slope with scattered juniper on it, I saw an excellent buck much too far away to shoot at. It was moving up the mountain. I watched it go to the top, where yellow-brown rimrock capped the ridge. Slowly, plodding along, it went over the top to the shady side. I marked the spot and began climbing. Three-quarters of an hour later I went over about where the deer had. The buck had bedded almost immediately after crossing. But I was looking the wrong way when it flushed. I heard a clatter and saw a streak going down the ridge. With a rather lucky shot I dropped it, happily 200 yards farther down toward the bottom!

Where rim-rocked ridges run north-south, bedded deer will sometimes get up in early afternoon, when the sun hits their side, and move across to the other. Watching the rim at that time of day, you may spot one. Later in the afternoon, following the daily routine of most big game, the deer move out to feed again, and from then until dusk is some of the best hunting time.

During the rut mule deer are seldom as aggressive as whitetails. The bucks fight, but sometimes almost playfully. When two do make up their minds to go at it, the result can be a wild battle. But they seem at any time more composed and deliberate than their relatives. Possibly because the battles are generally less vicious, calling mule deer by rattling antlers has, at

Small creeks and puddles should be checked, especially if other water is scarce.

Hunter approaches his desert muley. Lechuguilla (near deer's rump) is good forage.

least to date, not been very successful. I have experimented with it but I've not had the results that occur with whitetails.

Mule deer do at times come to mouth-blown calls with surprising alacrity. It seems almost as if they come out of curiosity. They will also respond to a coyote or fox call. Levi Packard, a game-department supervisor in Arizona and a friend of mine over many years, has experimented a good deal with this calling and has had mule deer all but run over him.

There is one aspect of mule-deer hunting in much of the range that is totally different from whitetail hunting. This concerns their vertical migrations, forced by weather. In the Rockies a major share of the mule-deer population summers up high. I've jumped big bucks while on trout-fishing pack trips way up almost to timberline. The deer summer in this high, cool country where forage is lush and the living is easy. I've often thought that this wilderness living is undoubtedly what fashioned the mule deer personality into the serene character it is.

When fall moves along toward winter, the first snows may blanket the high country, but they usually melt quickly. The deer are not too uneasy about that first snow or two. But presently snow piles up. Forage in the fragile heights is killed or covered and the deer must move to lower altitudes. The migration to the winter range begins. In numerous locations, deer herds have followed the same downward trails for many decades, and they have wintered on the same range likewise.

The quality and size of a winter range dictates how large a herd can grow. It cannot expand past the point where the winter range cannot sustain it. Some of the fall migrations are scattered out over a whole range of mountains. But in some the concentration of migrating deer funneling from a vast high-country range through rather narrow canyons to the lower country is phenomenal. Some of these, such as near Meeker, Colorado, have become so well known over the years that they are famous nationwide. For when the downward movement is in full swing, hunters can select stands along the route and sometimes see scores of deer passing in a day.

Not all mule deer make these migrations. Desert mule deer, for example, have no need to. And in some low mountain ranges, Rocky Mountain deer have no need for seasonal migrations. But in all the higher mountain country where deep snow is a part of every winter, hunting the migration routes is almost a surefire method. It requires exact timing, however, as related to the weather. During an unseasonably mild fall the deer may not move until very late in the season. Most game departments try to arrange for open seasons during the migrations, because this is the only way they can get a harvest of deer from the remote summer country.

After the migration, if there is a late deer season, some fantastic hunting can be enjoyed on winter ranges. Bear in mind that winter range is invariably much more restricted than the high-country summer forage area. Thus, a large number of deer may be forced to live on a comparatively modest expanse; they have nowhere else to go. I hunted one time in Colorado during a late, post-migration season when we looked over more than 40 big bucks in a day, simply picking out what we wanted. A caution regarding winter range is that a hunter new to mule-deer country should establish beyond doubt that, in early fall, he hasn't mistakenly set out to hunt what is winter range. He may find a lot of old sign from the previous winter, but few if any deer.

Hunting for blacktails on the Pacific coast is totally different from hunting other mule deer. The habits of these deer are a consequence of the cover in which they live. On the southern end of the range this may be brush so awesomely dense a man cannot walk through it, but has to crawl. Farther north in some of the coastal rain forest, the understory is like a wall. A good bit of blacktail hunting is similar to hunting whitetails, only in "thicker" country still.

As I mentioned, driving is used to some extent for this hunting, where high points allow stationed hunters to look down into cover. But the deer are inclined to lie as snug as a pointed quail, let a hunter go by, or quietly sneak out and double back. Another common trick is when a deer jumps near the hunter, bounds through brush around a corner of creek bed or rocks, and instantly lies down in dense brush. It simply disappears. Dogs have been used on blacktails in portions of their California range, just as they are on whitetails in some Deep South swamps.

There are places in blacktail country where one can take a stand. I remember a place where a large oak was loaded with acorns. It had a small patch of brushless ground under its shade, and there was a point up above that looked down into the small opening on a slant. Deer were coming every day to feed on acorns, and a man could have had no better opportunity. In the Northwest, in places where timber has been cut, the openings with much slash offer large amounts of deer forage. A stand in one of these is another good bet for blacktails.

Some hunters take great pride in their prowess at beating the blacktail on its own terms. They sneak and crawl through openings and trails in thick cover, sometimes even surprising a deer in its bed. This is tough hunting, however, and it is important to bear in mind that portions of the range have a substantial number of rattlesnakes.

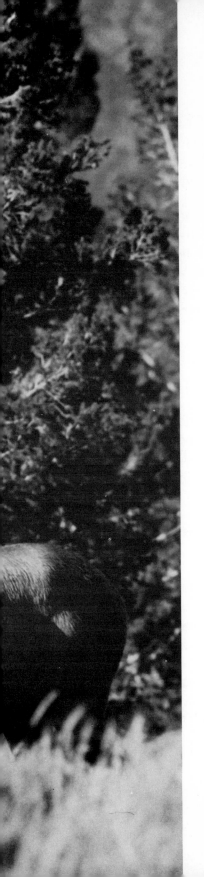

11.
ELK

Large bull bugles at Trinchera Ranch, Colo.

Although the elk belongs to the deer family, it is such a totally different animal from the viewpoint of the hunter that no comparison can be made. The bull elk is a true monarch of the forest, an authentic sultan. Among our horned and antlered game no other except the caribou gathers sizable harems. The bull elk brings together most aggressively the largest groups of females.

I have counted during the rut as many as 40 cows with a single mature bull. Harems larger than that have been recorded. The bull does not move across a mountain meadow with his cows following behind. He drives them before him, hooking at this one or that one to prod it into the group, grandly and arrogantly sweeping the members into a compact herd, and daring any bull hanging along the fringes to come near.

Elk are exceedingly wild, powerful animals. It is true that in some instances, driven by the need for food in winter, they act almost tame, accepting handouts from man, as at Jackson, Wyoming, or tearing some ranchers' haystacks apart. But the instant the need is gone, they revert to a true wilderness personality. It is a stunning sight in fall to watch a bull as big as a riding horse plunge across a mountain meadow, throwing his antlers back and bugling until the ridges ring. It is no wonder this animal appeals so intensely to hunters. Most sportsmen begin with deer, dreaming of the day they'll have a chance at an elk. But an elk hunt cannot be approached quite as easily as a deer hunt, or with so firm an assurance of success, or for that matter nowadays even of being able to obtain a permit. In addition, elk hunting can be rather expensive. So the prospective elk hunter needs to know all the facts he can gather—about the animals, about where his chances may be best, and what time of season to plan a hunt.

In the days of early settlement, elk were extremely abundant over a vast range. Modern hunters may not be aware that the Colonists found elk all the way from the southern end of the Appalachians to the Berkshires of Massachusetts. They ranged across the continent from far north in Alberta all the way to southern New Mexico. With the exception of the open plains, elk were abundant clear to the Pacific. A substantial number were even present along stream courses of the plains.

Unlike deer, elk consort most of the time in groups. When elk were taken for meat or hides in early days it was easier for a group of hunters to kill large numbers at a time. As the forests were cut and settlement pushed westward, elk disappeared from all of the East. They were slaughtered also in the more open country of the West, along the streams and in the foothills. Entire army encampments and forts lived on elk meat. The animals, because of their size as well as the fact that elk meat is excellent fare, were more desirable than deer.

Elk hides made tough, heavy leather. Hide hunters decimated the herds. One single river-boat shipment contained 33,000 elk hides! Finally the tooth hunters entered the picture. The so-called "tusks," which polished brightly, were a fad. Thousands of elk were killed for these alone. By the end of the last century elk had been totally killed off over 90 percent of their native range. The only ones remaining were on the Olympic Peninsula, in the Prairie Provinces of Canada, and in the Yellowstone region.

The re-establishment of elk is a remarkable story of protective legislation, enlightened game management, and concern by sportsmen and land owners. Today, although elk range is by no means comparable to the original, stable elk herds exist, by transplant and protection, on all range suitable for them throughout the country. The herds must be carefully cropped because there is only so much habitat, and animals this large, when over-populous, swiftly ruin their range. Presently the national elk herd is probably slightly below 400,000 animals. The annual harvest, made up of antlered and antlerless elk, reaches from 70,000 to 80,000.

There are three varieties of elk. The Rocky Mountain elk is the most abundant and has the broadest range, throughout the Rockies from northern New Mexico and northern Arizona up into Canada. On the West Coast the Olympic, or Roosevelt, elk ranges from a scattering in northern California up through Oregon and Washington, parts of British Columbia, and to Alaska by transplant. This elk is a subspecies generally a bit larger and darker than the Rocky Mountain variety. The antlers are usually shorter but heavier. The tule, or dwarf elk, sometimes called California elk, is a small species left only as a remnant on a small range in the Owens Valley of California.

A good many Western hunters are fortunate enough to live in states

Hunter employs simple but effective tactic in elk country: patient glassing.

where elk are plentiful. Even so, they may be required to apply for permits under a drawing and quota system. In most instances elk herds are very carefully surveyed and cropped, and there are few cases where unlimited licenses are offered. New Mexico has for some time been an exception during a special early season for mature bulls only. To date, unlimited licenses have been available. Of course that regulation can change at any time, depending upon fluctuations of the herd.

At any rate, particularly the non-residents of the elk states need to know where the elk are because success depends to a great extent upon selecting the proper place and applying in time for a license. Some of the top states where non-resident quotas are limited to only several thousand are generally sold out for the next season shortly after a current season closes. In addition, in several states, though not all, it is mandatory to have a guide for elk hunting, at least on specified lands. The prospective elk hunter has much to do in planning besides sighting in his rifle.

At least 95 percent of the total elk kill each season comes out of four states in the Rockies—Colorado, Wyoming, Idaho and Montana—and from the two Northwestern states, Oregon and Washington. Annual harvests are subject to fluctuation, but among those six states they average out surprisingly close. States in the Rockies get total kills of 12,000 to 15,000, and the Northwestern states average 10,000 or 11,000 as a rule. These figures show the total—mature bulls, spikes, cows.

Most of the remaining five percent of the continent's elk kill is about as follows: New Mexico, 1,000 to 1,500; Arizona about the same; British Columbia, 1,500 to 2,000; Utah, 1,200 (residents only); Nevada, a few (residents only). There are several other locations with low kills and each may be important to certain hunters. In Alaska, a few elk are taken in a limited range. Afognak Island, difficult to get to and hunt on, has some trophies. In Alberta the annual kill is low because few hunters go there, but there is some prime hunting in the foothills of the east slope of the Rockies. Saskatchewan has a few elk. There are also a few in Manitoba, but hunting in the past has been for residents only. There are several hundred elk in the Black Hills in South Dakota, and an occasional season with limited permits, for herd-cropping purposes. In Oklahoma, the elk herd on the Wichita

Mountains National Wildlife Refuge must be kept tailored to its range, and occasional and very successful hunts are held there, with a modest number of permits. Surplus elk from the refuge have also been transplanted into McCurtain County, and may someday be hunted. Michigan has a few elk in the northern Lower Peninsula; the state held a couple of hunts a few years ago, and may sometime again. There is also a small band of elk in Virginia that may someday need cropping, although that is doubtful. The few elk in California are no longer hunted and may never be again.

In all of the top elk states there are millions of acres of National Forest lands, and thus elk are in most instances well distributed over each state. I can point out a few prime locations here. This does not mean there aren't others. I would suggest to all elk hunters who do not have a specific area to which they return year after year that they contact the game department of the state where they propose to hunt, and get kill statistics for several years in various counties or hunting units set up by the department. In some instances, a low-kill unit may build up a herd that needs to be cropped. Checking the regulations carefully may allow you to get in on a spot where success runs high.

In Washington, there are Rocky Mountain elk in the east, Roosevelt elk in the west. As a rule, around 35 percent of the total elk kill comes out of the mountains of the south-central counties. Much of the remainder is split between the Olympic Peninsula and the mountains and National Forest lands of the southeast. Oregon also has both elk varieties, the Roosevelt in coastal forests and the Cascades, the Rocky Mountain elk in the east. The major Oregon elk kill is from the Wallowa Mountains of the northeast. For Roosevelt elk, the northwestern coastal counties, and Coos County in the southwest, generally turn up the highest harvests.

In Montana, elk are well distributed and plentiful on the eastern and western slopes of the Rockies. Both the eastern foothills and higher mountain meadows, and the southwestern area on the west slope, where terrain is fairly similar, provide the easiest hunting. The cover in the northwest is dense, so the hunting can be difficult. Wyoming has one of the continent's largest herds. For many years the most popular, and best, region has been out of Jackson, in the Hoback and Gros Ventre drainages. The Cody area is

Where elk have been stripping bark, hunter notes freshness of sign.

also excellent, as are the Bighorns. In the southeastern sector of the state, the Medicine Bow National Forest and Mountains vie with the others.

Idaho offers excellent opportunity over much of the state, but particularly in the forests of the northern and central portions. Some of the hot spots long famous among hunters are the drainages of the Lochsa, the Selway, the St. Joe, the Salmon and the Clearwater, plus the Chamberlain Basin. Colorado has excellent elk hunting throughout most of its National Forests, which cover much of the state's western half. Especially outstanding are the San Juan and Rio Grande in the south, the Gunnison and White River to the north, and the Routt still farther north, mostly in the county of the same name.

In Arizona the White Mountains and the National Forests of the central part of the state are considered best. And in New Mexico the Carson, Santa Fe and Cibola National Forests furnish the bulk of the kill. There is no point in trying to note the best elk areas in Utah, for units are opened periodically as needed for cropping; which ones may be open is not predictable. British Columbia has Roosevelt elk on Vancouver, but low success there. Chances are better for Rocky Mountain elk in the extreme southeast. There are a few scattered bands in the interior also.

In plotting an elk hunt, the sportsman should consider carefully what his chances of success may be. Elk are never as plentiful as deer and they need a big country. Lumping all elk hunters together, it is estimated that in any given year not more than one out of five, sometimes less, will bag an elk. But you may be able to beat that. Statistics kept by several game departments show that guided hunters are invariably more successful than those without guides. This can be translated generally to mean that non-residents, most of whom choose to use or must use guides, have a better chance than natives. Guides have to work hard to keep up their reputations. Success for guided elk hunters runs at least double that for non-guided hunters. Even within your own state, if you hunt strange country, an experienced guide may be worth the extra cost.

Further, you have to decide what sort of elk you will settle for. If you are after a trophy bull, obviously your chances are less than they will be for any bull—that is, a spike, small bull or trophy bull only if you chance upon one. If you can get a permit in an any-elk area, your surest bet is to go that route, settling for a cow if necessary. Trophy bulls never make up more than about 25 to 30 percent of the total kill. In some cases regulations will, of course, restrict you. In one state as I write this, non-residents are not allowed to shoot anything except a mature bull. In the special New Mexico hunt I mentioned, with unlimited licenses for mature bulls only, getting the permit is simple enough, but you cannot settle for a spike.

On occasion, success percentage winds up dependent upon how much money you can spend. There are a number of large ranches in elk country where you can book a hunt on private lands and be almost certain of success. But such hunts are sure to cost not less than $600 (which many guided hunts on public lands also cost) and they may run up to $1,000 or

$1,500, depending on what is furnished, and whether or not other game species are allowed. For example, I had the immense pleasure for two seasons of hunting in northern New Mexico on the huge Vermejo Park Ranch, west of Raton. It covers several hundred-thousand acres of stunningly beautiful mountain country, and has a fantastic number of elk. Over some years of taking hunters at a stiff fee, the ranch had 100 percent kills, all bulls. Unfortunately, this place has been sold and may not have fee hunting from now on. However, there are a number of similar ranches. Ads in magazines locate some. Queries to a game department may help locate others.

The beginning elk hunter quickly learns, often to his exasperation, two facts of the life of his quarry. First, it is inherently wild, and when spooked it doesn't just run over the ridge. A band of elk jumped by hunters may start running and go right on out of the country. At a distance-eating trot, these powerful brutes, used to mountains, may cover several miles before stopping. And they may move 10 miles before settling down again.

Second, although elk once were found on prairie edges and some today are found in easily negotiated foothills, the bulk of the continent's elk herd is in tremendously rugged terrain. An elk hunt is no jaunt after a woodlot deer. It may be extremely appealing but it is also exhausting work, whether you walk or ride a horse, or in a few instances hunt out of a vehicle. The altitude is always high, seemingly exaggerated if you are a visiting flatlander, the canyons and ridges are all too often stand-on-end. Further, when that big bull of your dreams hits the ground, you may be gloriously excited for a few moments. But whether you are alone or have help, by the time the brute is gutted and packed to camp, even if in quarters on pack horses, you may be wondering why you did it. This is not to discourage anyone, but you should know what your desire may be getting you into.

All the same, the thrill of collecting a trophy bull is worth the anguish. And if I had my choice of how to go about that tricky chore, I would select "whistling one up" during the rut. The meat of a bull elk just prior to and at the very beginning of the rut is excellent. The animal is fat from a lush summer of living the idyllic life up around timberline. During and after the rut, however, bull-elk meat is hardly fit fare for hounds. A few weeks later the old gentleman will be larded up again for winter, and so elk meat

Hunter whistles up elk in rut; best time is usually late September to mid-October.

Good pitch can be achieved with many types of whistle—from wood to hard rubber.

from the bulls in late season is fine. But I would gladly forego a prime piece of meat for the hair-raising thrill of watching a wild-eyed old sultan run at me ready to fight.

I remember a late afternoon in northern New Mexico with Ted Burt, who is chief of law enforcement for New Mexico's game department. Ted is an expert elk whistler, and he has had a few breath-catching moments with bulls that tried to remove the tree he took refuge behind. We were riding down a rugged mountain trail and distantly saw a good bull, off in a small valley meadow below us. There was a point of timbered ridge running out into the valley, and we made a fast, half-crouched, running sneak off across a small creek and then up onto the ridge and through the timber to the end of the point. Ted had his elk call, and I was armed only with a camera with a telephoto lens.

For those unacquainted with elk, let me explain that during the rut the bulls bugle. The sound starts with a low grunting cough, then ascends a couple of octaves in a scream that at close range will raise the hair on the calmest hunter. This is usually followed by several grating, coughing grunts. When you spot a bull with a harem, he probably won't come to the call, which imitates the ascending high-pitched portion of the bugling. He may reply defiantly, daring you to just try going after any of his cows. But he doesn't want to chance leaving them because a competitor may dash in. However, when you discover a lone bull bugling, it is obvious that he is harem-less and not happy about it. He comes to the call because he intends to have a go at fighting another bull and escaping with the gathered harem.

A very important point for an elk caller to learn is that the voices of bulls differ widely. The difference is mostly caused by age. Young bulls grunt and cough almost as if they're just learning. Then the up-scale whistle is thin and melodious. A big mature bull starts on the low end of the scale with a rasping, violent kind of "keough" sound and the upward scream is all rough edges and rasp along with the tonal quality. The coughs and grunts are hacking, chopping sounds. It is very easy to tell an unseen trophy bull by its bugle. If you'd rather have the meat of a young bull, it's easy to select one of these, too.

At any rate, Burt and I flopped on the ground at the point of the ridge, at the edge of timber looking into the meadow. Ted blew his call. The bull wheeled and simply filled the meadow with his scream. Without one moment of hesitation, he came on the run. I was focusing the big 300mm telephoto and shooting fast. Then, as the bull came on like a freight, I began to feel a little panic. I was afraid to lie still and afraid to run. He hauled up about 50 yards out and came stalking us.

A mature bull elk in the middle of the rut is not very couth. He smells to heaven. He is often plastered with mud from wallowing. He has often urinated and ejaculated all over his hocks and belly. He drools and grinds his jaws.

Ted crawled behind me to get the call some yards from the bull. He whistled with it muffled. The bull stared straight into the timber and let fly with a bugle that fairly rattled my brains. He came on. He was not quite

Trio of bulls head for thick cover in rough New Mexico habitat.

certain now. I touched off the shutter and realized he could hear it. He stood immobile, head high, scenting. He was now so close I could smell him, and I could not even get his head and antlers into the frame when I held the camera vertically. I guessed the distance at 25 feet, and I didn't much like our situation.

Stiff-legged, he circled the point of the timber. I kept shooting until I was out of film. About then he got far enough around to catch a whiff of us. He wheeled and galloped back around in a half-circle. At possibly 70 yards he hauled up spang in the open and stared back toward where we were. Several days later, when the season opened, we went back to the same area with rifles. We whistled up what we thought was the same big bull, and laid him on the turf. Such is the thrill of calling elk.

Where regulations permit, some hunters prefer meat of cow or spike bull like this.

There are many advantages to hunting during the rut. Most important, perhaps, is that you don't have to wear yourself ragged looking for elk. You get into elk country and listen for bugling. If you don't hear any from dawn until mid-morning, or again during late afternoon, you know you have to move. Once you hear elk, you can go to them. When undisturbed, a bull and his harem may hang around a mountain meadow and vicinity for several days. Other bulls are commonly drawn to the area, lone bulls or bulls with smaller groups of cows. A bugling bull may lead you right to a whole congregation of elk.

You do not even need to be a caller. If you don't trust your calling ability, you simply do some listening, and attempt to stalk the bugling bull. A friend of mine killed a handsome six-pointer a couple of seasons back just this way. I shot a lone bull by stalking his sounds, and when I knew I was close but he had quit, I whistled just once. He stepped out of the timber at possibly 100 yards. The rut is the easiest time to kill a bull elk. Its mind is on

This is nice Montana bull at start of rut, when animals are still in good shape.

other matters and there is always distracting confusion in the harem. It is also the easiest time to collect a cow if either sex is legal.

It takes some practice to become adept with a call, but it is not really difficult. Any sporting-goods store in elk country sells elk whistles. Recordings of elk sounds may also be available. On a rutting-season hunt, listen closely to the bulls. Practice trying to imitate them. Incidentally, most elk calls are made to sound like a young bull. The insistent bugling of a young bull is an infuriating sound to an old sultan with a harem. He interprets it as the challenge of some young gaffer with the gall to try to horn in. If you are purposely trying to lure a young bull, a spike, remember that a loud challenge from you may make it shy off. It may be timid, afraid to take on the old monarch. A subdued call will be more likely to attract it.

In regions where a lot of hunters keep elk stirred up, calling is difficult. You should try to get away from the crowd. Also, make as little noise as possible around camp or when driving in a vehicle. Elk are much more easily disturbed than deer. When calling, try to read the "sound signs" you hear. A bull that keeps answering but doesn't come toward you undoubtedly has a harem. One that bugles in reply but is moving away, you may as well forget. It probably is with cows, too.

Don't be too quick to give up on a bull that replies several times and then shuts up. Sometimes one comes sneaking and is suddenly right there. Very old bulls that still feel a breeding urge but are not very competitive are inclined to come cautiously and quietly. A young bull with its first branched antlers that has been run off a few times by bigger bulls is really feeling the urge and getting more frustrated every day. It may come screaming and on the run, figuring you are a spike bull and easy to handle. Bulls that have been soundly whipped in fights with superior bulls are mighty skittish critters. It is a good idea, when you are learning, to check the average length of time between the bugles of any bull. Then pace yours about the same. But don't call too much. When you get an answer, wait a bit and then reply. The answering bull has you marked down and if he is coming he'll know where you are.

A hunt during the bugling season has to be carefully timed. Timing differs somewhat with latitude, and the kind of weather of any given fall may influence it, too. In most of the elk country the peak of the bugling will be from about the last week of September through mid-October. But it is best to make a check beforehand with guides or local hunters or the game department, to be sure when it is most likely to come in the area where you will be hunting.

Two important signs during the rutting season are rubs and wallows. An elk often selects young spruce trees with trunks a couple of inches in diameter at the base. You can easily distinguish an elk rub from a mule deer rub by the height of it. A rub does not necessarily mean a bull is nearby, but a number of fresh rubs around a mountain meadow surely indicates a bull is hanging out there. Prior to and during the rut, bulls do a lot of wallowing. Sometimes you find old wallows from previous years. These will be depressions, usually in soft black earth, varying from the size of a lying-down elk to twice or three times that large. Grass may be grown up around, and the depression may have water in it. Old wallows, like the "barking line" de-

Though rut has subsided, winter range tends to concentrate groups of elk.

scribed in Chapter 7, are a good indication that elk have been using the region year after year.

A fresh wallow is a prime spot to watch if you want to try a stand for elk. Wallows usually are just at the edge of timber in a mountain meadow, or else in small forest openings. They will be in a place where the earth is soft, in most high-country elk range where the dirt is rich and black, and wet from a spring or seep. Flat ground without rocks or else small basin depressions among aspens and conifers are good spots to look for wallows. The bull paws them up and tears them up with his antlers. He lies down and rolls in the black mud until caked with it, perhaps cooling his ardor.

Hunters may be treated to awesome sight of bulls battling for harem rights.

Fresh tracks and droppings near a wallow tell you it is being used. Of course, tracks and droppings are important elk sign at any time of the season, not just during the rut. So are weather-whitened shed antlers. Elk make seasonal migrations from their high-country summer pastures to their winter range lower down, so numerous dropped antlers will tell you this is winter range. But there are exceptions. In a few places there is good habitat at altitudes or in protected mountain expanses where elk are able to stay either all year, or else into the period when antlers are dropped. It is possible to find abundant elk, and a number of shed antlers in these special habitats even in the breeding season.

It is possible that you might hunt after the rut, when elk have ceased bugling. If you don't hear any, and happen to see weathered shed antlers, and are unknowingly on a range that is used through the summer and on through the shedding period, you could wrongly assess the territory. So it is always a good idea to check on fresh tracks and fresh droppings. Any hunter in strange terrain—and most elk hunters are each season—has to piece together all the signs. As mentioned earlier, elk band together. There may be lone animals but most are in groups. One long valley may not contain a single elk on a given day, yet the next valley over may be swarming. Mountain country where elk reside is mighty vast. For that reason alone it can be confusing to newcomers.

The altitude is sometimes tough on those unaccustomed to mountain hunting, too. In the major share of elk range the animals summer very high up, even to 11,000 feet. Certainly they will be at least somewhere between 8,000 and 10,000. Only on a scattering of ranges are they at elevations of 5,000 to 7,000. They ordinarily stay on the summering grounds right through the rutting period. Only after the migration down to winter range will they be in the foothills. The high country is beautiful and very pleasant in fall, when the aspens clothe the ridges in gold set against backdrops of evergreen and towering peaks, some of them capped with snow. Certainly the hunting is easier at that time than after snowfall.

To be sure, late September and early October can be a period of unpredictable weather up high. On my last elk hunt before this was written, we had bright sun for several days, then fog and drizzle for several more. Incidentally, during rain or heavy fog elk do little bugling and do not react much to calling. Regardless of sun or rain, all elk hunters with experience hope for a steady temperature pattern. The animals tend to stay at one altitude level if this occurs. But if unseasonably warm weather hits an area where you are hunting, the elk will stay in dense conifer cover or will move up to a higher altitude. It is not difficult for them to shift to a forage ground a thousand feet higher. The hunter who doesn't realize what has happened may wonder why he sees no elk.

All the hunting methods used for deer can be used on elk. How you hunt, however, will depend a lot upon how many hunters are in the area, and also in your party. Elk harassed over a wide region by a crowd of hunters have an exasperating habit of getting into dense stands of timber and jackstraw blowdowns and staying there. It is virtually impossible to still hunt them in such places. Elk seldom bed like mule deer on open points or slopes. They get into the spruces and it is almost impossible to come up on a group and surprise them.

One of the best and most popular methods of elk hunting is to ride a horse across the territory, constantly glassing down into the valleys and draws. It is in such places, early and late, that bands slip out of the timber to feed. If snow is on the ground, tracks often point the way, and the animals may be out much of the day because they're having to work harder for their living. When hunted hard, elk may spot you at half a mile and run immediately. So even on horseback it pays to move slowly and always in the edges.

When a band is sighted and is unaware, a stalk can be made, minding the wind most carefully. Keep in mind that if you are in a valley or at mid-slope, jumped elk will invariably run uphill. If you are atop a ridge, riding around a valley, elk that see you from below will generally race wildly away up the canyon, or try to get over the first and nearest ridge in a hurry. Hunters who know these habits and have carefully appraised the terrain can occasionally make a successful drive. Sometimes even a couple of hunters can work out a drive.

I remember one situation when two men walked a strip of timber that ran out to a point and down into a valley where an elk trail ran. A third hunter sat quietly on a point overlooking the trail. The drivers moved slowly, not knowing if elk were in the timber. A trio of elk moved out the far end, trotted along the trail right to the waiting gunner. On the whole, however, elk are strongminded animals and don't drive very easily.

Some hunters are successful each year by taking a stand, in country where numerous hunters are operating. They watch a long valley or a saddle in a timbered ridge, hoping for someone else to move elk through. Using a horse and glassing the canyons and valleys is, however, a more successful routine, especially for guided hunters. Further, a man on foot who spots a moving bull out of range can seldom catch up to shooting range. Even when walking, elk move at a swift pace.

Hunting during the migration to wintering grounds is often successful. It requires close knowledge of the country and the routes. In certain places there are famous ancestral routes that funnel most of the elk from a whole range down only a few canyons, or through a series of ridges. Of course, you don't see streams of elk pouring off a mountain. It takes a substantial amount of snow in the high country to move them. But when they do come down their gregarious habits continue. A good stand on a migration route may show you numerous animals during a single day.

Although hunting in snow, after the breeding season, is never as pleasant as in early fall, it does have its advantages. A mounted hunter can ride up below a crest, keeping to timber if possible. He ties his horse, selects a place where he can see perhaps as much as a mile down a valley and both its slopes. Using his glass, he patiently scans the country. Against snow, bands of elk show up very well. Sometimes there are late elk seasons on winter ranges. They may be set in order to harvest a certain quota of antlerless elk. Obviously, on wintering pastures the animals are more concentrated, and hunting is at times easier.

When you hunt with a guide, presumably he will have all the needed equipment for dressing and quartering the kill. I want to warn the tyro who may be in an unguided party that he should realize what a chore it is to take care of the meat. An axe, a sizable meat and bone saw, sharp knives and a stone all belong in an elk camp.

Of all horned and antlered game on the continent, elk are the most difficult to put down for keeps. They are immensely tough-spirited animals, and they are also physically tough. A wounded elk may go for miles. In Chapter 5 there is detailed material about rifles and loads. I'll add to it here briefly. For many years the .270 and the .30-06 have been standard elk rifles. The '06 or the .308 with 180-grain softpoint is perfectly adequate. However, a great many elk hunters nowadays are turning to the Magnums, which are devastating even at long range. With any rifle, bullet placement on an elk, to anchor the animal right there on the spot, is quite critical. If you can handle it, the neck shot is far and away the best. If not, a shot fairly high in the ribs and slightly behind the shoulder is the next choice.

12.
MOOSE

Hefty bull crosses Fox Lake in Ontario.

O ne of the most dramatic hunting incidents I've ever experienced occurred on a moose hunt during an assignment trip I made for *Sports
Afield* Magazine. The setting was the wilderness region of the Wintering River in Ontario, far north of Lake Superior. We were some 40
miles by water from the nearest logging road. We had towed gear-laden canoes with small outboard boats, lake to lake, had set up camp, and were
hunting out of canoes.

On a still, frosty dawn my guide and I slipped quietly through a
channel between two lakes. The lake surface was without a ripple except for
the silent dip of our paddles, and the first rays of sun were touching the far
shore. When we were halfway across, from my position in the bow I saw
something move. I raised my glasses and was looking at a group of seven
enormous gray timber wolves, apparently on trail. We had heard them the
previous evening, their howls the most primitive sounds imaginable.

Instantly we pushed deep, racing for a possible chance to collect a
trophy. When we were roughly 75 yards from shore, an awesome racket
erupted back in the timber. The sounds of snapping sticks and saplings, of
something huge smashing through the timber, was accompanied by the most
hair-raising screaming and baying. The wolves had jumped their quarry.

In moments a moose came plunging out of the forest and down a
steep bank to the shore. Behind, snapping at its hocks and trying to bring it
down were the wolves, snarling and howling in frenzy. The moose hit the
water with an echoing splash and raced for deep water. Then it saw the canoe and turned broadside, running in knee-deep shallows. The wolves
would not swim after it, but were in the lake edge still wildly snarling. In total excitement, and no little confusion, my first impulse was to try to collect
the moose. I held for the shoulder, touched off.

The animal came to a stop, swayed, and fell. The wolves were still
on shore, startled as we were. I now swung on the biggest one as they
wheeled and bounded away. Naturally, I missed. I was shaking so hard I
could barely put down the rifle and pick up the paddle. That incident made
the trip one always to remember, but on occasion I have felt a bit uneasy for
having taken the moose when it was in such a situation.

Although moose do not have the supremely wild spirit of elk, and are in some respects rather stodgy creatures, there is nonetheless immense drama in hunting them, if only for their size (whether or not you happen to have a wolf pack drive one to you). The moose is the largest antlered animal on earth, and is found in northern areas almost around the world. Oddly, the animals of northern Europe and portions of Asia were called "elk"—in fact, are the true elk. During early settlement of North America there was confusion about the animals and the one we call an "elk" (the Indian *"wapiti"*) was given the name of the quite different European animal. "Moose" is an Algonquin name, and it has stuck.

There are three varieties in North America. Other races have been named by scientists in the past, but present views discount their validity. The moose known to most hunters is the common or Canadian species. Originally it ranged across much of the northern U.S. and across Canada, from New England and the Great Lakes region on west and north. A sub-species of the Canadian moose, generally somewhat smaller in both body and antlers, dips southward along the Rockies. This is the Shiras or Wyoming moose, with modest populations in Montana, Wyoming and Idaho and a scattering elsewhere in that region. The giant of the moose tribe is the Alaskan moose. The Kenai Peninsula is famed for it, and it spreads elsewhere into Alaska and the Yukon.

Moose are animals of cold climes, of snow country, and their domains are always based on abundant water. Lakes, and streams, are a kind of anchor in their habitat. Much of their feeding is done during spring, summer and fall in lake edges, on aquatic vegetation, or else along stream courses on willows and other browse. They may look ungainly with their extra-long legs, but they are able to wade deeper than other antlered game, and they can tolerate, and live in, depths of snow that would founder deer and elk.

It's interesting to note that the famed giant Alaskan moose was unknown during much of the last century. It simply was not there, had actually not yet evolved. Researchers are not entirely certain where the moose came from. It is odd to think of moose being abundant in the East, even in Massachusetts, Pennsylvania and New York. The animals were fairly easy to hunt, and early hunters after both meat and hides soon decimated the Eastern moose population. The same thing occurred in the Great Lakes area.

In the U.S. Rockies the population never has been large, but it has greatly increased since the days of early exploration in the West. In fact, moose were unknown in what is now Wyoming during the period when trappers and explorers first roamed the mountains. And it is certain that moose range expanded over vast areas of Canada during the latter part of the last century and the early portion of this one. As the animals spread north and west and thus into Alaska, it is thought that optimum habitat may have been awaiting them, and attracted them, where vast burns had resulted in moose forage such as young shrubs of birch and willow. Conceivably, it was the abundance of forage that influenced the size of Alaskan moose.

Today moose are hunted clear across Canada, in Alaska, in a few of the Rockies states, and just recently in Minnesota. A rule of nature, stated in an earlier chapter, is that the larger an animal is, the less abundant it is on any given range. Moose density is never as high on their quality ranges as elk density, for example. However, the range of the moose is so much broader than the elk's that the total continental herd is probably greater. Indeed, the annual bag, which of course fluctuates, usually runs 80,000 to 90,000 animals. The score on bulls is high, but nowadays moose are managed just as other deer, and in some areas they become so populous that antlerless moose are cropped. I hunted in Ontario one season in an area where any moose was legal.

Over the major share of the range, moose are hunted with guides. In quite a few instances this is mandatory. Further, in the lower states and in some instances in Canada moose hunting is by application and drawing for limited permits. A prospective moose hunter should check carefully when planning a hunt. In a few areas, moose hunting is for residents only. In any case, selecting a qualified outfitter is half the battle toward success. And moose success does run higher as a rule than for elk.

Average seasonal kill figures for the various states and provinces give a fairly good picture of moose distribution. However, many excellent but remote moose ranges in the Far North get very little hunting. They are either too difficult or too expensive for average hunters to get into. A case in point concerns both the Yukon and the Northwest Territories. Moose populations are excellent, but outfitters are few and visitors are restricted to hunting some of the least remote areas. The places easier to get to generally show the highest kills. However, this still means there must be an ample supply of moose present. Thus, the following figures, considered in light of the foregoing, may be helpful for planning. Keep in mind that they are averages over some seasons, and may change.

Average Seasonal Moose Kills		
	Harvest	*Success Percentage*
IDAHO	50	50–65
WYOMING	900 to 1,200	90
UTAH	5 to 15	50
MONTANA	400 to 500	75–85
ALASKA	10,000	30–40
YUKON	800	high
Northwest Territories	1,000 *(mostly natives for meat)*	high
BRITISH COLUMBIA	20,000 to 25,000	40–50
ALBERTA	15,000	35
SASKATCHEWAN	5,000	40–60
MANITOBA	4,000	50
ONTARIO	10,000 to 15,000	20–35
QUEBEC	8,000 to 10,000	12–25
NEWFOUNDLAND-LABRADOR	5,000 to 9,000	50–60
NOVA SCOTIA	300	30
NEW BRUNSWICK	200 to 600	20–60

Fluctuating harvests are sometimes due to weather, or to the number of permits offered. Some of the lower success percentages, where a spread is given (i.e., Quebec 12–25) indicate, on the low side, average resident success and, on the high side, average success for non-residents. This is because *guided* visitors always have a better chance. As this is written, Minnesota has had several recent seasons on moose. A fair number of permits have been allowed and success has been quite good. Maine also has a modest and expanding moose population. At this writing there is no season, but there may be in the future. Several other states have a few moose, but they allow no hunting and probably never will be able to. These states are New Hampshire, Ver-

Moose has vanished into timber, but hunter and guide watch for possible return.

Mature Ontario bull moose has left track almost as large as hunter's hat.

mont, Michigan (Isle Royale), Wisconsin, Colorado and Washington.

I want to repeat that prospective moose hunters should very carefully check all the regulations. In some instances where moose are few, if you manage to draw a permit it is the only one for a lifetime. In others, if you draw lucky you may not be allowed to apply again for several years, and if you fill your permit possibly not for a longer period. In the Far North only certain Hunt Units may be open to visitors.

Within the Rockies states, Wyoming has the largest moose population, with Fremont, Sublette and Teton counties the high spots. Montana probably has about half as large a herd as Wyoming. In Montana, the area above Yellowstone Park and that west of Glacier Park are among the top locations. In Idaho and Utah the permits dictate where the hunting will be done. In Alaska there is almost unlimited excellent moose range, from the Peninsula to the Brooks Range and the Arctic Slope. Guided hunts are the rule for visitors, and outfitters all have their favored grounds.

British Columbia gives you a choice of Wyoming moose in the extreme southeast, Canadian moose over most of the province, Alaskan in the far northwest. Some good locations: Skeena, Upper Fraser, Chilko, Peace River, Laird River, Wells Gray. In both the Yukon and Northwest Territories, where you hunt will be dictated by what areas are open to visitors, and by which outfitters are available and where they hunt. They are not yet abundant.

In Alberta the high population is in the northern forests and along the mountain slopes of the western border. For plotting a Saskatchewan moose hunt, it is a good idea to obtain from the game department a listing of kills by numbered hunting zones, to get an idea of current high spots of population. In Manitoba, the moose range over much of the wooded area. The hunting is good in accessible areas, such as the country bordering Ontario in the southeast along Lake Winnipeg, the lake region below La Pas, numerous lake locations above Flin Flon.

Ontario is moose paradise to a great number of hunters from the States. Good highways give ready access to a lot of excellent moose country and there are scores of fly-in camps and camps reached by rail. The Algoma Central Railway out of Sault Sainte Marie used to be dubbed the "Moose Meat Special" in fall. I went up and came back down through the bush on it one fall, a delightful trip from end of the line at Hearst; on my return trip there were 17 moose, including my own, in the baggage car. Central and western Ontario generally furnish the highest kills. Good reference points are Kapuskasing, Geraldton, Sioux Lookout, Kenora, and over in the east Sudbury, North Bay, Cochrane.

Quebec counties of Abitibi, Pontiac, Temiscamingue and Laviolette have high moose populations. In Newfoundland, where you hunt depends on your guide. There is much good territory. Both Nova Scotia and New Brunswick have low moose populations, and have recently had hunting only for residents. This, of course, may change.

Of all the deer family of North America, the moose has perhaps the most peculiar personality. Except for the Wyoming variety, it is a hulking creature of bogs and swamp edges, of willow flats seeping with moisture, of the deep "moose moss" of the Canadian bush. For all its awesome bulk—an

Canadian outfitter's moose camp provides comfort in middle of wilderness.

Alaskan bull may weigh anywhere from 1,000 to 1,800 pounds—it is an excellent swimmer, commonly takes to water and can run like a freight. Whether or not moose are a bit on the stupid side, or simply placid and not nervous, is difficult to say. At any rate, they are by no means as wary as elk or deer.

Sometimes they seem curious and perplexed by strange sights. I've watched one as it stared at a canoe going past. Yet old bulls can sometimes be very shy, running into timber at the slightest sign of what may be danger. Moose have an extremely sharp sense of hearing, and seem always to be listening for the crack of a twig or some other alerting sound. Their sense of smell is also keen, and a moose hunter must watch the wind as closely in this endeavor as in any other big-game hunting. However, the eyesight of moose seems to be average at best. It is possible that their affinity for dense brush and timber may have long made it unnecessary for them to see distantly. In hunting on water, from which the animals apparently do not expect danger, it is not at all unusual to spot a moose across a small lake and have it continue feeding or simply stare as a canoe moves in.

Sometimes moose can be dangerous. They seem quite unpredictable. During the rut, bulls are easily aroused to charge. And a bull moose is a formidable sight as it comes at a run, popping brush and with hackles up. Even outside the rutting period moose can be dangerous. A bull may decide to charge for no special reason. A cow with a calf or twin calves is a holy terror. Keith Stilson, a Wyoming guide with whom I hunted bear one spring, has been run right off a mountain on horseback by a cow guarding her territory and calf. He and I circled wide of a small, high lake in the Gros Ventre country several times on our horses because of a belligerent cow with twin calves that hung around there.

Every year there are newspaper stories of hunters or summer trout fishermen who were put up a tree by a moose, and stories of moose charging railway engines, or road graders, or automobiles. My boys and I, trout fishing, made an exhausting climb into down-timber country on a Montana ridge one summer because a bull blocked our trail and acted threateningly. My most memorable experience, however, occurred in a canoe back in the bush in Ontario. There was a fat yearling moose on shore that the guide wanted for meat. Any moose was legal. It was almost dusk and we had the canoe laden with moose meat from one I had shot earlier in the day. We were down almost to the rail and very gingerly paddling when we saw the big calf.

What we didn't see, in the dim light, was a huge old cow, her head underwater 60 yards or so away. At the shot, the calf dropped, and the hulking cow reared up, throwing water. We stared and she stared. The breeze was toward us. She could not scent us. But she looked toward shore, failed to see her calf, then stared at this strange object. And finally she came barreling down on us like a freight. We had stabilized the canoe for the shot by running the bow onto a mud bank. Desperately we tried to back off. No chance. The guide's rifle had held only one cartridge. I grabbed mine and trained it on the moose. She came to a halt roughly 30 yards from the canoe.

Several thoughts were tangled in my mind. This would be an illegal kill, since we had both filled tags. But I didn't intend to have that old hulk in any canoe with me. Fortunately, she snorted, turned her head toward shore where her calf should have been, and suddenly bolted away. It was a lesson.

For those who hunt moose in the Rockies, it is important to understand that they are seldom found as high up as elk. Like elk, they sometimes migrate down to the lower valleys when heavy snow comes. The river courses in Wyoming and Montana and the small streams, where willow grows profusely, show easily spotted sign of wintering moose, the willows stripped or chopped off close to where the top of the snow lay.

In the chapter on elk I noted that a hunter should go well prepared for the chore of dressing and transporting his kill. The task of moving a moose is prodigious. It's a good idea to try desperately to avoid dropping one in the water. Moving it to shore is a chore for several husky men. A long, strong rope is a mandatory piece of equipment in moose camp, and a wise hunter also has handy a winch of some sort or a "come-along" such as for unsticking a vehicle. Axes, meat saws, long, sharp knives and a big sharpening stone all are needed. Most moose are hunted where a boat, a four-wheel-drive vehicle or a horse can get to them for packing out the quarters.

Three main types of terrain are hunted. One is the mountains in the Rockies. The second is the dense bush of Canada. The third is the high, rolling to flat regions of the North and Northwest where timber may be meager but willow may be dense. This is in some respects similar to hunting moose in some of the short bush and tundra country of Newfoundland. Not a great deal of walking is done. In some places in Canada hunters walk old logging trails, watching for animals in the trails or near them. A tractor or other vehicle can be brought into such places if needed. Some hiking is done in far eastern Canada—Newfoundland—after the hunters have been flown in to camp and perhaps from it to spots where they'll hunt.

Most North American moose hunting is accomplished, however, from a horse, or a boat or canoe. Whichever way you hunt, scouting sign is important and can save much aimless riding or paddling. Moose are not the wild, long-distance travelers elk often are. If forage is ample, a bull will stay

Standing by custom-built snow vehicle, hunters study map of good moose area.

all its life in an area of not over four or five miles. Once abundant sign is located, persistent hunting of the area may well bring an animal into your sights.

Hunting from a canoe is in my estimation one of the most pleasant and thrilling methods. Obviously the best kind of country is the Ontario type where a welter of lakes with connecting streams and channels allows one to look over a vast amount of territory. The sandy or rocky beaches won't amount to much. The brushy points, the small bays and secluded pockets where forage may be abundant are the places to look, as well as open, swampy lake shores.

During hunting seasons, aquatic feed has been killed to some extent by frosts. This makes it actually a bit easier, since there are fewer good feeding spots. At this time of year, without the bothersome insects that often in summer drive moose into water all day, the animals will be most active from dawn until mid-morning, and again late in the afternoon. The canoe hunter should move always with the wind in mind, and paddle silently, without conversation. Sound carries far over water and in the stillness of the bush. Keeping in shadows along shore is always worthwhile. Constant glassing of the distant shorelines allows the hunter to spot his quarry far enough away to form a plan.

It may not always be possible to get within range in the canoe. But it may be possible to slip up behind a point, get out and make an overland sneak. This requires craft, however, and careful placement for every step. Some canoe hunters, when they have located a small inlet or other natural run that is filled with sign—tracks and droppings and possibly browse marks—take a stand. You judge from tracks about where the animals have been coming from, perhaps hide the canoe in brush and wait in the morning or evening for an animal to appear.

When hunting from water, always watch the weather. I have been far back in the bush via water when suddenly the October weather began to turn bitter. When ice starts to form it's high time to break camp. Getting frozen in by a series of unseasonably cold nights can be a serious matter when your transport is by boat. However, the chief reason for hunting via canoe or boat in the Canadian bush country is simply that in such dense cover this is about the only way ever to see a moose, or to get a shot.

Many native hunters in Canada like to hunt the log roads and other trails after snow comes. Some Canadian seasons are open at this time. The obvious advantage is that tracks show so well and fresh ones are easily discernible. If the going is not too tough, a moose can occasionally be tracked and jumped out of a thicket. Slow prowling on the track is needed, and absolute quiet. Even then it is easy to miss spotting what you're after. Even a trophy bull has an uncanny ability for getting into cover where he can see out and standing utterly immobile. A mean one can cause trouble. Or, it may simply slip away unseen. Many a hunter has marveled at the way a

Bull at Harvey Lake, Alaska, gazes at hunter; moose's next move is unpredictable.

heavy-antlered moose manages to move through the timber without a sound.

Horseback moose hunts in the West and in northwestern Canada and Alaska are extremely productive, because a tremendous amount of territory can be covered in any given day. It's a good idea in all this country to be on the lookout for burns. Where forest fires have wiped out timber several years previously, much forage comes up. These are prime spots for moose. It's routine to spot distant moose with the naked eye, just riding along. In wilderness country there's a good chance even if the animals see you that they won't run.

Glassing large sweeps of country is the best method on horseback. This is much like glassing for elk or sheep, only you don't expect to see large bands of animals. It is not uncommon to see several bulls or mixed groups together after the rut, or before. But moose seldom consort in large gatherings. The sharp hunter takes a stand up on a slope or just below a ridge crest, ties or ground-hobbles his mount and sits down to study the country. Where browse is dense, moose habitually feed without moving around a lot. Thus it takes careful glassing to pick them up. In willows or other such forage a large animal may go unseen until it finally raises its head.

Once the animal is seen, if you are trophy hunting you set up the spotting scope and study the antlers with care. From there on it's a stalk, and wind as always is important.

Moose can be called. Some hunters have in the past frowned on calling as an unsporting practice. I don't agree. In fact, I feel that, just as in calling elk or deer, it is a most dramatic undertaking when successful. Unlike elk, moose do not gather harems. Rarely a bull will be seen with two cows, but generally they consort with one at a time and after several days, with the cow bred, perhaps search for another.

There are several methods of calling. The tyro had best leave the calling to his guide. Trouble is, few average moose hunters have enough opportunity to hear what sounds moose make, so they have little idea how to imitate them. To my knowledge no moose call is marketed. Northwoods guides either call by mouth, or fashion various kinds of megaphone-like horns. There has always been a good deal of secrecy and mumbo-jumbo about the moose-calling horns made of birch bark or similar material, and also about the sounds different guides make. But they do bring in moose.

A rutting bull utters a hoarse grunting, barking sound. It is loud enough to be heard, by those who know what they're listening for, over a half mile or a mile, depending on terrain. A bull that hears the sound presumably considers this another bull intruding into its territory, and comes to the sound ready to fight. If you hear a bull distantly and try to make a sneak on him, chances are not always good. During the rut bulls are on the move constantly, seeking cows.

Using the grunting sound of the bull, and breaking branches before and after, adds to the illusion. Many a bull will come crashing through the timber. Another may try to take his adversary by surprise. Old bulls, in particular, will sneak around trying to get the wind on the location of the caller. Calling from a canoe is often successful because the hunter can watch a big arc without letting his scent blow into it. The bull is out in the open before it realizes it has been had. Or, the canoe hunters can quickly close the distance on him if he appears in an out-of-reach location.

The other method of calling is to imitate the whining, quavering, amorous bawl of the cow during breeding season. This is sometimes more effective than using the bull sounds. Further, quite often a bull will answer, uttering his barking grunts. This allows the caller to fix his direction. Moose calling is seldom used except in the heavy cover of central Canada, and almost never in the Rockies or the northwestern part of moose range. Calling seems to be most effective late in the day and on toward dusk, although occasionally an eager bull will heed the appeal earlier in the day.

There is really little moose range that can be hunted very effectively by today's average city-dwelling sportsman without booking an outfitter. There is just too much remote country to contend with. But the fact that getting into good territory is fairly expensive anyway, and that guided hunters are much more apt to be successful, even where they may hunt legally without a guide, makes the outfitter well worthwhile. If you are after a true trophy bull, you certainly need assistance and a guide who is a good judge of moose antlers. If you are willing to settle for any moose, then you can double your chances for success by seeking a hunting area where cows and calves are legal. There are not many. And in some instances non-residents are allowed to shoot only bulls, even when antlerless moose permits are available to residents.

In closing this chapter, I'd like to emphasize that the moose personality is quite different from that of elk and deer. The big critters do not seem to have the unbending will to live that is exhibited by an elk or mule deer or even a whitetail. Of course, it takes a husky whack to put one down. But a wounded bull often will stand right on the spot and finally keel over, whereas an elk shot so it is not instantly put on the ground may run several miles. This is not a matter of stamina. Certainly moose have plenty of that. It is a matter of spirit.

Yet this should not lead any moose hunter to go under-gunned. An animal this large has enormous bones, the hide is amazingly thick and tough, and there is a lot of muscle to go through before a vital spot is reached. As Hal Swiggett observes in Chapter 5, moose are often taken with .270's, 7mm Magnums and the like, as well as with the bigger calibers. You want a powerful load and a relatively heavy bullet. The .30-06 with a heavy loading has killed many moose, and I've shot a couple with a .308, using a 200-grain bullet. I had no problems, but there are more powerful cartridges to choose from. Undoubtedly one of the heavier Magnums is better suited to the job if, as Hal cautions, the shooter has time and dedication enough to learn to use it well. And just remember not to get excited and shoot one of those powerhouses broadside out of a canoe!

13.
PRONGHORN
ANTELOPE

Two especially fine bucks cross Wyoming prairie.

T he antelope of the Western plains really isn't an antelope. Like the elk and the moose, it was misnamed by those early American explorers who first saw it by millions on the plains. It is more properly called a pronghorn, but after all these years it's certain that hunters, though they use that name, too, aren't going to drop the name "antelope." This animal apparently evolved right here in America, and it has no known relatives anywhere else in the world.

Antelope are creatures totally tailored to their life in the wide-open expanses of the plains. In a vast land of little or no cover, they depend for safety on their amazing speed and on their astonishingly keen eyesight. I have clocked antelope on numerous occasions when they ran beside my pickup at 35 and 40 miles an hour. In Wyoming one time, a friend driving me raced a small band and was doing 55 miles per hour by the vehicle's speedometer when the animals narrowly crossed in front of us. When running all-out in that fashion, their front legs come clear up beside the head as they push the throttle clear down. They look rather awkward. But at 35, an antelope seems to float along with complete ease. Some antelope experts believe they can run 60 miles per hour for short bursts. Whatever their top speed may be, antelope are the swiftest of all our game animals.

Their eyes are extremely large, much larger by comparison than those of any of the other horned and antlered game, and are also set farther out to the side, giving the animal a larger sweep of vision. Unquestionably the pronghorn's speed and eyesight have evolved because of its open habitat. Antelope pick up motion or strange objects from extreme distances. It has been written in many places that their eyes are "telescopic"—equal to what a man sees through an 8X binocular—though to my knowledge there is no solid proof.

I hunted one time in west Texas with a Mexican ranch foreman, Feliz Valenzuela, who astonished me the way he saw antelope and distinguished bucks from does as far away as they saw us. He apparently saw as much unaided as I did with a binocular. I don't think he had telescopic eyesight, but he certainly had extraordinary vision. So does the antelope. And its whole life is attuned to watching distantly, and staying out where it can see distantly.

An interesting experience of some years ago concerns that point. Fred Bear, the renowned archer, and I were on an antelope and photo expedition in Wyoming. For days we watched a dry creek that had small waterholes along it. In the creek bottom, from which a gentle slope rose on either side, there were several high stands of sage. I presume it grew higher here because it sucked up more water. It was much higher than an antelope. There were several cattle trails through these stands.

Antelope coming down the grass-covered slope to drink would invariably stay wide of these clumps. For one thing, animals coming to water are always suspicious because at the waterhole is where predators often lurk. Those stands of high sage could hide some danger. After the antelope had jittered around, decided everything was all right, and had a drink, they would leave immediately. But, even though now settled down and having sensed no danger here, they would never pass into and through the tall sage. We decided it was because they did not want to let anything interfere with their sight. Since then I have observed this habit on numerous occasions. Antelope are uneasy if anything gets in the way of distant vision.

Excepting the small subspecies of whitetail deer, the pronghorn is the smallest of our native horned and antlered big game. The heaviest field-dressed buck I ever saw was bagged by the winner of one of the early one-shot antelope hunts annually held at Lander, Wyoming. It weighed 125 pounds. An on-the-hoof average for most bucks will run 100 pounds or less. The does are smaller, about 20 to 25 percent less in weight.

Both bucks and does have horns, but those of the doe are inconsequential. The pronghorn is the only animal in the world that annually sheds the outer sheath of the horn, leaving the core remaining, around which the new covering forms. Given proper forage, the horns of bucks continue to grow each year, often both in length and circumference. One of the reasons most antelope seasons are set early in fall is that the bucks begin to shed the horn sheaths quite early. I remember one year when an experimental season was set where I hunted, along in November. I shot a fair buck, and discovered the sheaths loose and about ready to fall off. My partner had worse luck. When his buck hit the ground both horn sheaths went flying. It wasn't much of a trophy that he picked up.

Sight of big band on the run is thrill every hunter waits for, but novices too often

The present-day national antelope population stands as a monument to modern conservation and game management. During the early days of exploration in North America the range of the pronghorn was immense. The eastern boundary was in Minnesota and Iowa. From there antelope were found clear to the Pacific. The north-south range extended from central Alberta, Saskatchewan and southern Manitoba far down into Mexico. I recently ran across a very old record of a hunt held in 1540 in honor of the first Spanish Viceroy in what is now western Hidalgo in Mexico, during which Indians killed several hundred antelope.

That was nothing to what was to come throughout the plains of the

fire at streaking antelope or try for one where there's danger of hitting herd-mates.

United States. Here antelope were present by millions. Some estimates—guesses, really—by early naturalists put the pronghorn population at a hundred million. They were as abundant as the buffalo. Whether there were that many or half that many no one knows, but it is certain that hundreds of thousands were killed by meat hunters to feed entire towns. Later, when fences began to cut up the plains and the plow broke the virgin sod, more hundreds of thousands died.

Some were cut off from waterholes or from migrations to wintering grounds protected from storms. The fences killed thousands, which hit them running at full speed. Antelope are not jumpers. They seldom learn to jump over a fence, even though they are capable of it. Eventually the animals learned to duck between strands of wire or crawl under. But vast numbers were eliminated during the conditioning. Landowners also rounded up huge bands and slaughtered them so that there would be no grazing competition with livestock. By the early 1900's antelope had disappeared from most of their original range. Surveys showed a meager 12,000 still in existence. The species was on the verge of extinction.

Last-minute protection by law, plus cooperation among landowners, hunters and budding game managers of the several states began to help the pronghorn hold its own. Soon several herds were building up again. Trapping and transplanting re-established the animals in numerous areas. Over the years, of course, suitable habitat was shrinking drastically due to settlement and farming and competition from livestock. However, today as a result of superb management, antelope are established on almost all range suitable for them. They are prolific, but they are also inclined to have erratic ups and downs, often because of severe winters. Although numbers fluctuate in different states from year to year, estimates place the total national herd at somewhere around half a million, and overall this is a fairly stable herd.

To keep the number of animals carefully tailored to their ranges, each year game managers make meticulous surveys, after which hunting quotas are set. In peak production years, severe cropping must be accomplished. In fact, a quota equal to the year's fawn production is often necessary to keep a herd on a given range from outgrowing its food supply, or becoming so large that landowners consider the animals a nuisance. Almost all antelope live on privately owned lands, and thus rancher cooperation is the key to their existence.

An antelope hunt is one of the most enjoyable and economical endeavors for any sportsman. Most states do not require that a hunter be guided. Permit fees in most instances are reasonable in cost. And landowners for the most part are cooperative, often going along to guide hunters, either for a modest fee or simply to help out. They want to keep the herd within limits on their property.

However, hunt planners should be aware that there are obstacles. Some states with low antelope populations reserve what hunting they have

Open pronghorn country makes stalking tough. Use every possible bit of cover.

for residents only. Some states offer permits by application and drawing, some by application on a first-come basis. In one recent instance—which may still be in effect—North Dakota allowed only residents to hunt antelope with a rifle, but non-resident archers were allowed to participate. There have also been regulations here and there eliminating any successful applicant from trying again for three years or more. Wherever one plans to hunt, invariably permit applications far outnumber available permits. In some low-population states, the season may be periodically closed. It behooves prospective antelope hunters to make a thorough check of regulations wherever they intend to hunt, and it's a good idea to start on this research a year ahead of time.

In Texas, for example, after a state survey has been concluded quotas are set by the game department on each ranch in the antelope country. The

Sometimes hunter can get within range by staying low and angling in gradually.

permits are turned over to the ranchers. They can do whatever they like with them—hold them back and kill no antelope, give them away to friends, sell them. The average going rate is $100 to $150. Under this system it is up to the hunter to find a rancher who'll allow him to hunt. Quite commonly groups get together, from some large firm, for example, and take as a party the entire quota from a large ranch. Thus, setting up a Texas hunt is likely to be difficult. This is one example of complications of planning.

On the brighter side, although antelope are extremely shy, the fact that they are almost always in bands, and in country where a hunter can find them without much difficulty, keeps the success percentage high. In the better ranges and hunt units, success often hits 100 percent. Seldom on any ranges does it fall below 50 percent.

A tip to hunters after presentable trophies is to make a diligent

After stalk, hunter rises from shallow draw to surprise unsuspecting band.

search for isolated spots that may have been "rested" for some seasons. These are usually found in some of the lesser pronghorn states, ranches or hunt units that have had no hunting for several years. In the states with the largest antelope populations, the ones with the greatest amount of suitable range, practically all of it is hunted each season. Obviously every hunter tries to find a buck with big horns. The result is that in those states few bucks survive to an age where they have real trophy horns. A 12- or 13-inch antelope is considered an average "mounting head" today. But 25 years ago when I was first hunting antelope, 15- and 16-inch horns, though not common, were not rare. And an occasional one beat that. In 1899 a head of 20-5/16 inches was taken in Arizona.

When a certain ranch of some state where antelope are not abundant has had no hunting for several seasons, there is always a chance that a buck may have become a real trophy. On a ranch in New Mexico several years ago, the state, with the landowner's permission, set a hunt after 12 years of no hunting. I saw two pronghorns collected there that were both just slightly under 18 inches.

Wyoming for a good many years has been the center of the best antelope range, and has had the largest number, probably about a fifth of the total national herd. Harvests, dependent upon number of permits offered, run anywhere from 20,000 to upwards of 40,000. It is interesting that in the second decade of this century Wyoming's State Game Warden said that quite probably antelope would never be hunted there again. In the intervening period around 750,000 have been taken! Practically all of Wyoming except the forested mountains has antelope. The eastern half of the state has the heaviest concentrations. Good focal points are areas surrounding the towns of Gillette, Sundance, Douglas, Glenrock, Casper, Lander, Kaycee, Buffalo, Newcastle, Lusk, Torrington.

Montana is second in number of antelope, permits and kills. Harvest averages from 10,000 to 25,000. All of eastern Montana and west to mountain foothills has antelope, with density highest in the east-central and southeastern parts of the state. I have already noted how antelope permits are handled in Texas, and they are never numerous. Ranches around Marfa, Alpine and Marathon, and a few in the Panhandle, usually get the major share.

The New Mexico antelope herd probably totals in average years not more than 15,000 although it peaks higher than that. Clayton, Raton, Wagonmound, Tucumcari, Roswell and portions of the southwestern plains are the high-density areas. Arizona hunting is quite limited. In the best years permits are seldom more than 1,000 to 1,200. The high plains of the central and northern parts of the state offer best opportunities.

Oklahoma has a few antelope in the western Panhandle. Permits are few, when a season is allowed. This is an illustration, however, of giving bucks a chance to grow up. Several years ago a buck from there went into the record book. Although Colorado pronghorn hunting doesn't get much publicity, it is fairly good, with kills running from 4,000 to 6,000. High-harvest counties are usually Moffat, Lincoln, Weld and Elbert, but the fact is in any county with permits the success tally is very high.

The Utah pronghorn population is low, with an extremely modest number of permits, presently for residents only. The same situation exists in Nevada. If you apply there, Washoe and Humboldt counties are a good bet, with most of the state's herd there. California has a small pronghorn herd in the extreme northeast, almost entirely in Modoc and Lassen counties. Permits, when there is a season, are quite limited. The Oregon herd, once very large, now is mediocre. The southeastern counties usually get a few hundred permits, but this state has had residents-only hunting for some time. The situation in Idaho is similar, with a modest herd, a few hundred permits. Butte, Lemhi, Custer and Clark counties get the most.

Nebraska usually offers a substantial number of permits, 1,500 or more. All hunting is north of the Platte River in the western half of the state. South Dakota has a fairly large antelope population, but it is subject to fluctuation, chiefly due to rough winters. As this is written, hunting is for residents only except in the case of archers. In the best years there may be 10,000 or more permits. The North Dakota situation is similar, although permits are fewer. Major share of the herd is in the southwest. Kansas has a small antelope population in the northwest, and transplants have been made elsewhere. There may or may not be token seasons. If so, they will undoubtedly be restricted to residents.

In the Prairie Provinces of Canada the antelope picture is not encouraging. Severe winters harm the small bands. Alberta has a minor number in the southeast, Saskatchewan in the southwest and along the southern border. At this time permits are few, and for residents only.

If you are willing to go out and truly *hunt* antelope, you'll find no big-game animal more sporting. Unfortunately, over the years there has been a great deal of rather unsporting hunting for pronghorns. The plains on which they live are in many places easily drivable, cross-country, via pickup or four-wheel-drive vehicle. An all too common practice has been to chase them. For some reason antelope have the odd habit of trying to cross in front of a vehicle.

In early days it was claimed that they loved to race trains, or mounted cowboys. This was supposed to be playful behavior. That's doubtful. A band put to flight by a moving rider or vehicle begins to run ahead to outdistance the danger. They seldom run away at right angles. Contrarily, they veer on a long angle toward and almost parallel to the moving danger as they attempt to outrun it. Then as they come close they appear to feel a desperate need to cross in front and get on the other side.

At any rate, chasing antelope with vehicles has long been common in some places, even though it is illegal in most states. Groups of hunters chase a band, then bail out and try to fill their tags on the running animals. Many are wounded this way, and many a buck, mixed in with does, has been missed and an illegal doe put down. Most states try to eliminate chasing. In New Mexico, for example, game department personnel really ride herd on hunters. Vehicles may be used to locate antelope, but they cannot leave a recognized ranch road. When a hunt opens in a specified area in New Mexico, you can bet there's a warden perched on practically every hill with his binocular.

Certainly I'm not against the use of vehicles. Driving the ranch roads and glassing the country covers much territory and is about the only way, on brief hunts, to locate the animals. But from here on, if no buck is sighted that will stand while a hunter gets out and off the road for a shot, then a stalk must be made. And that's where antelope hunting becomes a real sporting proposition.

One time, two of us hid our vehicle by some abandoned ranch buildings. From there we could see over a large expanse of rolling country. Glassing it, we found several good bucks. We then set up a spotting scope and checked them out. There was one that I decided to try for. My partner drove, and I got ready to roll out as he moved through a slight depression on the road about 400 yards from the buck.

I hit the ground and lay still. The vehicle went on. I could peer over a small bush and see the distant buck. It was watching the disappearing vehicle. Finally it moved and I could not see it. Hunched over in the small gully, I made 75 yards. There were a few small bushes from there on. The buck now had his rear toward me. Slowly I crawled from bush to bush, quite a trick while carrying a rifle.

At one point the animal turned and stared in my direction for a long time. I lay immobile. There were also several does a short distance from him. I didn't much like that. But to my great good fortune all presently drifted over a knoll. I went on the run, crawled up the knoll, leaving my hat behind. I now loaded the rifle and peered gingerly over the crest. The animals were within less than 100 yards. Instantly they spotted me. But their innate curiosity held them a moment, and I concluded my hunt with much satisfaction.

Stalking requires that a hunter utilize every small bit of cover, and that he look ahead to plan every move. It's best to study the terrain carefully beforehand, too. If there are rough places with hills and basins and gullies and rock outcrops, these will offer a better chance than the flats. Further, large old lone bucks or old bucks with small bands of does often lead secluded lives in the roughs. By climbing hills and crawling over to peer into the tight little basins you have a good chance of finding a real trophy.

When the season opens, however, it isn't always easy to pick out precisely what you want to do. Hunters in vehicles may be swarming around. Out on the flat country where they can drive, there may be abundant antelope, for they have not been disturbed all year. But they won't stay there long, if there is rough country available where the vehicles cannot handily maneuver.

One opening day a friend and I climbed up to a saddle in a high ridge at dawn. Behind us there was a huge expanse of flat country. Over the

Author grassed this pronghorn in Malpai country of northeastern New Mexico. Its heav

ridge were snug basins and extremely rugged hills. When the barrage started and the pickups and four-wheel-drives could be seen chasing animals several miles away, we watched with our glasses. Antelope circled here and there, sending up dust plumes. But they didn't stay out in the flat country long. Soon a scattering could be seen coming toward the ridge. The saddle where we sat was the natural cross-over. Several does passed us within mere yards. As several vehicles also headed this way, we prudently went over to the far side of the ridge, to get out of the line of fire. During the morning over 100 antelope came through the saddle, and we each picked off a good buck at short range.

...orns nearly qualified for record book. (Minimum Boone & Crockett score is 82 points.)

I suppose this could be called a form of drive. Where antelope have not been badly disturbed it is occasionally possible to make a successful drive. But the tyro should understand that in their big country antelope don't drive very well. Once I took a stand at a point where a woven wire fence, coming down off a ridge, cornered and the remaining fence was four strands. From much sign it appeared antelope had been used to crawling through the strand fence here. Some friends drove a ranch trail that circled over the hills. They moved a number of antelope, which came straight down along the woven fence as we had hoped. It happened there was no animal that I wanted. But this does illustrate one way a drive might be tried.

An open pasture gate may make a good stand, with hunters attempting to push antelope through it. The only problem here is that for some odd
reason they don't like to go through gates. Perhaps there is something about
a gate, out here in the wide-open, that looks dangerous to them. At any rate
I've seen a band, during times when we were photographing them while
producing TV films and purposely trying to push them past the camera, run
right by an open gate time after time.

Any attempt at a drive has to be set up with careful planning beforehand. If a lot of hunters are out, and the animals wild as hawks, there's no
telling where they'll go. But a band spotted in a valley, when hunters are
few and the animals not disturbed, just may be encouraged to move to waiting hunters. One time in Wyoming I dropped off with a first-timer friend
and lay in a small gully about two feet deep. There was a band at least half a
mile away that appeared to have several good bucks in it. There was no way
we could dope out to get near enough for a shot. The vehicle went back
away from them down the trail, circled far around past a windmill, and finally we could see it probably a mile up the valley, slowly drifting toward
us again.

We had an understanding that in no case would we shoot toward the
vehicle. The antelope, not very concerned, started to trot toward us the moment they spotted the pickup moving in their direction. They came on right
to us, crossed the very gully where we lay at no more than 30 yards. We
arose and each collected a buck. I would not advise anyone to plan on such
an occurrence, however.

Waterhole stands, where legal, make an interesting hunt. Although
it is not wholly predictable, in my experience I have noticed that most
pronghorns come to water shortly after sun-up, and again in the middle of
the day. But they do not seem certain to visit water again late in the day. In
photographing them at close range at water, I was on several occasions surprised that they seemed not to use their noses to any extent. Sometimes
they'd walk past our sagebrush and chicken wire blind only a few yards
away, look at it with curiosity, but go right on.

When actually hunting, I have several times taken a stand a good
long rifle shot from a ranch tank, or windmill, after first checking for tracks

and droppings near the water. The advantage of such a plan is that you are offered standing shots, or at least shots at walking animals. Running shots are always precarious on any game, and especially on antelope.

On one hunt I took a stand behind a wire fence, where I had a rest against a post. There were rough hills to my right, a flat in front of me with a dug tank approximately 200 yards distant. Shortly past noon, a stream of single-file antelope appeared coming out of the hills. I counted 40 and quit because I had spotted what I wanted. That buck, well back toward the rear and spaced so I'd have no difficulty with others in the way, stopped and stared down toward the water. Those behind him stopped when he did. At a guessed 175 yards I collected him.

In general the most popular method of antelope hunting is to cruise the ranch roads, pausing to glass distant bands, and then trying to make a stalk close enough for a shot. This is an endeavor in which a hunter must know precisely how his rifle is sighted, how flat it shoots, and he had better be able to judge range with fair accuracy. It is not easy on the open plains. Most shots at antelope are long.

If you use craft, however, the sport is enhanced and the satisfaction in outwitting a big buck on its home grounds is great. Knowing antelope habits helps. The country may all look alike. But bear in mind that all animals, whether of forest or plain, have their own bailiwicks. A band of antelope may run several miles. But to them the country doesn't all look alike. The place from which they started when first disturbed probably is within their home range. If left alone after their flight, they will be back.

One of the very best ways to collect a trophy pronghorn is to get on the ground well before season and scout the territory, making as little disturbance as possible. One of the finest bucks I ever shot was discovered prior to opening, hanging out in a small, snug basin where water was available. From no point except the rim of the basin could these animals be seen. When put to flight they had rough hills with rock outcrops on one side to dash up into. We saw the band with the big buck two days in a row, far out of range in the basin. Each time the animals raced up into the hills. The day the season opened we spooked them out again. Then I hiked up into the hills and sat down behind an outcropping of black lava rock. The others in the vehicle went on. Two hours later the animals drifted back home, following the identical route of their flight. The horns are in my office where I can see them as I write this.

In stalking there are two important pronghorn habits to keep in mind. Antelope are similar to mule deer in one respect. A band suddenly spooked by a hunter may race up a ridge, then do a kind of rally on the crest, pausing to look back. When a band or even a single buck runs away up a slope, get down into shooting position immediately and wait for the top-out. You may get a shot, and the fact that you are not standing now makes you harder to spot and arouses more curiosity in the animals.

The other antelope habit is seeming not to be able to judge the intent of a hunter who pays no attention to it. Much depends, of course, on how badly the animals have been pushed around by other hunters. I hunted in New Mexico one season with a friend who had never collected an antelope. We spotted an excellent buck too far away. But it was standing, looking at the vehicle.

I said, "When I leave, start walking, not toward the buck but on an angle as if you are going far past it. If you do this properly and it works, you'll close the range to about 200 yards way off there where that single green bush shows."

I explained that he was not to look at the buck, but to act as if he were unaware of it and just walking along leaving the scene, but actually angling all the time. I went on and over a ridge, then crawled back up to watch. The buck stood, intent upon the hunter, who did an admirable job. He did get within 200 yards by angling past while appearing to go away. Then he suddenly dropped to the ground, wrapped an arm in his sling and took a shot. Unhappily for him, he missed. But he had learned a good trick in pronghorn hunting.

The highest sport in this pursuit is trying to toll antelope into range by appealing to their curiosity. I cannot promise you that this type of "calling" will work once in a dozen times. I've accomplished it twice and have seen others successful twice. Badly disturbed animals probably won't let their curiosity get the best of them. But you never know. The idea is based on the fact that pronghorns easily see everything in their domain, and when they see something they don't understand they become extremely curious.

In early days Indians tied a cloth to a bush so it waved in the breeze, and lay hidden nearby. I read one time of a pioneer hunter who lay on his back and kicked his feet in the air to puzzle antelope. One recent season, I photographed a hunter who lay down in foot-high grass and waved a white handkerchief at two distant bucks. I sat behind a small bush with a telephoto lens. The bucks watched the antics of the hunter, and began walking toward him. They wound up no more than 50 yards away.

On another occasion I desperately wanted a big buck that had been spooked and was running down a slope. I lay behind some rocks with my rifle rested on my jacket upon them. The buck was going to pass at least 300 yards out. I picked up my Western-style hat and waved it frantically above the rocks. The buck instantly saw the motion, whirled and stopped, staring. With the variable scope cranked up to 8X, I put the crosshair on his chest and with a measure of luck brought him down.

On another occasion while producing a TV film in west Texas, in which I also had to appear as the hunter, we needed to put me in the foreground and an antelope not more than 75 yards away so that a short telephoto lens would still make the animal plainly visible. We had glassed a lone buck coming down a valley. I got down flat a few yards out in front of the cameraman and he flattened down behind. I waved my hat. The buck stopped. I waved again. Presently he started our way. It took half an hour to bring him in, a step or two at a time. But come in he did, exactly where we wanted him, and we had the entire sequence on film.

Indeed, tolling antelope via the curiosity route is worth trying. You can't stand up, for they know what a man looks like. But they do not always associate danger with something they don't readily identify.

14.
WILD SHEEP
by
Charles Elliott

Good desert bighorn has become rare trophy.

A t more than two miles above sea level, we crouched in a world of silence so intense that it poured against our eardrums. Far below we could see a ragged scar we knew to be timberline. Above that the earth stood on end, sweeping in unbelievable formations to a jagged skyline. It was a land done up in gray, brown and cerulean, marked at its outer limits with frosted mountains. No living creature moved, except a lone eagle, floating in tremendous circles above an alpine valley.

Along with the pleasure of this dramatic panorama around us welled a deep and excited anticipation. From every angle this was as perfect a situation as I'd ever helped arrange. For 10 days we had hunted bighorn sheep on the ragged back rim of Wyoming's Yellow Creek basin, had covered the tremendous scope of country by saddle as far as a horse could go and by boot into terrain marked only by wild animal tracks. We'd seen some bighorns but none we wanted until on a distant ridge my hunting companion spotted four rams. Three wore one-half to three-quarter curls and the fourth carried a set of horns that made the others seem insignificant. We set up a spike camp at the head of the valley and operated out of it.

Two days we hunted the ridge top but our sheep had vanished. We found a game trail, recently used, from one ragged spur of the ridge to another, and loaded with recent sheep sign. On the third morning we were studying this when my partner saw the sheep on our ridge, more than half a mile away, coming toward us. We remained still until they went out of sight in a hidden gap, then moved swiftly. My buddy, who had won the chance at the first big ram we saw, took his place behind a point of rock, no more than 50 feet from the trail. With my camera I moved to a position 30 feet behind him, set for the sheep-hunting photo of a lifetime, with my hunter in the foreground and the ram, when it stepped into sight, silhouetted against the big blue bowl of sky.

We must have waited more than a quarter of an hour and were beginning to think that perhaps the sheep had turned off on another trail when I heard a slight rattle of gravel. My partner put his rifle barrel up and I steadied my camera. One of the smaller sheep walked into perfect picture position, hesitated a few seconds, but with a cross-wind blowing, did not smell or see us. We held our breath as the second and third of the smaller sheep passed. In spite of the icy air current, I broke out in a sweat. This was to be one of my most dramatic moments; only it wasn't. Minutes and more minutes went by before I began to suspect that a part somewhere was missing. I suppose I'd have stayed there until I mummified if my companion hadn't suddenly jerked to his feet and turned to me.

"Hell! Where'd he go?"

I couldn't think of even a stupid answer. We're good trackers, and we went over that hillside several times before we were sure of the answer. That big ram, which had been following the trail with the youngsters when we first saw him, had simply turned off below where we were hidden and worked his way under the brow of the ridge past the top of the knoll on which we crouched, then rejoined his band two hundred yards beyond the knoll. Except for a vagrant wind current, which was not likely, he could not have scented us. The smaller rams had in no way spooked him, for they did not see us. We could only guess that his "ESP"—and animals have proved to me time and again that they do have some such perception—saved him from a bullet, as it probably had many times in his life.

"It only helps to prove," my partner said, with admiration, "why one of these critters is just about the top trophy on the continent."

I had to agree with him that this was one reason, but only one. I've been on the big-game trail for longer than half a century and have experienced unforgettable moments. Many had to do with the wild sheep and the places in which it made its home. At least a part of the glamor of an old ram is the magnificence of his estate, no matter where he is found from the Arctic to the arid Southwestern deserts, for he generally lives in the heart of desolation, at elevations beyond the comfort of most game animals, negotiating dizzy trails and stairways which only he and his agile counterpart, the mountain goat, are equipped to travel.

It is to these breathless heights, often standing on end, that a hunter must go if he wants to add the horns of a ram to his list of trophies. And no matter what the time of year, the weather there is almost as unpredictable as the horned quarry he is after. Weather at extreme altitudes is always fickle and frequently violent, especially in the more northern latitudes. In the Yukon we spent the larger part of a bright day climbing to a band of rams and were almost within range when a cloud mass we had been watching seemed to change course, blew in and completely enveloped us. The guide predicted it wouldn't last long so we put on the down jackets we'd packed along by hand and sat down to wait out the soupy mess. The guide was right. Within an hour it was gone—and so were the rams.

On those incredible heights I've been caught in rain storms, in electric storms that made hair crackle and stand on end, in wind storms so fierce that we had to lie flat and hold on and in sudden snow squalls that seemed to materialize out of nowhere. A partner and I kept hunting through one of these near-blizzards until he finally refused to go any farther.

"What the hell are you after?" he panted. "A damned yeti?"

This dramatic world above timberline—its drama somehow heightened by the fact that a hunter must be in superb physical condition to survive it—is the proper setting for one of our great game animals. No other type of home would fit his physical characteristics or his personality. Although he comes in a number of varieties, each in a location geared to his own particular type of domain, the basic anatomy of all wild sheep is similar. Size ranges from the massive bighorn, which stands 38 to 42 inches at the shoulder and weighs in at 200 to 300 pounds (though sometimes declared heavier by those who know it) to the smaller Dall sheep, about 38 inches in height and 180 to 200 pounds for a large specimen. The horns of the larger sheep are, as the name implies, massive. They are tightly curled, heavy and blunt to the tips. The more northerly Dall and his varieties carry horns with smaller beams and longer, more slender tips which flare outward on big rams. They are sometimes known as the "thinhorns."

Except for size, coloration and shape of horns, the body structure of all wild sheep is approximately the same. No wild sheep, for example, is covered with wool such as their domestic cousins wear, but rather with a coat of long, hollow hair that acts as insulation against temperatures which often plummet far below zero and remain there for weeks in more northerly latitudes. The sheep shed their longer hair and grow a shorter coat for the summer months.

The hoof of a sheep is of remarkable construction and well adapted to the land in which it exists. The edges are tough and sharp and the bottom made up of a concave cushion, forming a highly efficient suction cup—a combination that enables the animal to travel over incredible routes. I have seen sheep on almost vertical slopes, moving along as casually as I stroll down a country lane. They can swiftly climb or drop down a rocky face, utilizing almost invisible cracks or projections with great agility. They are not, however, perfect; I've discovered a few skeletons at the base of cliffs. The track of a sheep is less pointed than that of a deer and when it walks with its toes spread, as it usually does, the tracks appear more square in shape and can easily be confused with those of a mountain goat.

Both the nose and ears, as in most animals subjected to predation, are sensitive assets, but the truly remarkable organ of a sheep is its eyes. Mammalogists estimate that the animal has "eight-power" vision and most guides and experienced sheep hunters will agree. As one guide told me when I wondered if an old ram had spotted us from a couple of miles away, "He's counted the buttons on your coat and knows the make and caliber of the gun you carry."

The wild sheep is said to reach old age in about 10 or 12 years, but a few go as long as 15 before their time runs out. Age is indicated by the growth rings of the horns.

Most sheep of all subspecies spend their summers around the highest portion of their range. Winter usually drives them to lower elevations, to less extreme temperatures and where food is more easily obtained. This rule does not hold entirely true, for in the milder months of the year the bands often cross from one range to another. In Alaska we once took a good trophy by finding fresh tracks where the rams had crossed a creek valley and following them to the heights beyond. Throughout the range, hunters as well as biologists have reported sheep at much lower elevations than where they are supposed to live. I remember watching a band of bighorns for several autumns after they had moved off the top of the range to the lower slopes of the mountain above Valley, Wyoming.

How far the sheep bands range is thought to depend on the food and water supply and on how badly they are disturbed. Bands have been reported to remain within a mile or two of an established location, as in Yellowstone Park where they receive complete protection; and others cover a

Hunter glasses steep rock walls on far side of valley, where sheep feel secure.

distance of some 25 miles. The desert sheep is perhaps the widest wanderer, for he must travel far when rainfall is scarce and his seeps and natural *tinajas,* or water basins, begin to dry up.

How wild is the wild sheep? Some hunters swear that they are the most elusive of all creatures, and obviously such reports come from areas where the sheep are, or have been, heavily pursued. I have found them extremely shy in some places, almost tame in others (as in the protected region above Valley, Wyoming).

One of the amazing countries I hunted for Dall sheep was in the far northern part of the Yukon Territory, right up against the Northwest Territories line. We were two to three weeks beyond where the man-made trails ran out, and for a month we explored tremendous valleys and mountain summits where I am sure the game had never seen a human. We hunted by horse, but because of the round stones and boulders covered with moss, had to confine our riding generally to the valleys and lower slopes. From there my guide and I could spot sheep, but they were too high and far away for us to evaluate the heads through our glasses or, most of the time, with a spotting scope. We spent much time climbing afoot. For 19 days we climbed from six to eight hours a day to get close enough to decide on a ram, each of which we considered smaller than what we wanted. After a few days it began to dawn on me that those sheep were not afraid of us—only curious. Our movements did not seem to disturb them in the least.

The wild sheep is an old settler in America. Through geological findings it is estimated that this animal crossed the Bering Land Bridge from Asia about half a million years ago to make its home in the western highlands of our continent. The theory is that in the millennia since, the Asiatic sheep colonized western America from the Arctic to the tropics. No one knows how far the natural expansion of range had gone before the last glacial age, but this is thought to have been a factor in the colonization process. As the glaciers retreated, the sheep followed and the various forms developed to fit terrain, climate and habits, from the white sheep of the northern ice and snow to the desert brown variety of Mexico and the southwestern United States.

Although each may list a different number of varieties or subspecies which have developed from the original sheep, mammalogists generally agree on two main species which have evolved. These are the bighorn and Dall. Their subspecies run as high as 13 in number according to some of the experts, but the latest and most technical authority lists the Dall with three subspecies, the bighorn with seven.

If you really wanted to get technical about it, you'd therefore have to collect the heads of 10 different sheep to make a grand slam—if you could find and identify them all. However, on a practical basis of range, coloration, characteristics of horns and other factors, sportsmen and sportsmen's organizations settled on four distinct types for listing in the record books: the bighorn, desert, Dall and Stone. The difference in the bighorn and desert is mostly a matter of range and coloration, the former with usually a darker coat and a habitat from central British Columbia to central Colorado and eastern New Mexico; and the latter, ranging from the Southwest down into Mexico, sometimes toned down to a pale buff to blend with its surroundings. The Dall, of course, is the white sheep from the far north. Its horns are more slender and a bit differently contoured. Its body is also more slender than the bighorn, and although it stands almost as tall, its weight is normally about two-thirds that of its blocky cousin. Its range covers Alaska, extends over most of the Yukon and into mountainous Northwest Territories and takes in the extreme northwest corner of British Columbia. It has one recognized subspecies limited to the Kenai Peninsula.

As the Dall range extends east and south from Alaska through the Yukon and into British Columbia, the change of color phase begins slowly to show, with a few black hairs here and there, then all-black tails and dark colored saddles. This darkening continues, shading into the dark-colored Stone, which has a recognized range in the central southern Yukon and upper British Columbia. One of the color variations around this overlapping range is known as the Fannin, and is one of the trophies prized by many big-game hunters.

The most recent survey shows that sheep may be hunted in Canada's territories (both the Yukon and the Northwest Territories), the provinces of British Columbia and Alberta, and 11 states—Alaska, Arizona, Colorado, Idaho, Montana, Nevada, New Mexico, Oregon, South Dakota, Washing-

Hunters follow dry creek bed to get above band of Dall sheep in Far North.

ton and Wyoming. For desert bighorns, Mexico also has excellent hunting. In addition, Utah has had limited hunts for desert bighorns and will again, even though at this writing there is no open season.

To hunt in Alaska, British Columbia or the Canadian territories, you need only have a big-game license and a knowledgeable outfitter-guide who operates in sheep country. Non-residents need a permit in Alberta, and those who travel to Mexico for a desert sheep will also need a government permit. With the exception of Alaska, all of our states require a permit, and getting it is the first and one of the most difficult chores for the sheep hunter.

Just as soon as you decide you want to hunt sheep, and have picked a state, write to the game department there for information about the next season, plus instructions and application forms. All of this must be done far in advance. Your name will be thrown into the pot with hundreds, sometimes thousands, of other applicants and the odds are small that your name will be one of those drawn. I made application each year for 18 years in one Rocky Mountain state for a bighorn permit and, as far as I know, never came close.

Alaska is unquestionably our best sheep-hunting state. The Dall, or white, sheep is found throughout the state except in the Panhandle. Favorite hunting locations are the Talkeetna, Chugach and Wrangell Mountains, all in the southeast. The Brooks Range, far up at the northern limit of the Dall, is also terrific hunting territory but accessibility is a big problem. The fish and game department tells us the annual Dall harvest has been about 1,000 over the past dozen years or so.

The white phase of the Dall sheep extends over most of the Yukon Territory and is the most common there. Game authorities say this form "is found in the Mackenzie Mountains and Richardson Mountains along the eastern boundary, the British Mountains in the northwest, the Ogilvie Mountains in the central Yukon and the Dawson Range, the St. Elias and Coast Mountains in the west."

The darker form, the Stone, occurs in the central part of the territory, in the Anvil and Big Salmon ranges, and the Pelly and Cassiar Mountains. The sheep population is considered large throughout the territory and success ratio is high. With only a small fraction of the numbers of sportsmen who hunt in Alaska, the Yukon harvest usually runs between 250 and 300 rams a year.

In the Northwest Territories the Dall sheep appears in the rugged mountainous boundary along the Yukon, but as yet little trophy hunting has been done.

British Columbia recognizes four races of sheep in the province: the Rocky Mountain and California bighorns and the Dall and Stone, with the two bighorns in the south and the thinhorns in the north. Where you hunt in the province depends on what sheep you prefer on your den wall. A report from the British Columbia Fish and Wildlife Branch gives the following ranges: The Rocky Mountain bighorn is found in the Rocky Mountains and Rocky Mountain Trench from the international boundary to Golden, and in scattered bands from Mt. Robson to the Sukunka River. Two bands have been established from transplants, one at Squilax and the other at Spences Bridge. The California bighorn is found in the Okanagan, Similkameen and mid-Fraser River basins. Stone sheep occur on the Yukon and Stikine plateaus and the Skeena, Carriar and Omineca Mountains and from Peace River to the Laird River and the Boundary Ranges of the Coast Mountains. The Dall is confined to small, scattered bands in the Tatshenkini-Bennett Lake area.

No region holds a monopoly on record sheep, but one look in the record book might influence me to try my luck in Alberta. Although they go back some years, seven of the 10 top bighorn heads in the Boone & Crockett records came out of Alberta, and this province has produced more than half of the 271 record sheep listed in the book, many taken in recent years.

The Rocky Mountain bighorn is found on the mountainous western border of the province, and some of the top hunting is located in the mountain fringes bordering Jasper and Banff National Parks, as well as south of Banff and along the British Columbia border. Residents and non-residents may hunt for trophy sheep only in regular season, but recently there have been special hunts in which residents may make non-trophy hunts for ewes and young rams. Non-residents must hunt by permit in specified areas.

From the international boundary southward through the mountain states, getting a good bighorn ram or one of its related subspecies becomes a more difficult assignment. All sheep hunting, where allowed, is on a permit basis. Wyoming is the state probably most heavily populated with the Rocky Mountain bighorn, with its largest crop of rams extending through the northwest corner of the state. From these bands the game department occasionally traps a few animals to move elsewhere, hoping to establish new range. In addition to the vast ranges of the Shoshone, Teton and Bridger National Forests, a substantial population of sheep appears in the Big Horn Mountains and in the Laramie Peak area of the Medicine Bow National Forest in the southeast. The hunt is on a special permit basis in designated areas for both resident and non-resident licensees, and the current take usu-

After 10-day Wyoming hunt, sportsman is delighted with his ¾-curl bighorn.

ally exceeds 100 rams a season, which adds up to about 25 to 30 percent hunter success.

Idaho was one of the last states to have an open season for all holders of big-game licenses and hunters flocked there. The kill dropped alarmingly from 64 rams in 1970 to 12 in 1971. To save the herd, this state went to limited permits. Currently the total number issued is 89. The range of the Rocky Mountain bighorn is in east-central Idaho, mostly on the Middle Fork of the Salmon River. A small herd of California bighorns from British Columbia was transplanted to southern Owyhee County in the southwestern corner of the state, and these sheep have increased sufficiently now to provide a seven-permit hunt.

Montana has been busy building back its wild-sheep population and creating new sheep areas. The Rocky Mountain bighorn is well established in several ranges. Permits are, as in other states, limited. The largest sheep herds are in the south end of Ravalli County, the Clark Fork region of Granite County, the Sun River region in Teton, Lewis and Clark counties, and in the northwest in Sanders, Lincoln and part of Flathead counties. Permits are allotted for 10 hunting districts.

Washington shot out its native bighorns long years ago. In the past two decades or so, sheep have been introduced from British Columbia, and the animals are again on a huntable basis. Populated areas include Sinlahekin Game Range in Okanogan County, Tucannon Game Range in Columbia and Garfield counties, and Colokum in Chelan and Kittitas counties. Currently hunts are scheduled for five hunting units.

Bighorns also disappeared from Oregon in the distant past. For the past quarter-century, however, the game authorities have worked diligently to restore wild-sheep hunting. Bighorns were stocked on Hart Mountain in Lake County in 1954, and as this herd grew, excess ewes and rams from it were used to stock other regions in the state, among them the Owyhee and Steens Mountains in the southeast corner of the state. Since 1965, 57 hunters have taken 30 bighorn rams for a success ratio of 53 percent. Current season permits number 10, eight of them for Steens and two for Owyhee.

The game authorities tell us that Rocky Mountain bighorns have been successfully established in two areas in South Dakota—Custer State Park and the Badlands. The latter herd is small and has not been hunted, but five permits are issued annually for Custer State Park and "during the average year, hunter success there is 100 percent."

Colorado has a reasonably good sheep population in its high country. For more than 25 years, hunts have been held by permit in certain areas, with an annual harvest of 30 to 60 sheep. Some of the areas recommended are Poudre River and Pikes Peak, Sheep Creek and Cimarron Peak, Boiler Creek out of New Castle in Garfield County and Mount Evans.

Utah claims two varieties of bighorns. The Rocky Mountain bighorn appears in the northern part of the state on Willard Peak southeast of Brigham City. These animals are a part of the stocking program to bring bighorns back to their original range. Desert sheep are found in the southern part of the state. These are also the result of a stocking program and recently more transplants have been made from Zion National Park. Very limited hunts for desert bighorns have been held for a few seasons (about 10 permits and a harvest of four animals a year). Currently there is no season, but sheep hunters there have an eye on the future.

Nevada contains a good population of desert bighorns, concentrated in the central and southern portions of the state. All permits are issued for the south. The northernmost area open is in Units 21A and 21B, west of Nellis Air Force Range. The remaining 11 open areas lie in the extreme southern tip of the state. The number of permits vary, but are generally around 50 or above, of which only about 10 percent are allocated to non-residents. All permit holders must go through an "indoctrination period"—a short hunting course to determine if the hunter is capable and teach him how to judge a legal ram. Hunter success runs between 20 and 30 percent. Nevada is currently working to establish a herd of Rocky Mountain sheep in the northern part of the state, where this bighorn formerly ranged.

New Mexico contains both Rocky Mountain and desert bighorns. The original stock of the northern sheep came from Banff in Alberta; they were planted in the Sandia Mountains, east of Albuquerque, and thrived there. Sandia furnished stock for other regions such as the Pecos Wilderness, near Santa Fe, Glenwood in the southwest near the town of Glenwood, the Gila Wilderness above Silver City and certain portions of the Sangre de Cristo range in the north. Current hunting for the Rocky Mountain sheep is in Pecos (W1), Sandia Mountain (W2) and Glenwood (W3) Units. Of the 23 permits issued for these areas, only three are non-resident. The San Andres Refuge (W4) above La Cruces in the southern part of the state will be open for desert sheep, but with only six permits, one going to a non-resident.

Arizona is one of the better desert-sheep states. Hunting there is confined to the mountain ranges along the western boundary. About 70 permits are available for the management units named in the current hunting regulations. Annual surveys dictate where the hunts will be held. Normally the harvest is around 30 to 35 rams a year, which means about 50 percent hunter success.

Other states in the process of building their sheep herds for future hunting are California, Texas and North Dakota. California has not had a

Before making long climb, hunter uses spotting scope to evaluate ram's curl.

sheep season since 1873, but the game department is in the process of re-establishing its herds. The current estimate is 3,500 bighorns and desert sheep, chiefly in 16 scattered areas.

Texas is confining its sheep activity to the southwest corner of the state, which once had a sizable population of desert sheep. In 1957, six sheep from Arizona were stocked in the Black Gap Wildlife Management Area and kept in a 427-acre enclosure. By 1971 these had increased to 68 and in 1971, 19 of these were released in the 100,000-acre Black Gap region. These appeared to prosper and two years later, seven more sheep were released in the Sierra Diablo Wildlife Management Area in western Culberson County. Latest reports show that the herd is growing.

In 1956, 18 bighorns were imported from British Columbia into

North Dakota, and since then these have increased to more than 100 animals. The state looks forward to a season sometime in the future.

More than half of the 171 world-record desert sheep came out of Mexico, which boasts the first nine places in the record book. These nine top trophies were taken out of Lower California, Baja and Sonora. Getting a permit to hunt sheep in Mexico is not without its problems, but if you are lucky enough to secure legal permission, have the stamina to survive in that brutal range where the desert sheep live, and can find an honest, capable guide, there is a chance of putting a real trophy head on your den wall. The Mexican game officials will give you all the necessary details.

A sheep hunter is not born, he is made. He may have all the basic qualifications such as good eyes, strong legs, patience and a blazing ambition to collect a trophy head, but he just doesn't jump up from his desk, run out and knock over one of the big four like a cottontail on the rim of the nearest swamp. Even though he may be lucky enough to get teamed up with the best guide in the business, a man must make certain preparations of his own if he expects to be a successful sheep hunter.

Assuming that he has had a certain amount of experience outdoors, that he knows how to adjust a binocular, read a compass and handle a gun, the most basic need of any sheep hunter is superb physical condition. Endurance is more important than strength, and endurance means stout legs, and lungs and heart in peak condition. In the high elevations where sheep are found, the oxygen is thin and both the heart and lungs must often do double duty to properly supply oxygen to the blood stream.

Unless they live in high country or travel it constantly, most ram hunters I know go into a period of physical training that would do justice to a pro football player. One important thing I do before I start my training for sheep is to go through a complete physical examination to determine that all my organs are sound and can take the punishment I know they will get.

Those who do not have the privilege of much exercise must start slowly, even if it's only walking a mile or two each day for the first few days. I usually graduate from the walking into jogging, by jogging a hundred steps (or until I breathe hard) and then walking the next hundred steps. I gradually lengthen my periods of jogging until I can go half a mile, then a mile without a strain on my heart and lungs. I increase the pace until within a few weeks I can do a mile in 10 minutes or less. But I don't stop there. I build toward two miles and then three, for I know how badly I'll need that endurance at high altitudes.

During this period I also spend as much time as possible on the rifle range. It's important to know what the rifle of my choice will do and to know what I can do with it. The shot I get at that prize ram may be a long one and I want to have a good chance of scoring.

I also spend much time getting my equipment together and in shape for the hunt. They say anticipation is half the delight of realization and this must be true, for I get many a pleasurable hour gathering those items I will need for my hunt and boiling them down to the essentials which must be packed in by horse or afoot to sheep country.

Naturally, I suppose, my first consideration is my gun, with its carrying case or saddle scabbard if my outfitter or guide does not furnish one, and with ammunition, oil, rod and cleaning equipment. I have killed sheep with my old .30-06, the .270 and .300 H&H Magnum, and I prefer the .300 H&H because of its flat trajectory as well as its power. I prefer the 180-grain bullet weight and have always found it completely satisfactory. Since I believe that most of my shots at sheep will be long, I like a variable 2½-8X scope, which also makes a good glass for studying a head. I don't depend on the scope altogether, but carry a pair of binoculars. Some of my hunting acquaintances like their field glasses up to 12 power, but anything larger than a 7x35mm tires my eyes and even my arms after continuous long use. With this average glass, I can sit on a mountain for long periods, look the country over and remain relaxed. Many sheep hunters I know pack along a 40X or even larger spotting scope to save a bit of climbing.

My choice of hunting knives is one with a five-inch blade and, either in my hunting-coat pocket or the shoulder bag that I ordinarily use on any hunt, I carry a whetstone, compass that I hope I'll never use, a small roll of friction tape, a length of stout cord that comes in handy for many purposes, a waterproof matchbox, films for my camera, extra shells, as well as light, tightly rolled rain gear.

In sheep country the right clothing is important. Next to my skin I like light cotton underwear. Some ram hunters I know use heavy flannel or thermal underwear in every kind of weather, but where climbing is involved (even when it's very cold) I have found this heavy cloth next to the skin induces perspiration and then is uncomfortable when I am faced with long waits or other inactivity. My best trousers are heavy, close-knit virgin wool, and I wear a heavy virgin-wool shirt. Even wet, these are warmer than most other materials. In severe weather a second wool shirt, cashmere sweater or down underwear over the shirt makes good insulation and I top these with a down hunting coat. For moderate weather I have a lighter down jacket that I can roll into a small bundle, tie with a piece of cord and sling over my shoulder while I'm climbing, then when I sit on a high, windy knoll to glass, the jacket keeps me comfortable.

Heavy virgin-wool socks are my choice for the feet. Where there's any danger of sweating, one or two hunters I know pull on loose cotton socks over these, saying that the moisture will osmose through the wool to the cotton. The choice of boots varies with the individual hunter. One will tell you he prefers metal caulks—and these are all right for traveling over logs or windfalls in the timber or on glacier or other ice at higher elevations. Another hunter likes the leather pac with the lower or foot part made of rubber, which is good for slush or soggy ground, but under hard exercise or in warm weather will often sweat your feet. For normal sheep hunting I wear a medium leather 10-inch boot with a composition sole with its pattern engraved deeply enough to give me secure footing on almost any type of terrain.

I pack both virgin-wool and heavily insulated gloves for the extremes of weather. The wool is usually enough when the weather is dry. My choice of headgear is a heavy wool cap with ear flaps, and I carry along a down-insulated cap as a spare. In the rain I can protect either of these under the hood of my rain jacket.

The final step to actually hunting what is perhaps the trophy of a lifetime depends to some extent on what part of the continent you hunt and which of the big four you are after. Basically, of course, certain fundamentals apply to all species: Find the largest head on the range, stalk it, then down it with one well-placed shot. A lot of sheep hunters I know wish it

Tired but exuberant hunter kneels with Yukon trophy that has nearly full curl.

were that simple. If you have your license or necessary permit, and your guide has brought you to where the sheep are, it boils down to finding the best legal head, stalking it successfully and, if possible, downing it on the spot.

Finding the head of your dreams is not always possible. Once in sheep country I had rams all around me for eight days and passed up at least a dozen legal ones while I continued my search for that one to go in the record books. With so many sheep in the country, I figured I could wait until the last day to settle for just any head. The biggest I saw during those eight days was badly broomed on one side. As all sheep hunters know, a ram will thrust the tip of his horn in a crack and break it off when it grows long enough to obscure his vision in that direction. So I waited until the last day. And you already know what happened. Every sheep in that country simply disappeared. All we could find were tracks and droppings. You can't eat or mount and hang those on the wall. I got no sheep that year.

Almost always the stalk is a necessary part of the game. A few times I've walked up on sheep in a pocket when I was hunting them or other game, but those are rare occasions. Most sheep are seen at a distance, must be approached close enough to evaluate a head and then stalked close enough for a shot. The spotting scope helps in this evaluation.

Most guides will tell you that sheep are more easily approached from above, but sometimes this is not possible unless a guy is equipped with wings. After you decide on a ram, the trick is to make a circle detour and put a ridge or other massive formation between you and the sheep, then approach upwind on the blind side to a point preferably above the sheep.

The biggest Dall I ever killed in Alaska lay on the edge of a tremendous open slope where he could see for miles in three directions. The only approach was behind the band of rams and luckily downwind, so the guide and I circled in that direction around a slope that ate my lungs out until we came to a point where the blind side of the slope was a vertical cliff. There simply was no way to get to those sheep. We had watched them trail single-file across the rim of the cliff to where they lay down, and we knew they would probably return along the same route. I concealed myself above the trail in a clump of rocks and the guide circled away from the sheep, made a hazardous detour through the canyon below and almost two hours later came out on the ridge about a mile below the sheep.

They spotted him instantly, got to their feet and slowly backtracked around the top of the slope toward me. They were within 40 yards when I took the big ram. I sprinted downhill to him. The other rams, their leader gone, just stood and looked at me, a couple of them close enough to touch with a long fishing pole.

Every stalk is different and must be laid out according to terrain; most of them take patience and determination as well as tremendous physical endurance.

15.
MOUNTAIN
GOAT

Goats often bed on high, wind-swept slopes.

I t is difficult to find a mountain-goat hunter who is a true enthusiast, as sheep hunters invariably are. The mountain goat is indeed one of the most interesting of creatures, but as a trophy it is not especially exciting. Most hunters who collect a goat do so while on a trip for other game that was the main attraction, or else they decide to collect a goat simply to fill out the list of horned and antlered North American game.

As I mentioned in my earlier discussion of how to judge trophies, there is very little variation in horn length among mature goats. Both sexes have horns, and at a distance and sometimes close up it is not easy for the tyro to tell a billy from a nanny. Generally the horns of the female are more slender, but they may be just as long. In fact, a female head held the top record for a number of years.

At maximum, goat horns grow to be about a foot long, but that's rare. That record nanny had horns slightly exceeding a foot. Under the present scoring system, horns of greater diameter and other desirable features, though shorter, put her out of the top spot. Eight-inch horns are common in mature animals. Though an eight-incher is hardly a trophy of consequence, horns nine inches long can be considered pretty fair. Those more than nine inches automatically fall into the trophy class but they'd have to be more than 10 inches to have a chance at the record book. The chance of finding a head with 11- to 12-inch horns is not great, for one reason because a hunter is not likely on a given hunt to be able to look over many heads.

Thus, what we're talking about is a trophy with horns that are not especially impressive, and further, the difference between a book head and a so-so head or one to pass up is a matter of an inch or two. The judgment is difficult, and there is so little variation that competition among hunters is not remotely like that which exists among sheep hunters.

In attempting to judge length of mountain-goat horns, several guess-measurements have evolved. Visualize a horn as detached and laid along the bridge of the nose, with its base at the tip of the nose. If the horn appears to be long enough so that the tip would reach to the eye, it is probably about nine inches long. If the horn is long enough to reach beyond the eye, to a point between the eye and the actual horn bases, it's a very good specimen, and if the horn would reach from the nose tip to horn bases, it is exceptional.

Old billies have the heaviest horns. The trick is to find one, and be certain of it. Goat seasons in various places run from as early as mid-July or August 1 on into November or in a few instances to the end of the year. If you plan to hunt in August or September you are sure to have the best chance to spot old males by themselves. Any large, lone goat is likely to be a mature billy. If the distinctive hump above the shoulders is unusually pronounced, it's all the more reason to judge this as a big old male. Exceptional males will weigh as much as 300 pounds, but 200 to 250 is more common.

Where a group of goats is seen and the individuals differ in size, it's a pretty good bet that they are nannies and kids. However, experienced hunters always comb the surrounding country. Now and then a billy will be in the vicinity, though not consorting with the others. By November, however, judgments become more difficult, for this is the breeding season. The sexes now intermingle, and lone animals are seldom spotted.

Although the name "goat" has always been in common usage, the animal is not a goat at all, but a curious variety of highly specialized antelope. Or perhaps one should visualize it as one of a number of links between the goats and the antelopes. In this group of mammals are several oddities— the chiru of Tibet, the saiga of central Asia, the goral of Siberia, the serow, or "cliff donkey," of eastern Asia. Scientists believe that forerunners of the North American mountain goat filtered onto this continent eons ago via a land bridge with Asia. However, there is no animal elsewhere in the world like it. Presumably one of its closest relatives is the chamois of Europe.

One of the most interesting items of goat lore is that they seem unable to extend their range downward, and thus are restricted to a rather limited amount of territory, chiefly above timberline. To be sure, transplants have been made out of the original range, which was in the northwestern portion of the continent, from central Idaho and western Montana into Washington's Cascades and north into Alaska. And transplants have been made from range to range within states, such as in Montana. But the mountain goat is fundamentally an animal of the highest, most desolate crags and pinnacles and slopes. On its own the species was able over the centuries to extend its range only so far as it could do so by following the high ridges from peak to peak.

Mountain goat habitat is without any question the most severe of any on the continent. Winters are violent and bitter. Food variety and supply are at minimum. Lichens and scrub browse of numerous varieties make up goat diet. Nonetheless, the animals have the ability to lay on awesome amounts of fat for the winter, and to tolerate constant blizzards and far-below-zero temperatures.

These animals never have been numerous, by comparison with other horned and antlered game. Their reproductive rate is not high, possibly because they are so closely attuned to a sparse habitat. Usually only one kid is born annually, although some twins do appear. Predation, from eagles and bears for example, may account for some cropping of the population. Disease takes some. There is a great deal still to be learned about these animals, but it is believed that avalanches, rock slides, and other phenomena common to their range take numerous individuals annually. Though this is the most sure-footed species on the continent, accidental falls are more common than one would believe from watching the fantastic agility of goats on steep faces and ledges.

Despite the severity of conditions on their ranges, goats require little "management" in order to keep their population levels relatively static. For that matter, management on their home grounds, except for trapping and transplanting, is not very practical. Nonetheless, mountain goat populations exhibit few drastic ups and downs. While this means that the mountain goat is certainly not an endangered species, it also means that goat hunting unquestionably will always be quite limited. The only way to enlarge it is to transplant and form new populations. But the amount of suitable unpopulated range today is minimal.

Planning a hunt should be done carefully, with a survey of the possibilities and weighing of chances. Many hunters try for goat permits when going on hunts for grizzlies, sheep, caribou or moose within goat range. Even if the goat is somewhat an incidental, this takes even more careful planning, to make seasons and possibilities dovetail.

Alaska has long been an excellent bet. The Alaskan goat population is estimated at between 10,000 and 15,000. Contrary to popular notions, goats do not range throughout Alaska. They are, in general, confined to the

Hunters pack out mountain-goat cape in high Sun River country of Montana.

coastal mountains, from the southern Panhandle north and then northwest to the Talkeetna region above Anchorage. From there the range extends southward into the Kenai Peninsula. Transplants to Kodiak Island have done well, and hunting is open there also, as well as throughout most (but not all) of the range mentioned. There have also been transplants to several islands off the Panhandle.

Laws may change from year to year, but for some time Alaska has allowed the taking of two goats in some areas, and of either sex. Even with such liberal regulations the annual bag is not very high, at most only a few hundred, chiefly taken by non-resident trophy hunters. Natives are seldom interested, because goat meat is not highly regarded, and the flesh of old billies is often next to inedible. Probably it would be possible for authorities to extend goat range in Alaska by transplants, but with hunter demand as it is, this seems rather pointless.

An interesting hunting method peculiar to coastal Alaska (and portions of coastal British Columbia) is via boat. A substantial percentage of the goat population ranges on coastal slopes within sight of salt water. A coastal cruise combined with glassing, then a tough climb, often is successful. Chances of success, especially for the guided non-resident, are high in Alaska. If one simply wants a fair trophy, and has the steam to get up where it lives, there is seldom reason to go home without one.

Like Alaska, British Columbia allows hunting by non-residents (and aliens) as well as residents. The goat population here, as in Alaska, cannot be accurately estimated, but is certainly substantial. For some reason a good many residents hunt goats in British Columbia, an average of three or four thousand each season. Records show that over the past decade they've often taken 1,400 to nearly 2,000 animals a season, with a low of roughly 1,000. Non-residents bag another 300 to 700 each season.

Goats are found in most of the mountainous portions of British Columbia, from the far northwest to the southern border. In fact, some excellent hunting can be found in certain management areas of the south. Overall, you can figure on somewhere between 30 and 40 percent chance of success. But success is much higher in a few specific management areas, particularly in the northwest, for guided non-residents. It has run 100 percent.

As this is written, non-residents must have a guide.

There is a modest amount of goat hunting in the Yukon, particularly in the southeast. But there are several difficulties, and the kill in some recent seasons has been less than 50. A hunter must book through an outfitter and be guided; outfitters are limited in number and assigned territories. This is also very rugged hunting. Canada's highest peaks are in the Yukon.

There is fair opportunity in the Northwest Territories, but here again regulations are quite restrictive. Non-residents may hunt only in a couple of specified zones, must employ registered outfitters and be guided. The kill to date, since the zones were opened to non-residents, has been very low.

There is quite good goat hunting in Alberta, but at this time it is for residents only, and probably will remain so, although a few years ago non-residents were allowed. It is not on any large scale. In a recent season 50 permits were offered via drawing. The average kill runs around 20 animals, with success for those who use their permits slightly better than 50 percent. Hunting area is specified in the license-application instruction, so there is no way for any "best location" to be noted.

Within the contiguous U.S., Washington has by far the largest goat population and the highest kill. Goats are rather actively "managed" here, because the state has ample high range for them. They are quite widespread, and have been transplanted here and there. One aspect of management is the opening of designated hunting units to only a specified number of permits. In a recent season, 30 specially designated Goat Management Units were open. The permits were so distributed as to eliminate any concentrations of hunters and, by figuring past success percentages, to crop the goat population properly in each Unit.

Fortunately, non-residents are allowed to hunt. Although permit offerings may fluctuate, in the past they have run around 1,000 or more per season, and the total goat population is estimated at 7,000 to 8,000. Success runs from 30 to 40 percent, with a bag of 300 to 400 each season. This makes Washington one of the best bets for a hunter. With a guide he can be assured of better than average chances of success. For those who might want to go back a second time, however, it would be wise to check current regu-

Colorado goat poses common dilemma: Long fall will break horns and ruin trophy.

lations. In the past those who drew permits were not allowed to apply again for several seasons.

Oregon began a modest goat program over 20 years ago, when a few animals were brought in and released in the Wallowa Mountains in the northeastern portion of the state. Several small hunts were allowed between 1965 and 1968, with 20 animals collected for a success of 87 percent. However, at the time this is written no season has been held since '68. The estimated goat population is only 35 animals, in the Eagle Cap Wilderness Area. The seasons that were held were for residents only, with a drawing for permits. Undoubtedly if there are seasons in the future, the same situation will occur.

In Idaho goats are found in several high areas. These include the drainages of the Salmon, Clearwater and St. Joe rivers, and down in the southwestern part of the state the upper Boise and Payette. The animals are fairly plentiful, and there are open seasons each year in which both residents and non-residents may participate. Presently 10 percent of the permits issued by special drawing may go to non-residents. Hunter success runs at least 50 percent and up to 60 percent. The annual harvest is from about 100 to 160.

Idaho's goat population appears to be stable. There are no "best areas." Hunts are set by unit or portions of certain management units, with a specified number of permits for each. Currently no guide is required. It is important for hunters to check regulations carefully, for they may change in some details from year to year.

Montana is also a good bet. This state has been very active over a number of years in goat trapping and transplanting. The animals presently are found in numerous locations. There are substantial populations in the high country to the north of Yellowstone National Park. Others are found in the high ranges of northwestern Montana, and still others far down in the border region of the southwest. There was even a successful transplant to a high plateau jutting up out of the farm country not far from Fort Benton.

As a rule, some 800 to 900 permits are available by special drawing. These are spread over a large number of hunting areas or units, and 10 percent of the total may be taken by non-residents. Presently goats of either sex

Trim-looking goat shown here has not yet grown thick, shaggy winter coat.

are legal. The kill has run as low as 200 and as high as 500. Ordinarily it is about 300, with the success percentage between 30 and 40.

There is a small amount of goat hunting elsewhere. Wyoming has a small but stable goat population, with a season most years, but with a very few permits offered—four so far each season, three of them for residents, one non-resident. The total goat population is probably no more than 75. They are found in the tremendously rugged country of the northwest, above the Clark's Fork River and in the Beartooth Pass region that is reached out of Cooke City, Montana. Even with only four permits, the chance of all four hunters filling their tags is precarious. Over a period of several years success has averaged out to about 80 percent non-resident and 66 percent resident.

The state of Utah brought in a few goats some years ago from Washington. They were placed in the mountains east of Salt Lake City. To date there is no hunting. However, in Colorado there is an open season each year. The state estimates its goat population at around 400, with an upward trend. Permits are issued by special drawing. The average kill is about 10 each season. However, this hunting is for residents only. Open areas pres-

Winter pelage can make goat look deceptively large. This one is Alaskan.

ently are Mount Evans north of Grant, and the Collegiate Range northwest of Salida. Hunters on Mount Evans have chalked up 100 percent success. Average overall success is around 75 percent.

Possibly the most interesting goat population within the contiguous states is in South Dakota. Some Canadian goats were brought into Custer State Park in the Black Hills way back in the early part of the century. A half-dozen animals escaped over 50 years ago and launched populations in two high, rugged areas of the Hills: Harney Peak and the Needles. These appear to be the only places the goats are capable of colonizing, for they have never spread from these locations after original establishment. A population of 300 to 400 has been attained, but it cannot go beyond that because of lack of forage and living space. Occasional token seasons are set. For example, in 1973 there were 15 permits, all for the Harney Peak Area. Hunting is for residents only, no guide is required, and success runs very high.

The man from whom I learned most about mountain goats is Jimmy McLucas, who for many years has trapped big-game animals for the State of Montana. Over a period of 20 odd years he live-trapped and transported somewhere near 15,000 big-game animals. During this experience, needless to say, he was able to probe animal personalities very thoroughly.

Jimmy and I have been friends for a number of years. He told me much about his early days of trapping, when the game department's goal was to transplant goats to practically every suitable peak in the state. That goal, incidentally, they accomplished long ago. Jimmy discovered early in the game that a goat, caught and thus cornered in a corral-type trap, would often charge him. Hunters have discovered the same thing. A goat stalked along a ledge that happens to dead-end can stand up on its hind feet and turn around in a place too narrow to accomplish a turn otherwise; and it won't always tolerate having its retreat cut off. In the open, of course, goats will run away with their rather awkward gait, invariably moving uphill.

McLucas told me he has seen a big billy, when excited, penetrate an inch-thick pine board with its stiletto-sharp horns. He has also seen one in a trap ram another and kill it instantly. He learned to get in with them, rope one, pull its head down and grab it by the horns. Then he devised the idea of shoving a length of garden hose down onto one horn, looping over and doing likewise on the other. The goats couldn't get it off, and it blunted their weapons.

Some things McLucas learned while trapping goats are well worth remembering when you hunt. Goats are always scattered over their rugged alpine terrain. They are invariably found in places far rougher than where sheep like to roam. For example, sheep will graze and bed down in saddles and on ridges. Although sheep will often move into broken, rocky country, they are not the ledge-and-crag dwellers that goats are.

Because of the way their hoofs are fashioned, goats can move up or down rocky outcrops or faces that are almost sheer and smooth. They will commonly select a high pinnacle to bed down on, sometimes where a portion of the animal literally dangles off one edge. Goats are phlegmatic. Often an animal will stand or lie for hours in the same spot, hardly moving a whisker. Jimmy was never certain that goats were very intelligent, whereas sheep, of which he trapped and handled many, were superbly so.

"Goats don't seem to have any fear of their own surroundings," he once told me, "like of falling off a cliff. And they don't have many enemies.

An old billy might grow up having never been in danger from any predatory source, and few ever see a man. His cliffs and top-of-the-world peaks give him a sense of security. He gets sort of dumb from never having to elude danger. He might fall off a cliff to his death but he never believes he will, or thinks about it."

A help to hunters, which McLucas discovered in his first trapping experiences, is the fact that goats must have salt, just like other animals, and salt licks up in the high country are at just a few locations. McLucas located a salt lick used by goats, and that is where all of his first trapping was done. Find such a lick and you increase your chance of seeing goats.

A salt lick is a magnet for goats in any of their ranges. Of course, glassing is an easy way to find goats, for their white coats stand out plainly. But when planning a hunt, if there is a chance to discover from old-timers, trappers, guides or others where salt licks are located, the process of finding a target may be shortened. The animals do not make daily visits, but periodic trips. McLucas tagged some with red plastic streamers in later experiments, and discovered that certain individuals, located by plane, were living as far as 15 miles from the lick.

There is really no long list of fundamentals that must be learned so far as goat hunting methods are concerned. The fact is, the most difficult part of collecting a goat is getting up to where the animals live. Stalking an antelope or a whitetail deer is much more difficult. Once a possible target is sighted, there is usually a way to approach to within range without spooking the goat. In all rough terrain, stalking is much easier than on flats or in gently rolling country. By keeping out of sight behind rocky outcrops or ridges, though the route may be circuitous an approach can ordinarily be made without showing yourself. Fred Bear, the famed archer, once stalked and shot a goat with bow and arrow from a distance of 15 paces.

An advantage for any hunter operating at the highest elevations is that here the air movement, whether a stiff wind or a mild breeze, is in general quite constant. A little lower down, air currents are whimsical. They may seem to move from every direction as a breeze whips through and around canyons. But higher up at the top of the peaks there are few obstructions to bend the wind.

The eyesight of the mountain goat is undoubtedly efficient, but by no means like that of the sheep. Or perhaps it is simply that the goat isn't as easily disturbed by what it sees. Sound is no problem. I recall a friend telling me that he was making a stalk on his first goat and at short range he slipped and sent rocks rattling and crashing. He lay flat and immobile, watching the target and expecting it to flee. All the goat did was turn to stare placidly in the direction of the sound. Rocks are constantly falling or rolling in goat terrain, where only modest vegetative cover ties them down. The sound isn't very disturbing to an animal used to hearing it every day.

Almost all goat hunts are begun on horseback, often while the hunter is on a trip for sheep or bears or caribou. As the hunting party moves into higher and higher country, serious glassing begins. Goats can be spotted rather easily at extreme range. When one or more have been located, the riders can move on, contriving to get into snug valleys or draws that take them higher and closer under cover.

The daily routine of the mountain goat is to begin feeding early in the morning. It may travel a fair distance as it feeds. But once you've located an old billy, or a group, you know that this is where the animals live. Most goats spend their entire lives in a fairly small area, never moving—except to salt—more than a few miles in any direction. By mid-morning, as a rule, the animals seek a bedding spot. Because goats are adapted to a cold domain, it does not take a very warm day to send them to the shade of a cliff or some scrub vegetation or even into a cave to rest and chew their cuds. But on most days they'll be out in places where they are easily spotted with a glass. The high open slopes with scattered rocks, or places where a bench catches the breeze and allows a survey of a vast domain, offer good bedding spots. Always during midday also check the high peaks and pinnacles thoroughly, and the ledges along cliffs touched by cool breezes.

Goats spotted any time from mid-morning until early afternoon can just about be depended upon to stay put until at least middle of the afternoon, so this is a good period to make a stalk. The stalk may take a long time, and call for rest periods because it is physically so taxing. Thus it's a good idea to be at least reasonably certain the quarry will be in the same spot when you emerge within range.

Montana sportsmen pack in for early hunt, while large billies still wander alone.

Because of the ardors of the climb, an exceedingly careful appraisal should be made with a spotting scope beforehand. And any hunter with an experienced guide will do well to listen to his advice. Many a goat has been stalked by an over-eager tyro who discovered when within shooting range that he was looking at no trophy at all.

Goats are used to looking far off and down. Any time a mountain goat raises its head from feeding, or beds down and lies calmly chewing its cud, it is staring into space, across toward some cliff or peak, or else down some steep slope. There is little to fear from above, and in fact in many instances there *is* very little above except the sky. Thus, one technique of goat hunting that outfitters have evolved over many years is to attempt an approach from above.

When an animal is found by glassing, the spotting scope is brought into play. If the goat appears worthwhile, a closer approach may be made and again an appraisal is in order. Finally, if it is agreed to make a try, the stalk is planned so the hunter comes out above the quarry. It's the same technique often employed in sheep hunting. It may take a full day, or most of it, to make a goat stalk. But if you have spotted a bedded animal, moved close enough to ascertain that it is shootable, and then continued the stalk during the bedding period, you may come into a shooting position above the goat and yet not be able to see it. This is the time, depending on terrain and cover, when it may be necessary to stay put and wait. After an hour, perhaps, the animal arises and begins feeding again. This is the late-afternoon feeding period before the animals retire for the night. Now the trophy comes into view and the shot is made.

One of the great exasperations of goat hunting is that shots on excellent trophies often place the hunter in an awkward dilemma. Charlie Schreiner, owner of the famous YO Ranch in Texas, was on his first goat hunt in Montana a few years ago and saw a good specimen standing on a ledge. Eager to collect, he touched off and made a solid hit. But he had not considered what might happen thereafter: If he killed the goat, how would he get to it? And, if he killed it and it fell off the narrow ledge, how far and where would it fall? He did kill it, but it jumped at the hit and fell over the edge of the precipice. After many hours of anguished labor he and his guide retrieved his animal, somewhat pulverized in body but fortunately not in horn. Many times, good trophies have been picked up at the bottom of a cliff with one or both horns snapped off.

A mountain goat is cool and stoic always. It is also physically tough. Many a hunter has made a solid hit on a goat and not observed the slightest flinch. A hunter should go well gunned, and should make certain whether his shot has or has not connected.

A friend hunting in British Columbia had an intriguing experience with a big billy. At his shot, the goat snapped its head around to look in the direction of the sound. It then very calmly turned around on the ledge where it had been and walked away. He shot twice more. His guide saw the bullets hit the rock wall. The goat passed from view. The guide had a hunch. They climbed up to the spot, about 250 yards straight-line as the shots had traveled. The goat was there. Dead.

16.
CARIBOU
by
Charles Elliott

Mature bull and cow cross Newfoundland muskeg.

We were hunting the far northern part of the Yukon Territory, up where the Bonnett Plume River flows toward the mouth of the Mackenzie on the Arctic Ocean. When we'd first ridden into that country, we had seen caribou singly and in small groups every day but had made no attempt to seek out the trophy bulls, having what our guide considered more noteworthy game species on which to concentrate. When we had collected fine specimens of sheep, moose and grizzly, and turned our attention to locating a caribou rack as creditable as the other trophies we'd taken, every one of the tundra deer seemed to have disappeared. We covered miles in every direction and even set out two spike camps. We found tracks and droppings that were not too old, but sighted not a single caribou for five days.

We made ever-widening circles from camp, but not until the sixth afternoon did we come on fresh sign of several animals traveling in a southerly direction through a long valley between massive ridges. We dismounted and examined the tracks.

"Nothing especially large here," Louie Brown commented, "but from the deep-cut trails this appears to be one of the main migration routes. Let's work up the valley and see what we can find."

I had put one foot in a stirrup when he said, "Hold it a minute."

Four bull caribou stood on the side of a low ridge sloping into the valley. They were watching us from about three-quarters of a mile away. Through the glasses one appeared to carry a good rack. While the guide was studying the lay of land and contemplating whether the best plan was to waylay or stalk them, the caribou solved his problem by turning tail and disappearing over the hill.

"I guess," he said wryly, "it's best to go after them."

We dipped into a shallow, brushy canyon. Holding to low ground, we came to the point of the ridge where we had seen the bulls, and tied our horses. Crawling to the point, we located the caribou in the bottom, above a gravel bar we estimated at about 175 yards. The biggest bull carried a nice rack. On my belly, I put the crosshairs behind his shoulder and low enough to hit the heart. With the gun blast, the bulls jumped and looked uphill in the direction of the echo. I tried again for the same spot and again missed. Louie gave me a queer look.

"You nervous?"

"Hell, no. I've killed these critters before."

At my third shot the bulls turned and trotted with the long, swinging stride characteristic of the clan, and disappeared into a hollow that ran at right angles to the creek bottom.

"They'll swing around to get behind us," the guide opined, "and continue on their way. I didn't see where a one of those bullets hit. When your horse slipped and fell against that tree the other day, he must have knocked your scope out of line. Let's sight in the gun. Maybe the sound won't spook those bulls too far."

We tried the rifle. I couldn't believe that both my shots were in almost the same spot—about 12 inches low. We screwed up the scope to a couple of inches above the target and went after those bulls again, making a long circle downwind to get in front of them. Before we moved, Louie had studied the lay of the land and he used every bit of cover available to put us in a spot where he figured the caribou would cross the bottom of a side canyon. They fooled us and crossed above us and when we saw them they were making fast tracks along the ridge crest 150 yards away.

"Either we or something spooked them," he said. "Better try the big one."

This time when I pulled the trigger, my big bull staggered and went down.

As if that had been the signal, the whole wilderness around us suddenly erupted with caribou. We saw more that afternoon, and the next day when we rode up the river to fish for grayling, we counted sizable bunches on a number of slopes. For the next week we were in sight of bulls and cows most of the time. We saw some larger racks than the one we had taken, but I had filled my license.

Louie shook his head and sighed. "If I live to be a hundred, I'll never understand a stupid caribou."

What we had witnessed has for uncounted generations been a problem with Indians of the north country, who depend on the herds for their winter meat. For a few weeks each year for many years the herds may stream by in migration, and then suddenly for no apparent reason, the migration course is changed and the caribou do not come. The tribes who have counted on them may then face a starvation winter. This behavior continues to remain a mystery.

Depending on the subspecies and where it ranges, the caribou stands from 3½ to about five feet at the shoulder, and weights run from 300 to 400 pounds for the smaller varieties, up to 600 for the mountain caribou and even occasionally 700 for the Osborn caribou, which is close kin to the mountain race.

The caribou is perhaps the most strikingly handsome member of the deer family. Throughout the range, each subspecies has its own color characteristics, most marked by summer coats that shade from mouse gray to chocolate brown, with lighter-colored neck and cape. The winter coat is much more striking. Over the main body it is lighter in color, with the neck, cape and long throat ruff or mane extending from the chin to the chest, turning from a light gray in some subspecies to pure white in many barren ground bulls. Each kind of caribou has its own color peculiarities which help to identify it; the mountain variety, for example, is often called the black-faced caribou.

The caribou's hooves are uniquely adapted for a habitat encompassing vast regions of swamp, marsh, mud and tundra, all boggy through the warm months and frozen in the winter. The caribou has the biggest foot in proportion to its size of any hooved animal. The hoof is cleft almost to the hock and he can spread it until his track is often wider than long. Before winter, the rim of the hoof hardens to tough, sharp horn that gives the animal a better footing on ice.

One of the most peculiar things about the foot is that the ankle bones are so constructed and arranged that when the caribou walks, it makes a clicking sound loud enough to be heard for some distance. A number of times I have heard this sound before I saw the animals.

Who could ever aptly describe the configuration, much less the majesty, of the rack that a bull caribou carries high and at such a regal tilt?

In remote caribou country, hunters may have to work out of primitive spike camp.

Technically the antlers have been described as "bifurcated, palmate, wide and branching with many points, and with brow tine compressed laterally." As apt as that may be, it hardly expresses the eloquent beauty of a trophy head. Both sexes wear antlers, but those of the female are much smaller. They are shed and re-grown annually, as with all the members of the deer family.

Unlike the antlers of most other deer, caribou racks tend to be extremely variable. The headgear of almost every caribou is unique—with its own shape, size, number of points and degree of palmation. The brow tine, which parallels the top of the face and often extends beyond the nose, is called the "shovel" and gives a rack distinction. An especially attractive trophy may have a double shovel. No one seems to know what utility the shovel has. One theory is that it's used to clear away snow above the ground plants, but this is generally discarded by the experts, who point out that the shovel is not much longer than the nose—if that long—and most of the low-growing vegetation for feed is uncovered by pawing.

The caribou is well dressed for the bitter winters it must endure. Its short summer coat is replaced by a garment of long thermal hair, which is hollow and excellent insulation, and beneath this is an undergarment of fine, curly wool. The hollow hairs provide the buoyancy of a life jacket. A caribou swims with the upper part of his body out of water. With his broad hooves going like a paddle wheel, he makes surprising speed crossing a river or lake on his migration route in late summer or early fall.

Over many years I have talked with guides about caribou and never cease to marvel at the difference of opinions regarding its status as a game animal. A few guides, like Louie Brown, look upon it as a rather dull-witted species and not too difficult to add to a trophy list. When the herds are on the move, they say, the only question is finding a rack that suits your fancy and shooting it in the right spot. I have never found this opinion quite accurate. With one exception I've had to work for those heads I've taken, as Brown and I did in the far corner of the Yukon. The exception was a nice bull in Alaska's Talkeetna Mountains. We rode through the willows of a wide creek bottom and to within 30 yards of a bull that stood in the open on the far edge, watching us. The animal continued to stand while I slid out of the saddle, pulled my rifle from its scabbard, threw a shell into the chamber and broke its neck. I had a guilty feeling, as though I'd just slaughtered a heifer in a farmer's pasture.

One of my outdoor partners, Dempsey Cape, hunting on the other side of the continent, found a far different situation. He went to Newfoundland with his hunting bow, to add to his growing list of trophies with that weapon.

"We saw some nice bulls," he said, "but they were as spooky as whitetail deer."

The first two bulls they tried to stalk got a glimpse of Dempsey and

While hunting sheep in Alaska, guide glasses lower slopes for big bull caribou.

Reindeer moss (also called caribou moss) is vital food for barren ground caribou.

his guide and left the country. They worked on the third bull for a full day and finally out-guessed it by making a footrace to a spot where the animal would pass if it held its course.

"It was more a matter of luck than of outwitting him," Dempsey admitted. "He passed within 40 yards of where we thought he would."

Dempsey put an arrow in the bull and his broadhead sliced through an artery. The rack turned out to be even better than he and the guide expected. It landed first in the Pope & Young records and 12th in Boone & Crockett.

"It was one of the toughest hunts I ever made," he said. "Don't let anybody ever tell you that the caribou is easy game."

I've found that they come easy and they come hard, depending on hunting pressure and on the individual animal. Consensus among the guides is that the caribou is often very excitable, especially if alarmed by some unaccustomed sight or sound. Biologists have told me of seeing a group, suddenly frightened, run in circles or bound back and forth without leaving the immediate vicinity, and they say that now and then an animal will get so wrought up that it dies of a heart attack.

A caribou is said to have as much curiosity as an antelope and will come to a red or white flag waved by a hidden hunter. I've never decided whether my experiment with this was a failure or success. In the Northwest Territories I crawled to within 200 yards of two small bulls and, completely hidden, I slowly waved a handkerchief. They stared for a long minute, then whirled and made tracks as if they had only a short time to reach the next province.

I sat there ruminating on this for a while, then put my glasses on the bulls; they had stopped on the brow of the next ridge to stare in my direction. I heard movement behind me and froze for an instant, hoping it wasn't an old grizzly that had sneaked up on me and scared off the two caribou, then turned slowly, my rifle ready. A bull caribou stood there, not 50 feet away, looking me over, though I sat in plain view. He seemed completely unafraid—almost disinterested—and then he grazed slowly on by. Long ago I had made up my mind that those critters are entirely unpredictable and that incident did nothing to change my mind.

Almost everyone who has heard the name of the animal knows of the migration of the vast herds and what an important part it has played in the economy of the North, but so far no one has been able to explain the mechanism of this migration, which seems to be as notional as the animals themselves. They may follow a route for years and suddenly abandon it, or they may appear in entirely unexpected places. Almost everyone familiar with the caribou has his own theory. There are those who say that in summer the herds seek open spaces where the wind blows, to help keep off the flies and other insects, especially while the female is bearing young and the male is growing his new set of antlers in a soft-velvet-like cover. The barren ground caribou goes to the treeless tundra and the mountain caribou climbs above timberline.

Both food and shelter are also thought to motivate migration. Winter is a lean season and with the open tundra locked in ice and bitter cold, the herds trail south to the tree line for protection and for food, which consists of moss, lichens, grass and willow and birch twigs where they are available.

Authorities differ on the number of species and subspecies on the North American continent. One of the earlier mammalogists listed three distinct species and broke these down into 15 subspecies, extending from the Alaska Peninsula to Newfoundland and as far north as the tip of Ellesmere Island, within a few degrees of the North Pole. Many of these were thought to be closely related forms, with only subtle technical differences. The most recently recognized work on the subject, however, has boiled this down to one caribou with seven living subspecies, including such forms as the "arctic," which covers most of middle-northern Canada from James Bay to the mouth of the Mackenzie River, and apparently is a general race that contains both barren ground and woodland caribou as well as the *"pearyi,"* the northernmost form on Ellesmere Island and named for the explorer Admiral Peary.

For the purpose of keeping adequate records on trophy heads, the Boone & Crockett Club recognizes four kinds of caribou. These are the barren ground (across far north and northwest Canada and Alaska); the mountain (which includes the Osborn—largest of all caribou—with ranges of the two forms in British Columbia and extending up into the Yukon Territory); the woodland (across southern Canada); and the Quebec-Labrador form (from the upper portions of these two provinces, and thought to be a woodland-barren ground hybrid).

To be on the safe side and possibly to keep down any confusion which might result in wrong identification of a trophy head by an outfitter or hunter, Boone & Crockett not only lists the form, but the region from which it may be considered. The exception to this is the barren ground, though all but a few heads in this listing (which includes the subspecies Grant) have come out of Alaska. The others are listed as: mountain caribou from British Columbia; Quebec-Labrador from Quebec-Labrador; and the woodland from eastern Nova Scotia, New Brunswick and Newfoundland.

A matter of interest to a vast number of hunters are the minimum scores necessary for registration in the Boone & Crockett records. Seventeen measurements are needed for the total score, and for the smallest recorded head of each recognized form these are: barren ground, 400 points; mountain, 390; Quebec-Labrador, 375; and woodland, 295. If an official measurer of Boone & Crockett adds up more points than needed for one of your trophies, it will go into the book. To give some indication of how large your antlers must be to make the records, here are eight of the 17 measurements which will help you decide whether you should take further steps to have it officially measured:

	Length of Main Beam		Inside Spread	Length of Brow Points	
	right	left		right	left
Barren Ground	57⁴⁄₈	56⅞	37⁴⁄₈	18⅞	19
Mountain	41⅛	50	40⁴⁄₈	17⅛	6
Quebec-Labrador	55⅞	54⅛	55⅜	19⅝	10⅜
Woodland	41⅝	41⅛	28	16⅝	14⅝

	Width of Brow Points		Number of Points	
	right	left	right	left
Barren Ground	12⅜	11⁶⁄₈	14	16
Mountain	14⅜	⅛	21	16
Quebec-Labrador	12²⁄₈	2⅞	15	12
Woodland	12²⁄₈	9⁶⁄₈	18	14

These caribou were released on Adak, in Aleutian Islands National Wildlife Refuge, t

Once, the U.S. Government tried an experiment in stocking caribou. Accounts of this experiment vary, but the general theme of the story is about the same from all reports. Around 1890 the Eskimos and Indians of Alaska were thought to be starving, and the solution concocted by bright political minds was to stock one part of the territory with Asiatic reindeer. What we call the caribou is simply the reindeer of the North American continent, so why not import reindeer from elsewhere? From 1891 to 1902, between 1,200 and 1,800 Siberian reindeer were released in southern Alaska, mostly on the Seward Peninsula. With them came Lapland herders to tend

uild up herd there. Earlier experiments with Asiatic reindeer were less successful.

the animals and teach the natives to manage and profitably use the herds.

In the decade of the 1930's the herds increased to numbers estimated between 250,000 and 600,000 and were doing so well that more of the Asiatic deer were stocked at the mouth of the Mackenzie River in Canada.

By the late 1940's, however, only a fraction of the vast herd remained. The quick decline was blamed on many factors: government inefficiency, lack of interest by the native tribes for whom the reindeer were originally intended, profit-taking by non-native businessmen, overbrowsing of range which resulted in disease and starvation, wolves and other predators, the tendency of the animals to scatter among with native herds, etc.

Except for recent transplants of native caribou to a few localities where they normally ranged, little has been tried in the way of further stocking. One experiment was tried in Michigan in 1922, but it ended in failure. Both Maine and Nova Scotia have made successful stockings.

Outside of covering a country by saddle or afoot, looking over the herds in migration or an occasional bunch of bulls, picking out the best possible head in the period of time allotted to you, then making your stalk to a shootable position, there is no set procedure for taking a trophy caribou. All of those I've bagged followed this ritual. I have never gone exclusively for the purpose of finding a record head, as have some of my outdoor acquaintances. A few of them have come home without firing a shot, and others were able to take an average head or better in the final days of the hunt.

Most of my caribou kills have been made when I was on a hunt for several big-game species, such as bear, sheep and moose, as well as the big Northern deer itself. No matter what trophy we were after, we stopped to study heads whenever we saw a group of caribou bulls. The best rack I ever took was above Chickaloon in southeast Alaska while the guide and I were concentrating on sheep. During our course of looking over the country, we often paused to glass other big game and we studied dozens of caribou without seeing one we wanted. We were afoot in high sheep country when we spotted two bulls a thousand feet below us on a barren ridge. We hadn't seen anything in the Dall line we wanted, but one of those bulls looked mighty good to me.

With our glasses we studied the best approach to get within range without disturbing the animals should they happen to be spooky. When we moved, the caribou saw us and stood with heads up, watching us walk away from them to the crest of the ridge. We ducked out of sight and they went back to grazing.

We made a wide circle of perhaps two miles to come in on the downwind side of the caribou, and crawled within a hundred yards. The largest bull was even more magnificent than he had appeared from above. He was close enough to down with a neck shot and I was lucky enough to place my bullet in just the right spot.

On their migration routes, caribou have favorite crossing places over rivers and the narrow necks of lakes. Long before the white man introduced the rifle, Indians used to wait for caribou at those spots so that they could get close enough to use primitive weapons—even spears—to collect their winter meat. The hunters would lie in wait until the animals were caught way out in the water, then push off in a canoe, chase the quarry and spear it.

Scouting migratory crossings can be worthwhile, of course, and if the herds haven't changed routes unexpectedly you might on occasion be able to watch for a good head as animals funnel across. But since man no longer gets his winter caribou meat with spears, a much more satisfactory hunt today is by conventional methods, horseback or afoot, with a modern rifle. Any caliber above a .30-30 will do the job, but most hunters prefer the more high-powered guns with long range and flat trajectory, since one never knows when he must make a long shot for an exceptional head.

Other standard equipment for the Far North includes wool and down clothes for sudden cold weather or storms which may blow in during the late summer or early fall, a good binocular, hunting knife, compass and the essentials one needs in a hunting camp. I covered clothing and equipment in greater detail in my chapter on sheep hunting, and I recommend the same gear when you're out for caribou. In fact, as I mentioned before, you're likely to be looking for sheep or other trophies on the same hunt.

The caribou, in its various forms, occurs all across the continent, but for a number of reasons the population is lower than it was some decades ago. Some of this is due to abuse by both the native and the invading hunter. You hunt a certain kind of caribou either because it's the closest one to you or because you have an eye on the record books. The following reports from Alaska and certain Canadian provinces may give you an idea of where to go.

Alaska possibly has the best caribou hunting on the continent. This northern deer is the state's most abundant big-game animal, with the total herd estimated at more than half a million animals and with an annual kill of 20,000 to 30,000. The barren ground caribou is the main type; the lesser-known Grant's (in the southeast corner) is included in Boone & Crockett records together with the barren ground. Of the 11 recognized herds in this state, one of the most accessible is the Melchina, which ranges chiefly in the

Talkeetna Mountains north of Palmer and Anchorage. The Arctic herd, far off the beaten trail, has little hunting pressure, and that's also true of some of the smaller isolated bands scattered through the state. Game officials feel that the caribou is much underharvested, for meat as well as for trophies, and they worry that some of the faster-growing herds may cause a depletion of their natural food supply.

The Yukon Territory is also a top caribou spot that gets too little hunting. The record books show a number of barren ground heads out of the Yukon; one from Great Salmon River stands 14th on the list and another from Pelly Mountain is in 16th place. Included in the book also are two mountain caribou, one from the Cassiar Mountains and the other from Snake River. Range maps show the barren ground caribou across the western half of the territory and the mountain (the Osborn subspecies) through the east and southeast portion. Native and visiting gunners take both forms each season.

Traditionally in the Northwest Territories, because wild meat has been the lifeblood of this tremendous region, hunting was reserved for the Eskimos, Indians and long-time residents. In recent years, however, a few permits have been issued to non-resident sportsmen on an experimental basis for the far northwest corner of the territory, and there may be a time when the regulations are more liberal and the average sportsman can hunt reasonably virgin lands in and around the Mackenzie Mountains for a mountain-caribou or in other portions for the more widely distributed barren ground.

In British Columbia, caribou are found most abundantly in the northern, upper central and mountainous eastern portions of the province. The upper third is inhabited by the Osborn, with the woodland caribou occurring down to the international boundary. For record purposes, both are listed under the woodland heading.

British Columbia is divided into management areas. A map is available showing the locations. The largest harvest of caribou usually comes from the tremendous triangle formed by Management Areas 27 and 28 around the Laird and Peace Rivers and their tributaries. Atlin-Stikine Management Area 26 in the northwest corner of the province is said to be good, but has fewer hunters, most of whom employ outfitters and guides. Those

Photo of Manitoba bull shows outsized hooves, ideal for walking on muskeg or ice.

Hunter poses with outstanding rack that will dominate his trophy room.

familiar with the province also recommend Big Bend (MA 9) and West and East Kootenay (MAs 10 and 11) in the southeast corner of the province as good, easily accessible hunting territory.

In Alberta, caribou hunting is rated as fair and at present the animals are huntable only in Zone 1 in the northern part of the province and in Zone 6 along the western boundary north of Jasper National Park.

In far northern Saskatchewan and Manitoba there are few caribou and hunting is very light, usually by the natives for meat. Recently limited non-resident permits have been issued in Manitoba but the take is negligible by comparison with the big kills each year in both western and eastern Canada. The woodland caribou is found in both of these provinces and a few barren ground caribou show up in northern Manitoba.

Not until the past few years has the Quebec-Labrador herd been "discovered." Only 15 records of this big animal appear in the books, and all but one were taken after 1964. Hunting is done in Zone 0, above the 50th parallel, and the best heads are said to come out of the Ungava and Whale River regions.

Newfoundland has long been a mecca for caribou hunters. The earliest record shown in the B&C book is 1881, and several others go back half a century or more. The record head, taken in 1910, scored 419⅝ points. The caribou population deteriorated there for a while, but is said to have been making a strong comeback over the past few seasons and now numbers more than 15 herds. Hunting is by permit and the season lasts about six weeks. The two top regions are reported to be Area 1 (LaPoile, in the southwest) and Area 2 (Buchans, just to the north, between Grand and Red Indian lakes). Other recommended areas are 3 (Grey River, in the south central portion) and 4 (Middle Ridge, a large eastern area).

Caribou were once common in both Nova Scotia and Maine, but disappeared from both places decades ago. In 1963, 23 woodland caribou were stocked around Mount Katahdin, in Maine, and recent stockings have been made on Cape Breton Island in Nova Scotia. There is hope that, in the future, caribou hunting may be possible again in both the state and province.

17.
BEARS
by
Erwin A. Bauer

Downed grizzly requires cautious approach.

During the early spring of 1965 in a remote valley of northern British Columbia, a lone Indian trapper had spent the morning splitting firewood and repairing his beaver sets beside his crude log shack. The evidence revealed that much. Perhaps the sled dog that was his constant companion gave him some warning of danger, but no one will ever know for certain.

Several days later another Indian passed the camp and found both the trapper and the Malemute dead, torn limb from limb. The shack was totally destroyed and even the tins of food inside had been ripped apart for the contents. It was a scene of horror. In the soft earth everywhere were paw prints of a grizzly bear.

That same springtime produced similar tragedies elsewhere. A bruin just out of hibernation in Alaska ambushed and killed a hunter and his guide who were tracking the animal near its den. At about the same time in the Yukon, two trappers sat skinning a wolf when a grizzly surprised and mauled both of them fatally. Then later in Montana's Glacier National Park another grizzly savaged a man and his wife who were on a hiking trip.

Such incidents are not unfamiliar to anyone who has lived long in grizzly country. While the incidents related above are true, most of the stories you hear are not. Each story teller has his own version, and the versions are usually expanded and colored as they are repeated. Fact eventually blends into nearly pure fiction.

But exactly what kind of creature is it that inspires such stories—and occasionally does such evil deeds? Where does it live? Why does it behave as it does?

Some member of the bear family *Ursidae* inhabits almost every temperate corner of the earth. But nowhere do so many, of so many different species and subspecies, exist as in North America. There is the black bear, for instance, which once inhabited all of the United States and southern Canada from coast to coast. Across the polar and sub-polar regions roamed the great white or ice bear. King of Alaskan coastal areas was the "brownie"—the Alaskan brown bear. And once roaming over a far greater portion of the North American continent than most people realize today was at least one of the several varieties of grizzly bears. Together they thrived in the plains, prairie, tundra, woodland, foothill and high mountain habitat.

Perhaps no animal has excited man's fear and imagination more than bears, particularly the grizzly bear which is still the subject of legends today. From the grizzly's first confrontation with man, it has been regarded as a challenge and, of course, has become a matchless game animal. Here potentially is one of the most dangerous creatures to walk on four feet. It is therefore easy to understand why the species is abundant no more.

The grizzly is bordering on oblivion in the United States, except in Alaska where a fair number remain. Remote and mountainous portions of western Canada also contain sizable populations. South of the Canadian border, no more than 300 odd animals survive, nearly all in Yellowstone and Glacier National Parks. If the Mexican grizzly is not already extinct, a mere handful may remain in the Cerro Campano fastness, about 50 miles north of Chihuahua City.

Perhaps grizzlies will continue as legal game animals for another decade or so if the harvest is carefully managed by competent big game managers rather than by politicians and barber-shop biologists. Everywhere, nowadays, a grizzly hunt requires an outfitter and packing into bear country. There the animals are hunted very much like any other mountain big game—by riding out and thoroughly scanning the lonely, lofty landscapes all around. When an animal is spotted, usually at long range, it is carefully stalked, taking advantage of all terrain features, staying downwind of the animal and always trying to approach from above rather than below. There are enough exceptions to prove the rule, but it is far safer to approach from above.

Though many who are experienced with grizzlies and their ways will not agree, the concensus is that grizzlies have comparatively poor eyesight and only fair hearing but excellent scenting ability. They may readily spot a moving object, say an approaching hunter, yet even at close range a bruin seems unable to distinguish something that does not move from its background.

But are grizzlies really dangerous to hunt? The best (or most conservative) answer is probably yes. But incidents between bears and bear

Huge pit gapes where grizzly dug out marmot—one sure sign of bear.

hunters are very, very rare. Those clashes which do occur involve hunters who are either careless or stupid, who wound bears rather than dispatch them outright, or who blunder onto an angry female guarding small cubs. Although grizzlies have immense potential to be killers, very few of them go around looking for trouble, and unprovoked attacks by these animals are extremely uncommon.

A good bit of bear hunting still exists across America, thanks to one of our most misunderstood animals, the black bear. It is often pictured as very dangerous, an enemy of mankind and his livestock, but this is almost the exact opposite of fact. Some people see all blacks as the panhandling bruins along Yellowstone Park's highways, or as an animated character out of Disney, or the friendly animal wearing a ranger's hat on forest-fire posters. All of these images also are preposterous. The black bear is a shy and re-

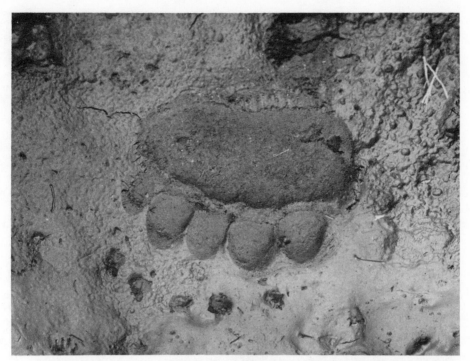

Track shows marks of very long claws, indicating grizzly rather than black bear.

tiring resident of deep woods and swamps. It is next to impossible to see a really wild black bear anywhere outside a national park. Most are known only from roadside zoos or TV animal shows.

The original range of the American black bear was probably the most extensive of any native big-game species. Today its range is restricted to Appalachian hardwood highlands, swamp forests of the Deep South, remotest wooded New England, the northern Midwest, the Rockies, the Cascades, and all of Canada and Alaska except the Arctic. Although that area is only a fraction of its original range, the species has fared rather well against the spread of "civilization" and is fairly abundant. Thanks to its shyness, adaptability and (some say) intelligence, the black bear has been able to cope where other big game has not.

As in all hunting, success may first depend on knowledge of the

Sow black bear leads three cubs. No bear with cubs should be shot, as orphaned young

quarry—and that is especially true of the black bear. To begin with, not all "blacks" are black. An equal number are of various shades of brown. Add to these also a tan and cinnamon phase, as well as the rare blue subspecies of Glacier Bay, Alaska, and the cream-colored Kermode bear, also of the Northwest.

At first it may be easy to mistake a black for a grizzly and vice versa where both share the same range in the West. Color, especially, can be confusing. But keep in mind that grizzlies have wide, dishfaced profiles; blacks have thinner "Roman" noses. Grizzlies have very pronounced humps over the front shoulders, blacks do not. Grizzlies walk with a more pronounced

won't survive. Also keep in mind that sow guarding cubs is especially unpredictable.

pigeon-toed swagger which has been described as "menacing." When surprised, alarmed, or to test the wind, both blacks and grizzlies may briefly stand erect on their hind legs to look around, but this is far more characteristic of grizzlies.

Everything about bears is likely to be exaggerated, but two characteristics of the black especially are enlarged: the animal's size and ferocity. Sportsmen are likely to overestimate any bear's dimensions and behavior. In the Northeast and northern Midwest, especially after feeding around garbage dumps or on some abnormal diet, an odd black bear may reach 500 pounds or even more. But the average, large, fully grown animal is much smaller. Figure a good one to measure 30 inches tall at the shoulder and to weigh 250 to 300 pounds. Its green hide will stretch five to six feet from tip of nose to rump.

For the record, the largest known black bear was a 605-pounder live-trapped near Tupper Lake by personnel of New York's Department of Conservation. The animal had been living and growing fat near a garbage dump. The trappers estimated this big male's age at between five and 10 years. A hunter looking for a really large black might consider that same area, because Adirondack bruins tend to reach better than average size, a good many over 400 pounds having been taken there in recent years.

Black bears are omnivorous, but of necessity thrive almost entirely on grass, nuts, berries, bulbs, roots and perhaps more other plant foods of the forest than have ever been listed. Not many other mammals relish such a variety of edibles, which also include small reptiles and amphibians, insects and insect larvae, mushrooms, ferns and, on those rare occasions when it somehow becomes available, meat, either fresh-killed or carrion. There have been instances when bears destroyed livestock, especially sheep, and wrecked apiaries. Almost any bruin will rob any beehive it encounters. Although each season produces its quota of bear-versus-human incidents in our national parks, there are almost no completely authenticated records of wild black bears attacking humans without provocation. All of the park incidents are a result of visitors illegally feeding or teasing the bears, or otherwise treating them like docile pets, which they are not.

Hunting black bears can be a fascinating sport because here is truly a fine game species. It lacks the size, aura and reputation of the grizzly, but in my opinion the black is a far more difficult trophy to obtain in fair chase—unaided by mechanical devices, baits, dogs or cars—than the grizzly bear or than any other North American animal except the mountain lion or jaguar.

Most—an estimated 90 to 95 percent according to one game biologist—are taken incidentally by hunters after other big game (mostly after deer, which share black-bear habitat). Almost all the rest are tempted by baits or pursued by dogs. Very, very few are taken by the hunter alone, on foot, deliberately seeking a bear and nothing else; the odds of success are too low to make it worthwhile, even in regions where blacks are most numerous.

Brought to bay by hound pack, black bear can kill any but the best dogs.

The black bear is a remarkable creature. Not as powerful as the grizzly, it does have better hearing and a better nose, plus vastly better eyesight. It is fast afoot, has tremendous endurance, can swim well and because of semi-retractile claws, can climb trees (which an adult grizzly cannot). Even though (in whitetail country) bears often follow the same trails and crossings as deer, they are much harder to ambush along these trails.

Any outdoorsman can improve his odds, no matter what part of America he is hunting, by concentrating on those places where blacks are most likely to be during the shooting season. With the advent of winter, its deep snows and low temperatures, bears begin a period of dormancy—or "hibernation." Only in the South do they remain active throughout the winter. To prepare for hibernation, bears spend the autumn on one large feeding binge, cramming themselves with the ripened foods of the season, storing up fat for the long cold sleep. A wise hunter will seek out the places where fruits, berries, acorns and other mast have fallen to the ground in greatest quantities. That's where the bears will be.

Another way to seek out bears is to keep in contact with landowners (particularly any who keep bees) living on the fringes of forestlands, or with professional foresters and timber cutters. All of these men may at least see fresh sign, a good indication of bears feeding in the area.

Ursus americanus has one great weakness very significant to hunters, and it originates in the animal's stomach. Very few bears—even the oldest, wariest individuals—can pass up a free meal, as the habit of hanging around garbage dumps will attest. That is the undoing of more bruins nowadays than any other cause of mortality. Some are shot by hunters who also wait around garbage dumps—or who simulate these dumps by putting out their own baits. Reduced to simplest terms, the surest way to obtain a bearskin rug is to hunt whatever way the local law allows.

In some states baiting is legal; elsewhere it is not (or is regulated in some manner). In certain states and provinces, the use of hounds is permitted; in neighboring areas it is outlawed. First step, then, is to be acquainted with the law, as well as all the fine print about details, wherever you plan to do your hunting.

If baiting is legal, the technique begins with locating areas that bears are using, by the presence of fresh tracks or stool, by territorial claw marks etched into tree trunks or by actual sightings. Nearby, establish bait piles, which can consist of almost anything edible, whether fresh or decaying. Entrails from packing plants or fish-processing plants are excellent. Speared suckers during spawning runs are good. Or find an old rotting log and thoroughly saturate it with fish oil or something equally odoriferous. Chances are good that eventually a bear will show up, probably at night. Later on, as it gains confidence in being safe, it will begin to visit a frequently replenished bait in the daytime. That's when the hunter should have built a blind nearby—and he should be prepared to spend long hours there on stand and downwind from the bait.

In a few areas (particularly in the West and Canada) there is a spring open season as well as a fall season. Often it is possible then to employ a natural bait—say a winter-killed deer, elk or moose, or even livestock. Upon locating such a bait, build a blind close by and begin the vigil. But be prepared to have coyotes and several species of carrion birds visit the bait. Do not discourage these competitors, because the commotion they make may help to attract bears.

Possibly the best, most certain way to bag a black bear—at least for the typical city-dwelling hunter—is to contact an outfitter in one of the eastern Canadian provinces. The outfitter, in this instance, usually is the owner of a summer fishing camp who also caters to springtime bear hunters on combination fishing-hunting junkets. Since bears are plentiful in Manitoba, Ontario and Quebec, many of these operators become extremely good at baiting, and their clients have a high degree of success.

A good many baits are set out over a wide area, often around spots accessible by boat, at just about the same time the bears emerge from hibernation in May or June. As soon as a bruin begins to visit a bait, a blind is erected within short rifle range for the guests who begin to arrive.

Shooting a bear over bait is far from the most exciting sport, but it is not quite the cut-and-dried proposition it may appear. On the average, the hunter sits long hours, completely still and cramped, usually tormented by clouds of mosquitoes and black flies since this is the insect season. Suspense builds up and at last turns into boredom. Then suddenly, unaccountably— just at dusk when all hope has been abandoned—there's a bear tearing into the bait. It is easy enough to miss a shot under such conditions.

Another kind of bait, also natural, is used to hunt black bears during the Alaskan springtime along the coast. This begins when salmon surge into freshwater streams to spawn and bears come to gorge on the vulnerable salmon. The hunters either live on boats and cruise until they find game, or they walk along stream banks looking for a suitable target. Black-bear hunting in coastal Alaska is extremely good and, incidentally, here also is a chance to bag a brownie. Most outfitters who deal in springtime bear hunts are looking for both species, hoping for a brownie but quite willing to settle for a black.

Next to hunting over bait, the most common method of pursuing black bears is with hounds, usually a pack of them. Several different hound breeds—Plott, black-and-tan, redbone, Trigg, bluetick, Walker, redtick, even beagles—are used, but not all hounds are willing or able to run bears. Most of the really good bear dogs are especially bred and trained. The most promising are kept, the others disposed of.

A good bear dog must have several important qualities. First is a keen enough nose to follow even a cold track several hours old. Second, the dog must have sufficient stamina to last through a long chase; mature bears are long-winded and can cover a lot of landscape when pushed by dogs. Finally, a hound must be willing to fight if necessary—to help tree a bear or hold it at bay until hunters arrive. Sometimes the toll in inexperienced dogs can be high during a bear season. Dogs that survive a number of bear chases and are still willing to hunt are usually very valuable allies.

The first step in bear hunting with dogs is to locate the target. This is often done by driving back roads or logging tracks to find where the animals have crossed. Another way is to put out baits and then inspect these for bear sign. When it is found, a strike dog—one with an especially keen nose—is put down. If that dog takes off confidently, the other hounds are put down and the chase is on. It may end quickly, but it may be still in progress a whole day later.

Once dogs are in full cry on a track, strategy depends on terrain and topography, as well as the number of hunters participating in the chase. In country broken up by rivers, roads, forest openings and meadows, hunters can be stationed near places a pursued bear is likely to cross, in the hope of getting a good killing shot as the target passes. Stands and stations are likely to be changed during the day as a hunt progresses and the quarry dodges to elude the dogs. At times the chase can be followed by listening to the baying of the hounds; at other times it will fade and disappear in the distance. Placing the hunters on stands is the normal technique when there is a large party, and is typical of bear hunting in the Smokies, the swamps and lowlands of the Southeast. Waiting on stand, especially as the action approaches a climax nearby, is certain to make anybody's adrenalin begin to pump.

Elsewhere, in unbroken wilderness or where only one or two hunters are involved, a bear hunt must continue to its natural conclusion. Either the bruin outwits or outruns the dogs, or they bring it to bay. Either way, the hunters must somehow manage to stay within hearing distance of the pack, and that is rugged business, across inhospitable country, even on horseback. In much of the West's canyon country, following the dogs entirely on foot is impossible. Most of the time, a treed or bayed bear is a well-earned trophy. Following bear dogs anywhere—whether through a Southern cypress swamp or deep in Utah's box-canyon country—is no pastime for the timid, the weak of heart or those fragile afoot.

Where are black bears most abundant, and therefore chances of hunting success best? The best advice generally, if you live in the Midwest or East, is to head westward. The largest populations of bruins and the largest annual kills have for many years been in several Western and Rocky Mountain states. Washington is tops, with an average of nearly 3,000 animals collected annually, all in the high country. In Oregon, Idaho and Montana, the kill each year may reach 2,000 bears. Alaska officials figure that between 1,000 and 1,500 black bears are shot there each season (meaning spring plus fall) and in California the annual estimate is about 900. Good to fair hunting exists in Wyoming, Colorado and New Mexico. Some low-odds hunting is possible in mountainous Arizona and Utah.

But the West has suffered a steady decline in black bears because of the indiscriminate use of poison for coyotes over a period of years. Perhaps the highest percentage of success exists in Ontario, where about 1,250 or so blacks are killed each year. As many as 75 percent of all non-resident hunters have scored in a single season, and the figure is about 65 percent over several seasons. Quebec offers bear hunting nearly as good as Ontario, and Manitoba reports 350 to 400 taken annually. Of the Eastern United States, Maine is by far the best bet (about 1,500 annually harvested) and upper New York State's forest reserves are a surprising second. Some hunting is possible in Vermont and New Hampshire.

There is fair bear hunting in the Great Lakes states of Minnesota, Michigan and Wisconsin, in each of which a few hundred animals are taken. Michigan once was a very good destination for bear hunters, but now all hunting is restricted to the sparsely inhabited Upper Peninsula.

In Appalachia, central and northern Pennsylvania has the only significant black-bear population, and the annual take is between 500 and 600.

Nearest hound keeps its distance as hunters approach bear cornered under ledge.

North Carolina reports a similar average harvest. Some hunting also is possible in the swamps and hardwood highlands (the National Forests) of neighboring Virginia and South Carolina. Florida offers the only bear hunting in the Gulf Coast states, and the kill averages less than 100 per year, mostly in the northern portion.

Today a limited amount of hunting for Alaskan brown bears—commonly called Kodiak bears—still exists. These are the largest carnivores in the world and are extremely desirable trophies. They may tower higher than nine feet when standing up. A very large old male may weigh a half ton, and in the past rare individuals may have attained a weight of 1,400 pounds. There have been claims of even more extravagant dimensions, but these must be taken with a grain of salt.

Biologists disagree on the exact status of the brown. Some claim it is simply a larger race of grizzly—one that grows bigger faster because it lives in coastal areas where an abundant diet of salmon is available throughout a good part of the summer. Other big-game experts believe the brownie is a separate species. In any case, the Alaskan brown bear is one immensely impressive beast, and it lives amid some of the most magnificent scenery on the face of the earth.

Most brown-bear hunting is done in spring, cruising by boats among the islets, bays, inlets, fiords and stream deltas along southeastern Alaska's coast. Even if no bear is sighted, the cruising alone is high adventure. The biggest brownies by far have always come from Kodiak Island. Some excellent trophies also roam the length of the Alaska Peninsula. Formerly Admiralty Island was a good place for many bears of smaller size, but in the last few years an absolutely insane and destructive policy of clear-cutting timber for a quick-buck sale to Japan has radically changed the picture. The U.S. Forest Service has recently been guilty of tragically excessive timber cutting in many parts of America, but few match the ugliness on Admiralty, where important salmon-spawning streams (important to brown bears as well as salmon) have also been eliminated by erosion from the timbered areas.

Brown-bear hunting can be a mixed pleasure. The living aboard a boat can be comparatively easy and snug, but coastal weather in the 49th state can be dreadful for long periods. A sportsman must be prepared to hunt in constant dampness. And once he wades ashore in pursuit of a bear, he will encounter some of the densest, most impenetrable cover he is likely to find anywhere.

As recently as a decade ago, a big-game hunter with time and money to spare could hie himself to Alaska and be reasonably certain of going home with a trophy rug he could brag about. The big bears were plentiful. But hunting in the future will be much harder and the success ratio lower. Also, heads and hides are averaging smaller, a result of cropping the population as close as it is safely possible. Few bruins are reaching ripe old age. No longer is it possible for outfitters to take hunters into nearly virgin territory where the bears have never known much hunting. Such places no longer exist.

How much longer our hunting for grizzlies and browns can last depends a good deal upon the hunter himself—or at least on how stringently hunters are willing to restrict themselves by law. There is, for example, a

This grizzly was taken in British Columbia, where huntable population exists.

Long non-retractile claws deter adult grizzly from climbing trees like black bear.

movement to limit the number of browns or grizzlies any hunter can ever shoot to just one in his lifetime. Besides guaranteeing a more equitable harvest of a valuable resource, this would encourage *trophy* hunting—rather than just shooting any bear that comes along. If a man is limited to only one animal, he is much more likely to look for a very good one and pass up the others. Guides and outfitters also have an important role in the future of bear hunting; their policy should be quality bear hunting and nothing less.

As recently as the mid-19th century, a polar explorer wrote in his journals about seeing white bears "roaming over the ice floes like sheep on a commons." Today, international wildlife authorities estimate that there are less than 10,000 of these great mammals left in all the polar regions of the earth. Of course, polar-bear hunting is pretty much a thing of the past except for subsistence-hunting by a few Eskimos and other native peoples of the Far North.

According to a few authorities, such as Jim Brooks, Commissioner of the Alaska Fish and Game Department, polar bears still might be hunted on a limited, strictly regulated basis (for trophy males alone). There is apparently still a surplus of the big bears off the coast of northern Alaska. But the greed and behavior of a few outfitters and their clients killed a good thing for everyone.

In no way can hunting polar bears be considered a lark or even a safe activity. In Alaska it always (and necessarily) was timed when the animals were roving the shifting ice pack in search of seals and other forage. Temperatures then rarely rise above zero and are often far below. There are two possible ways to hunt them—by sled and dog team across the ice, or by using aircraft. To go out and bag a bear in traditional Eskimo style was a genuine challenge and a rich experience, but rugged. Few, if any, chose to hunt by dog team, and during recent decades flying out across the polar ice to spot the targets, then landing as near as possible to shoot same, became big business out of such Arctic villages as Kotzebue, Wainright, Nome and Barrow. Normally two light planes, each with a guide-pilot and hunter-client flew parallel courses in case of any kind of emergency. It was a fairly sticky business. Hunting this way, a polar-bear rug would cost at least $3,000, not including transportation to Alaska.

But, perhaps obviously, it couldn't last. More and more bears, once sighted, were hazed or driven by one of the planes toward a hunter waiting in ambush on the ice. It became execution rather than sport. More bears than the legal quota were shot, and skins were shipped illegally to destinations in the lower Forty-Eight. During one recent winter, federal wardens were kept busy across the country intercepting the contraband and apprehending the hunters. The result was that public pressure (from such groups as the prestigious National Rifle Association and Boone & Crockett Club, and not just anti-hunting groups) caused the complete closing of polar-bear hunts in the United States, probably forever.

In Canada, as a rule, only the native peoples may shoot polar bears, but I understand that sport hunting has recently been permitted, on an extremely restricted basis, in the Northwest Territories. Since each native village is allowed a yearly quota of the white bears, the authorities worked out a system to let the Eskimos fill part of that quota by guiding non-resident hunters for a rather high fee—part of the money going to the guide and his assistants, part to the village. When the game authorities decided to give this system a trial, they made a point (a good point) of stipulating that travel must be by dog sled: no aircraft, no snowmobiles. Perhaps, just perhaps, such restrictive arrangements will eventually bring back polar-bear hunting, at least in the most remote fastnesses of Canada's Far North.

Today there are no better symbols of the American wilderness than the wild bears, some of which are too rapidly vanishing. Let's hope we will always have the bears and the wilderness for those who love the outdoors and hunting. The future is up to us.

18.
HORNED
AND ANTLERED
EXOTICS

Author hunts mouflon at Marble Falls, Texas.

Several years ago, on a number of large Texas ranches, live-trapping operations were set up for blackbuck antelope. The original stock for these fleet, handsome antelope on Texas lands had stemmed from surplus zoo animals years before. Blackbuck antelope are native to India and Pakistan, and those being rounded up in Texas were shipped to an ancestral homeland—to Pakistan—in an attempt to replenish native stock, inject new blood lines and possibly prevent extinction on their home grounds.

This paradoxical situation came about because while the blackbuck has drastically declined on its ancestral ranges, it has thrived thousands of miles away in this eminently suitable portion of Texas, roaming wide expanses of private lands along with native whitetail deer, and numerous other introduced exotics.

When I first came to live in Texas, we settled in the region of heaviest private-land experimentation with exotic big game. The first ranch, I believe, to advertise nationally the availability of hunting at stipulated per-trophy prices for several species was the Rickenbacker Ranch owned by the late, famed Eddie Rickenbacker and operated by his son Dave, some miles from the village of Hunt, Texas. I was mesmerized by the idea of blackbuck and the stunning spotted chital, or axis deer, of India, the sika deer from Japan and Malaysia, ponderous sambar deer from India, mouflon from Sardinia and Corsica, the aoudad from the Atlas Mountains of North Africa—all right on my doorstep.

I hunted on the ranch dozens of times. I also rode along with the first load of exotics (axis deer) delivered live to the 70,000-acre YO Ranch, which has become famous throughout the continent for its highly varied hunting. Thus I enjoyed a kind of ground-floor introduction to the phenomenon of exotic big game in the United States. Its importance has grown so swiftly, even though the range of these animals is extremely restricted, that the subject deserves a full accounting in a book of this kind.

Already some thousands of hunters from all over the nation, as well as Mexico and a number of European and Middle Eastern countries, have made pilgrimages to Texas to hunt the exotics on the big ranches. It is possible to collect a better blackbuck in Texas nowadays than in India, and the aoudad world record has been broken by a Texas specimen. But that is only part of the picture. The Texas experiments are entirely on private lands, the game actually privately owned, with the exception of a successful introduction of aoudad by the state to the Palo Duro Canyon of the Panhandle. (Even these animals are on private lands, but the state sets the seasons and permits.) Thus the Texas situation should for all practical purposes be termed preserve hunting, and it will undoubtedly stay that way.

But in New Mexico, the only other state where introductions of consequence have been made, the situation is different, and, for the average hunter, perhaps more interesting because there the state launched the experiments, except on one or two ranches where some exotics were stocked under a state preserve license system. New Mexico's Department of Game and Fish has made tremendous strides in the study and successful introduction of varied exotics. When and if several of the species become numerous enough to be huntable (the aoudad already is) the animals will be under state control, and on public lands.

It should be explained that foreign animals cannot simply be purchased in their homelands either by individuals or by game departments for import into the U.S. All exotic big game presently here originated in zoos. Surplus progeny of zoo animals can be sold to individuals. Or a state beginning an exotics program can arrange for a zoo to bring in animals of a certain kind, with the understanding that offspring will be turned over to the state. There is a substantial traffic presently in Texas and elsewhere in exotic game animals from preserves and ranches, sold to stock other preserves and ranches.

I must also emphasize that the exotic trophies you hunt in Texas or New Mexico are descendants of the zoo stock—not the original zoo animals themselves. They have lived in the wild and they behave as wild animals. The fact that their ancestors weren't native to the United States doesn't mean that they're tame in any sense or that hunting them is just a matter of walking up as you'd walk up to a zoo animal, and then shooting it. On the contrary, these are truly game animals, worthy of the sportsman.

Now, since my experience with the horned and antlered exotics has been chiefly in Texas, I'll discuss hunting conditions there and then turn the rostrum over to an authority on such game in New Mexico.

Exotics in Texas

There are several reasons why Texas has become a focal area for exotic big game. One is that the ranches are large, and a number of land owners are wealthy enough to be able to afford experimentation. In the beginning, of course, it was not a matter of commercial hunting but simply an enjoyable hobby. Later, when large surpluses of animals were on hand, friends of ranchers were at first allowed to take one or more trophies, and finally the demand by hunters willing to pay became so great that the exotics joined the native deer in the fee system. The prices have been going up ever since.

The chief reason for success in establishing several species is that both climate and vegetation in portions of the state, especially the Edwards Plateau region, closely approximate those of the African and Indian homelands of those animals in question. Most of the introduced animals have proved extremely hardy and adaptable. A few have difficulties when the winters, usually mild, are severe. During the winter of '72–'73, for example, when several most unusual snows swept the region, blackbuck were decimated. They are thin-skinned, thin-coated creatures, and highly nervous. On several ranches the loss was staggering.

No one knows exactly how many horned and antlered foreign game animals are in the state. But the aggregate of all species probably runs somewhere between 40,000 and 50,000. Among the most numerous presently are the mouflon and various mouflon crosses. The mouflon is a sheep with large, curling horns, originally from Corsica and Sardinia. Pure blood is difficult if not impossible to find. For centuries this animal has crossed here and there with other sheep. The Barbado sheep is a rather similar looking West African domestic sheep which crosses readily with the mouflon. Most of the Texas "mouflon" are mouflon-Barbado crosses. Some nearly pure mouflon specimens are found here and there, and the YO Ranch has bred a pure white sheep from various crosses that is a stunning trophy. When left to themselves in pastures of several hundred acres, all these sheep remain very wild and wary.

Author walks up on his trophy blackbuck, taken on ranch in Texas.

Next in numbers to the sheep are the axis deer, from India. This big reddish-brown species is covered with white fawnlike spots that are retained in the adults. The antlers of good specimens are extremely long and sweeping. They have a brow tine and a single fork at the top of the main beam. The blackbuck antelope from India has black spiraling horns. Blackbuck does and young bucks are light tan with white underparts, but mature bucks become black with white underparts and white inside the front legs and around the eyes. They are beautiful trophies.

The nilgai, or blue bull antelope, of India is probably next numerous. But it is not generally distributed. The King Ranch has a large herd, and there is some experimentation with these animals—and the eland—as meat animals. Nilgai have short horns and are not very prepossessing trophies. Fallow deer, in brown, white and spotted variations, are common. These originated in Europe. Sika deer from Japan are numerous and there are several races, some small, some almost as large as mule deer. Sika are very dark, look chocolate black at a distance, and have light-colored, slender antlers.

The aoudad, as I mentioned, is found both in private ownership and state ownership. In the late 1950's a group of aoudads, big, heavy horned sheep of North Africa, was released in Palo Duro Canyon in the Panhandle. It is estimated that now there are some 600 or more of them. After annual surveys, permits are issued by the game department to the landowners on whose premises they range. The landowners are then free to dispose of the permits as they wish, giving them to friends or selling them. Hunting aoudads, whether state or privately owned, where they have opportunity to live totally wild in canyon country, is a rugged proposition. I've made two hunts, the last one on Dolan Creek Ranch on Devil's River, in country horribly rough and stand-on-end. These big animals are adept at hiding by simply standing immobile among rocks, and they can go up a practically sheer cliff to escape when necessary. As I noted earlier, Texas now has the world record, an animal taken on a ranch in Bandera County.

Those are the animals that figure in almost all of the fee hunting presently available. The established system is to make a per-trophy charge, and to take hunters out (guide and transport furnished) on a no-kill-no-pay basis. Exotics hunting has received a bad press in some instances, with re-

Eland in Texas

Fallow deer in Texas

Sika deer in Texas

Axis deer in Texas

Young Persian ibex bounds over flat in New Mexico's Florida Mountains.

porters claiming it's a "fish-in-a-barrel" proposition. It is certainly true that in small pastures with gameproof fences certain of these animals will become quite tame, especially if regularly fed. So will whitetail deer. It is also true that where acreages are large and the animals roam entirely wild, they are just as wild as native game.

I remember well a tough hunt I made, on a magazine-story assignment, for a trophy blackbuck. They do not jump ordinary ranch fences very readily, and I was put into a pasture containing one section—640 acres. That's a square mile. Most whitetail hunters don't realize that they seldom hunt more territory than that. There were 30 to 40 blackbuck in the pasture, which was scrub live oak and shin oak—scattered cover. At least four or five of the animals were mature bucks with horns 18 to 20 inches, which is excellent. There were also a substantial number of whitetail deer on the same range. In three days I could have killed a dozen of the whitetail bucks—

but I had not blown a cap at a blackbuck. I *saw* them often enough, but always running like the wind, distantly. I finally got my trophy one chill morning with a stiff wind blowing, but I knew I'd been hunting.

On the old Rickenbacker Ranch some years ago I was determined to bag a sambar. This big, rough-haired deer from India would seem to stand out so a hunter would see every one on a given acreage in an hour. I hunted on an 800-acre pasture with a high fence. Much of it had heavy juniper cover, and there were deep, rough canyons. Three afternoons a week for almost two months I drove out from my home and hunted until dark. In that time I saw sambar half a dozen times, got one shot and missed. They were not numerous, but there were probably 40 of them. They simply knew how to hide in the thickets. By the time I finally connected I wasn't sure I wanted any more sambar hunting!

Sambar, incidentally, have not done well in Texas. They are also so large they require much room and browse that can be better utilized by smaller species. Furthermore, it takes so long to allow a sambar to become a true trophy that in the present-day situation the price would have to be very high, probably $1,000 to $1,500. As this is written, average prices for successful hunts are about as follows: mouflon-Barbado, $100 to $300; sika, $300 to $500; axis, $300 to $750; blackbuck, $300 to $750; fallow deer, $300 to $500; aoudad, $300 to $750.

Many other species are on Texas ranches in small numbers: sambar and barasingha deer from India; red stag from Europe; eland, oryx, impala, kudu, sitatunga, sable antelope from Africa; tahr from the Himalayas; ibex from Siberia. There are a few others, difficult to obtain, carefully nurtured in very small groups in the hope of building up future herds.

Although this ranch-preserve hunting may sound expensive, the fact is no hunter could collect these animals on their original ranges for anywhere near the same cost. Further, several of them, such as the aoudad, blackbuck and axis, are in better supply and are larger trophies in Texas than in their native countries. There are some exotics on preserves in other states, for example Tennessee, Pennsylvania, Michigan. But some of these operations are quite small, and the hunting somewhat less than "wild." A few of the preserves advertise in outdoor magazines.

Not just exotic but majestic and handsome, oryx graze at Red Rock.

There is also a scattering of exotics here and there under state or federal control. On the Chincoteague National Wildlife Refuge in Virginia there are sika deer. Hunts have been held to keep them under control. Maryland's Dorchester County has sika established, and they're hunted along with whitetails. There are also a few fallow deer on Mills Island in Chincoteague Bay. In the Land Between the Lakes region in Kentucky, and also at Fort Campbell, there are fallow deer that are hunted. Modest numbers of fallow deer are also found in Wilcox and Dallas counties in Alabama, and a few in Nebraska that are legal game during the regular deer season.

In Texas the present spread and growth in raising and hunting the various introductions continues at an astonishing pace. Many believed a few years ago that this was a fad that would soon level off and pass entirely. But it hasn't. Foreign big game has become an important segment of Texas hunting, and of our national hunting picture because so many hunters from throughout the nation book Texas hunts. It is necessary on most of the ranches to make hunt reservations, stipulating what species are desired so you'll know whether certain trophy animals are at that time available. Most of the preserves belong to The Exotic Wildlife Association, from which a list of addresses may be obtained; address Box 1365, Kerrville, Texas 78028.

There are game-management experts in New Mexico who probably know more about a number of exotics they work with than anyone else on the continent. I'm referring to William S. Huey, Chief of Game and Fish Management for New Mexico's Department of Game and Fish—and the people working under him on the state's exotics programs. I asked Mr. Huey to provide information regarding his state's non-native big game, and he has graciously contributed detailed coverage, including the history of the New Mexico exotics program, the present situation and some predictions for the future. His New Mexico account follows.

Exotics in New Mexico
by William S. Huey

A fascination with exotic animals has affected man since the beginning of time. This interest, whether motivated by utility or simply a desire to look at something different, was demonstrated by Hannibal's elephants and by the pheasants of the English countryside. Does this fascination have a place in the program of a modern natural-resource agency? The biological purists among us say no—that biological contamination of any ecosystem is intolerable. The realists among us point to modern man, domestic livestock, countless plant, insect and higher animal species that have been spread around the globe by man's activities, and they note that contamination of the ecosystem by various biological forms has become so extensive that purity is not possible, and for this reason, the enhancement of our environment should not be set aside because the enhancing feature is not native to the immediate habitat. Controversy surrounds the introduction of exotic, or non-native, species and this controversy is served best by discussions of introductions which have had unfavorable or at least unpopular results.

In the United States we talk about the English sparrow, the German carp and the European starling. In these discussions, seldom mentioned are the German brown trout, the Chinese ringneck pheasant, the Hungarian partridge, or the Indian chukar. The unfavorable effects of imported pests can in most cases be attributed more to environmental degradation by man than to the importation of the pests that took advantage of the degradation. The English sparrow, for instance, has come to occupy a unique habitat that never existed in the United States before the coming of the white man. Without the filth of the cities, the English sparrow, as we know it in the United States, would be without a home. We might also speculate, with some justification, that had the English sparrow not been imported, native species, perhaps the house finch, would have occupied this man-made habitat in sufficient numbers to create a situation as unfavorable as that created by the English sparrow.

The German carp shares a degraded low-quality habitat with native sucker-type species that are fully capable of occupying this habitat if the carp had never been introduced. Here again, the habitat was created by man's activities which reduced the amount of oxygen in the water, increased the chemical pollutants, diverted the flow, increased the temperature, or in some other way adversely affected the quality of the water as habitat for those fish which we considered desirable.

The argument that supports the introduction of foreign, or exotic, big-game animals into native habitats is the possible presence of the *vacant niche*. A niche not occupied by native wildlife and capable of supporting some other desirable animal should not be left vacant. It is also argued, with support of reliable data, that most of the introduced wild mammal species can more efficiently convert forage to protein for human benefit than can the domestic livestock now used to supply the meat requirements of our diet.

Meanwhile, back at the ranch, the first introduction of exotic mammals into wild habitats in New Mexico occurred in 1950 with the release of Barbary sheep into the Canadian River Canyon in the northeastern part of the state.

The Barbary sheep, or aoudad, is native to the mountains of North

Africa. Its range once extended from the Atlantic Coast to the Red Sea. To-day its range is pretty much limited to the mountains and buttes of the Sa-hara Desert and to the coastal mountains of North Africa.

During the 1800's there were many introductions to European parks, and the descendants of those animals are now widely distributed in zoos and parks throughout the United States.

The Barbary is a mixed feeder, taking advantage of browse, grasses and forbs, but it is primarily a browsing animal. It appears that a free range in New Mexico has agreed with Barbary sheep, as they attain larger size in the wild than that normally found in captivity. Mature rams weigh in excess of 300 pounds. Although the Barbary is called a sheep, it is not a true sheep but of the genus *Amotragus*. The horns are not as tightly curled as those of our native wild sheep, but have a more sweeping character. Large sets some-times measure up to 33 inches along the outside curve. The ewes also have horns, but their size seldom exceeds 20 inches. The color of the Barbary sheep is light tan to rufous, lighter on the back and darker under the belly. A mane and chaps are found on males and females alike, although they are much more pronounced in the males.

The initial planting of these Barbary sheep came from a local ran-cher, Joe McKnight, of Picacho, New Mexico, who had established a herd in his private game park. Preliminary evaluations to determine the effect of this release were based more on the speculation that they might do well in the selected habitat than on assurance that they would have no adverse effect on the native wildlife and that a beneficial effect could be expected. The re-leases were made, supplemented with animals obtained from the Hearst Ranch in California and, after five years, the first hunting season was permitted.

Hunting continued on an annual basis until 1962 when a com-bination of factors resulted in a sufficient decrease in the population. Hunt-ing was discontinued until 1967. Annual hunting seasons have been permit-ted since that time and the Barbary sheep has developed considerable popularity as one of New Mexico's big-game species.

An intensive research project was conducted to examine the "after-the-fact" effect of the Barbary sheep on New Mexico's habitats. No nega-

Dalrymple glasses band of aoudad on Dolan Creek Ranch in Texas.

tive results were turned up by this research. The area used by the Barbaries for foraging is too rough to accommodate the domestic livestock that also use the area. The native mule deer in the area increased significantly following the release of the Barbaries. It has not been speculated that the Barbaries contributed to this increase, but at least the conclusion can be drawn that they have no adverse effect on the mule deer. The palatability of the meat of the Barbary and its elusiveness contribute the primary factors required of a top-quality big-game animal.

In 1961, the New Mexico State Game Commission decided that the exotic experience should be expanded. The Commission selected ibex, gemsbok and greater kudu as the initial species for experimentation. The ibex first selected was the Nubian. Due to difficulties in obtaining stock of this species, the Siberian ibex was substituted. In order to accommodate United States Department of Agriculture's import requirements, an agreement was negotiated with the Albuquerque Zoo, which provided for housing the initially imported animals. Pens were constructed and in September of 1962 the first Siberian ibex arrived after a 60-day European quarantine followed by 30 days of United States quarantine. These periods of quarantine are designed to guard against the introduction of foreign animal diseases into the United States.

The Siberian ibex, as the name implies, is a native of Russia and the mountain plateau areas of Siberia. Its adaptability to the extremely cold winters and the equally hot summers of Russian Siberia apparently make the species well suited for New Mexico's varied climates.

The ibex is primarily a browser, although grasses and forbs are used. The Siberian ibex is grayish-brown, the older males having a dark beard. Their long sweeping horns are triangular in cross-section, with distinguishing nobs, more or less equally spaced, on the front edges. On fully mature adult males, the horns may reach a length of 60 inches, while the horns of the females are about 10 inches. Weights of males are about 150 pounds. Twin births are not uncommon.

The arrival of the ibex was followed in 1963 by the arrival of gemsbok and greater kudu from Southwest Africa. The gemsbok is an oryx of southwestern Africa; one of the large African antelope. It is a peculiar pinkish-gray in color with black and white face markings, a black stripe at the base of the tail, and a black tail similar to that of a horse or a mule. It has long straight horns that may reach 45 inches in exceptional specimens. The horns of the females are normally longer than the horns of the males, although more slender. Large gemsbok may weigh as much as 600 pounds. The gemsbok is primarily a grazer, although studies show that they do take some native New Mexico browse species. Reproduction is limited to a single calf per season.

In order that field testing of these introduced species could be accomplished prior to their release in the wild, the Department's Red Rock exotic-mammal experimental area was established along the Gila River in southwestern New Mexico, with the construction in 1964 of the first in a series of experimental pastures.

Offspring produced from the imports at the Albuquerque Zoo were transported to the Red Rock area and released into these pastures. Contracts were developed with New Mexico State University for research to determine the adaptability and the effect that these imported species might be expected to have on New Mexico's habitats, native wildlife species and domestic livestock.

In 1965, Persian ibex were imported as gifts from the Governor of the Province of Kermanshah in Iran to Governor Jack Campbell of New Mexico. These were supplemented by importation of additional females—gifts to the Department by the Shikar-Safari Club during the summers of 1967 and 1968.

The Persian ibex is smaller than its Russian cousin. It is lighter in color and its horns are dorsally compressed, or knife-edged, on the front. The horns on a good trophy may well run from 40 to 50 inches. Horns of the female are only about seven to nine inches. Weights of mature males go up to 130 pounds and females 90 pounds. Persian ibex commonly have twins, and triplets are not uncommon. It is yet to be determined, however, what level of survival may be expected of these multiple births in wild herds.

During 1967 and 1968, Persian gazelles, also gifts of the Shikar-Safari Club, were imported from Iran and added to the species under consideration for introduction into New Mexico's habitats.

These Siberian ibex seem right at home on Red Rock range in New Mexico.

The Persian gazelle is a small tan or brownish gazelle, smaller than our native pronghorns. Adult males weigh less than 100 pounds. They inhabit high prairie areas in Iran, quite similar to the upper Sonoran life zone in New Mexico. They also have twin births. No life history of food-habitat data has yet been obtained for the gazelles.

The last addition to the species for consideration was the markhor. Four of these, donated by the Southern California Safari Club, arrived in the summer of 1968.

The markhor is a dark gray goat with creamy gray markings. It is another species found in the higher mountains of Asia. It has long spiraling horns. The size of the animal is about comparable to the Iranian ibex. Markhor have single or twin kids. Very little life history of food-habitat is available for this species.

It was realized from the beginning that all of the candidate species would not be adapted to our New Mexico conditions and that suitable habitats were probably not available for the total number of species under consideration. In spite of this, there is still agitation created by those afflicted with the "Noah's Ark" syndrome to flood New Mexico with an unending number of imported big-game species. The Department has attempted from the beginning to pursue the exotic project with biological responsibility, hoping that in doing so, the final results would be beneficial and without any uncontrollable adverse effects.

From the time of the first introductions, production of gemsbok, ibex, kudu and gazelle has been transferred to the Red Rock experimental pastures, where their numbers have continued to increase and where research by New Mexico State University has continued. Arrangements had been made with the U.S. Bureau of Land Management for the release of ibex into two locations—one in the Florida Mountains, south of Deming, in the southern part of the state, and the other in the Ladron Mountains in the central portion of the state between Albuquerque and Socorro.

Studies conducted at Red Rock indicated the desirability of additional field testing with the gemsbok on a larger scale than was possible at Red Rock. Arrangements with the Army resulted in an agreement for the release of gemsbok onto the White Sands Missile Range between Las

Cruces and Alamogordo in south-central New Mexico. In the summer of 1969, the first releases of gemsbok were made into the White Sands area. These releases have been supplemented, and more detailed behavioral research has been conducted in cooperation with Colorado State University. Considerable production has taken place on the area, and it is expected that hunting of this species will begin in the very near future.

In December of 1970, Persian ibex were released for the first time into the Florida Mountains. This release has also been supplemented and follow-up research has been conducted. The response of the Persian ibex has been as satisfactory as that of the gemsbok and, as a consequence, ibex hunting is also planned in the near future.

Production of Siberian ibex was not as rapid as that of the Persian species, but sufficient animals have been produced for a release planned at the time of this writing for sometime in 1974. Studies comparable to those conducted in the Floridas will follow, and, barring the development of adverse situations not anticipated, the Siberian ibex will also become huntable in New Mexico within a very few years.

Continued difficulties with reproduction and deaths at the Albuquerque Zoo have slowed our experimentation with the Persian gazelle and the markhor. The Persian gazelle, a potential replacement for native pronghorns on ranges where domestic livestock use has resulted in the elimination of the pronghorn, is still a possibility which we look forward to with enthusiasm.

The kudu has been eliminated from the program since studies at Red Rock have indicated it is doubtful it would adapt to New Mexico habitats.

As our knowledge of the non-native big-game species increases, it becomes more and more evident that some can be established in various of New Mexico's habitats, to the benefit of recreational hunting and without any significant uncontrollable adverse effects upon the native wildlife species or upon domestic livestock grazing.

19.
OTHER
ANIMALS

State-managed bison sometimes require trimming.

A book of this kind would not be complete without touching upon a few animals that attract fewer hunters than the major species but nevertheless may be considered big game. One of these which has some importance to a limited number of hunters is the wild boar.

The term "wild boar" today has a wider meaning than it did when the European or Russian boar was first getting publicity in Tennessee and North Carolina. Hunters have discovered over past years that in out-of-the-way places there are a good many more feral swine—domestic hogs living wild for many generations—than most people ever realized. A 200- to 300-pound feral hog can be just as tough a proposition as the true Russian boar. In some instances the foreign boars, ranging where feral swine also are found, have interbred. Some odd trophies have come from these matings, big spotted specimens and varied colors.

The first fame came to boar hunting in the U.S. when Russian or European stock held at a private hunting lodge in North Carolina, close to the Tennessee line, escaped and took up residence in the Cherokee National Forest. A population built up quickly to huntable proportions. In recent years there has been a general open season in fall in several Tennessee counties—Sevier, Blount, Monroe—and several state-managed hunts on the Tellico Wildlife Management Area. These hunts are varied: for archers, for gunners, a hunt without dogs, a hunt with dogs. Information can be obtained from the Game Commission. As a rule, anywhere from 100 to 250 animals have been bagged each year.

Across the line in North Carolina, where the stock originally came from, an almost identical situation occurs. There are general hunts, and state-managed hunts by drawing. The bag runs about even with that in Tennessee. Graham, Cherokee and Clay counties are the top locations, with the Santeelah Wildlife Management Area furnishing much of the total kill. In both states the European boars have interbred, especially along the wilderness fringe, with feral hogs.

There are a very few European boars, also from escapees, in Sullivan County, New Hampshire. Feral hogs are abundant in some parts of South Carolina, Georgia, Florida, Mississippi and Arkansas. But it is a good idea to check the laws carefully. In some instances wild feral swine may not be considered fair game even when you find them on public lands. In Arkansas, for example, wild hogs found in forests and bottom lands are in a kind of legal limbo with neither a closed nor an open season. The state takes the stand that they are the property of someone.

Texas has numerous feral hogs, some in coastal swamp country, some down in the southern brush country. I've hunted them several times. Wherever you find these hogs under wild conditions, it is uncanny how wary and secretive they are. Most of their foraging is done at night. Texas also has a fair number of Russian or European boars in parts of the hill country of the Edwards Plateau. For many years, most of this area has raised sheep and mohair goats. A big boar is pure murder when it gets into the flocks, and it can go through a woven-wire fence as if it weren't even there. Very large boars are occasionally taken in the Comfort and Leakey areas.

For many years there have been European boars in California's Monterey County. The stock was brought in from North Carolina. They have spread their range and have interbred with feral swine. Guided hunts out of King City, Paso Robles and elsewhere have been available for some years, but check the game laws. For some time Monterey County has had a season and bag limit, while elsewhere wild swine were unprotected.

A few boars are killed each year by still hunters, but in heavy cover this is a long gamble. Wild hogs of whatever breeding are extremely sharp animals, with an excellent sense of hearing, fair eyesight and noses. They're extremely wary and retiring. A rancher friend of mine saw tracks and rubbing sign of a big Russian boar on his place for several years, had innumerable goats killed by it, yet never saw the animal in days of prowling its domain. Finally some deer hunters happened to move it from cover just as my friend drove a ranch trail in his pickup. He jumped out, grabbed his rifle, shot across a canyon at the running animal and put it down. It was enormous, almost 400 pounds.

The most successful and popular way of hunting boars is with a pack of specially trained dogs. They have to be plenty tough, and know enough to stay out of the way of the tusks. There are a few such packs in boar country, but of course all hunts with them are either guided or on a friendship basis. Thus there is little to say further about boar-hunting methods—except

Surprised and cornered, javelina boar pops its tusks and backs up against rock.

to advise a prospective hunter that he had better be in good physical condition. This can be an exhausting endeavor. It pays also to be able to shoot fast and accurately and be fast on one's feet. An aroused boar is not choosey about whom or what it charges.

Not a true swine but distantly related to the boar is the javelina, or peccary, of the American Southwest and Mexico. At one time these little animals, sometimes called the "smallest of big game," ranged up into southern Arkansas, but farming and ranching practices severely reduced their numbers, as did the attitude of ranchers who considered javelina pests to be killed on sight. Some ranchers still have that attitude, and there are some Texas counties that impose no closed season or bag limit. However, there are also ranchers who now realize that the javelina is a game animal, and they conduct fee hunting for the species or allow their deer-hunting clients to shoot one as a kind of bonus. Only three states—Texas, Arizona and New Mexico—now have peccary hunting.

Texas has the largest number of javelina. There are three main regions of concentration in the state. One is the vast, rolling brush country—densely covered with cactus and various tough, thorny shrubs—south of San Antonio and stretching along the border roughly from Del Rio down the Rio Grande to McAllen. Prickly pear, one of the mainstays of javelina diet, is abundant in this region. The animals rip off the pad and dig up the roots. Freshly ripped prickly pear is a good sign that game is nearby. Obviously, rooting is another hot indication.

Walking in this region is a scratchy proposition and not very productive. It's better to check ranch tanks for the small, blunt-toed tracks. Taking a stand and watching a tank is often successful. And any wash or draw leading from a tank, or a trail below the dam, is a likely travel route for bands of javelina coming to drink. Most of the ranches in the brush country have grids of roads that can be cruised slowly in a vehicle. The best times are from dawn to mid-morning and from mid-afternoon to dusk. Javelina often cross the roads. If you want to get out and walk, investigate the areas around the tanks, and at mid-day get into the creek bottoms. There are also ridges that offer broad views of valleys and draws. On overcast or chilly days, the pigs may be on the move at any time. They dislike a biting wind and will take shelter from it in a draw. They also dislike heat. Gage Holland, a very observant rancher in the second good region—the Big Bend country of western Texas—has noticed that when the temperature climbs above 70 the javelina bed down along the rims or other cool, shady places.

The big problem about hunting the brush country is that it's almost solidly leased up by groups of hunters, and fee hunting for javelina hasn't made much of an impression there. However, local chambers of commerce can sometimes supply lists of ranchers who will take hunters.

That second region is across the Pecos River, spreading north out of Big Bend National Park. The vistas are long, the mountains high and rough but with broad valleys between them. The javelina population is large and the cover is much more open. Animals are sometimes spotted hundreds of yards away on slopes. Hunting is usually done by cruising the ranch roads, glassing the slopes and brushy draws. It's a region of big ranches, where the owners have begun to accommodate javelina hunters for a fee. I've often hunted on the Gage Holland Ranch and the Catto-Gage Ranch, both at

Marathon. In towns like Alpine and Marfa the chamber of commerce will be helpful. Fees may be relatively stiff but success hovers near 100 percent.

The third recommended range is chiefly in Val Verdy County—in the rugged mountainous region based on Devil's River. Here again the cover is different, although it's on the western edge of the brush country. There is much cedar on some of the slopes, and the cover on the low desert mountains makes the animals hard to locate. But several ranches there have started offering package hunts for javelina as well as deer. I've hunted on a typical one, the Dolan Creek Ranch, owned by John Finegan, about an hour's drive north of Del Rio.

No one knows exactly what the state's overall success ratio is, but it's probably rather high because of the large number of animals and the relatively easy access to hunting territory on ranches, plus the guiding services of ranch hands. The only hurdle is doping out the Texas laws. Some counties regulate the hunting and some don't; some show open seasons (or no closed seasons) but haven't had a javelina in them for years.

Arizona also has a very good javelina population, and vast public lands on which to hunt. The species is highly valued and carefully managed as a game animal in this state. The season is usually in February. The number of permits depends on surveys of the herd, and in one recent year 26,000 were offered. By the way, javelina may breed at all times of year, so take care not to shoot a sow that's still nursing a piglet. The sexes look alike and the animals travel in bands, but piglets tend to stay so near their mothers that it's usually easy to avoid orphaning one.

My first javelina hunt was made south of Tucson, where there is plenty of good but rugged hunting land. The finest hunting is in the desert foothills. Roads in a lot of the best habitat are strictly for a four-wheel-drive vehicle. You may have to do a lot of climbing, and then pack your pig out. It's an excellent idea to hire a guide. They can be found in Phoenix and Tucson and other Arizona cities, and the game department may be able to furnish a list. The chance of scoring on Arizona javelina is about 20 percent.

New Mexico has only a small population, and has had to close the season in some recent years. Lately, however, a season has been opened again, usually in February or March, and limited numbers of permits have been issued. All of the hunting is in the southwestern counties. Whichever of the three states you try, don't overlook the possibilities at medium altitudes—around 5,000 feet. The javelina is so often pictured as a purely desert animal that newcomers tend to search only the flats. I've seen bands at nearly 6,000 feet in western Texas.

There are other misconceptions about the javelina, of which the most drastic concerns size. A mounted head, with the mouth open in a snarl and the bristles standing out, looks like it came from a great big boar. But the javelina is a slim-hipped, stubby-legged little creature, shaped almost like a miniature buffalo. An average javelina weighs less than 40 pounds.

A second misconception concerns the meat, which is excellent unless you shoot a tough old boar. If you want a mounting trophy, try for the largest specimen you see in a band. But for good meat, pick a medium-sized javelina. The species is sometimes called a musk-hog, in reference to a gland among the bristles high on the rump. When a peccary is excited, the bristles stand out and the gland emits an unpleasant odor. But before you start field dressing your javelina, you can simply cut out the gland, removing it and the patch of hide around it without touching it. If you do that, it will not taint the meat, contrary to some stories you may have heard or read.

And that musk gland can be a definite help to a hunter. You can often smell a band of javelina and follow the scent into some shady draw or to caves in the rimrock where the animals are bedding at midday.

The third misconception regards the javelina's supposed ferocity. It has a sharp upper and lower set of canines—tearing teeth—but not really big tusks like those of a boar. When angered or alarmed, it may raise its coarse bristles, pop its teeth and utter short, explosive grunts. And if wounded or cornered it can certainly do a lot of damage. But it is not a ferocious animal, and the "charges" you hear about generally amount to no more than an effort by these weak-eyed animals to get away. Occasionally javelina are hunted with dogs. Unless a dog is big and tough and knows its business it can get cut to ribbons, but the javelina—unlike the boar—can't be classed as dangerous to man under normal conditions. It has excellent senses of hearing and smell to offset its poor eyesight, and sometimes it can be a very wary animal. But at other times it can be stalked to very close range. It's a gregarious animal, occasionally seen alone but usually found in groups of six to a dozen, and occasionally droves of more than 20. Since it doesn't like to wander much, the presence of abundant fresh sign means you'll probably find a band nearby.

There is currently so much controversy about the big cats that it is not predictable how long any of them may be classed as game animals. Jaguar hunting below the U.S. border has been cut off for U.S. citizens, at least legally, by banning import of the hides of any Mexican cats.

For many years the mountain lion was considered a "varmint" throughout its range, which has dwindled over two centuries or more from most of the contiguous states, parts of Canada and all of Mexico. Then slowly game departments began to convince stockmen and others that bounties should close and the lion should be placed on the game list. In cases such as this some of the current crop of urban conservationists cause great harm because of their ignorance. In a state where lions have long been bountied and killed indiscriminately, the species suddenly appears on the game-animal list and the all-out protectors wail in anguish. Now hunters will kill them! Placing an animal on the game list is a long step toward saving even an endangered species, because from there on it receives legal protection, a limited harvest or none, and it can be properly managed.

The mountain lion is not yet endangered in the U.S., but it certainly is in scant supply compared to what it once was. Texas has a few, but biologists studying them believe probably less than a hundred. In this state at this writing the lion still does not receive protection. New Mexico has a fair number, and the animal is no longer bountied there. The state holds seasons for hunting with dogs and without. Arizona was the last state to keep a bounty on lions, but has established some protection now. In a recent season sport hunters took 120 Arizona lions, and ranchers (legally able to kill stock-killing lions) took 48. This indicates a good population.

Lions are quite plentiful in Utah's rough country and hunting is regulated. The same is true in Nevada. In Colorado there is a stipulated season, and the kill has been averaging 50 or 60 annually. Lions are scarce in Wyoming. In Idaho the annual bag averages 100 or more. Several years ago California authorities estimated that no more than 500 to 700 lions existed there. Oregon now accords the lion status as a game animal, but it is not plentiful. In the 1972 season, 75 tags were offered in the northeast, where predation was evident on livestock, and 22 lions were taken. Washington has the lion on the game list, but here also the animal is far from abundant. British Columbia, particularly Vancouver Island, offers good opportunity for lions. The animals come under regulations there, too.

Without any question there are a few mountain lions in places where they are not now supposed to exist. These animals, near civilization, are masters at keeping their private lives private. Our own small Texas ranch is rather remote and wild, in the hill country. A non-hunter friend has an isolated cottage near us, which he uses only occasionally. He swears he saw a lion walk down across his creek and move onto our property. It may be. The cougar is a most intriguing puzzle in the wildlife scene. It may be more abundant—or less so—than even the knowledgeable authorities believe.

Attempting to still hunt a lion, under present distribution and low incidence, is a foolhardy endeavor. Some animal callers have been successful occasionally at bringing in lions. I was with the Burnham Brothers of Marble Falls, Texas, well known for their animal calls and their calling ability, in Mexico one year when we called up a lion at night. Elsewhere, several instances have been authenticated of calling them even in the daytime.

The only way to assure yourself of a reasonable chance of success in lion hunting, however, is to use a trained pack of lion dogs. Obviously this has to be a guided hunt. There are outfitters with dogs in several of the better lion states. Game departments or guides' associations can furnish lists.

Now and then a hunter becomes interested in trying to collect a buffalo as an unusual trophy. A few surplus animals are offered here and there by preserves, or by ranches that raise them. Arizona has had very limited resident hunts under state supervision but may not as this is read. An attempt to establish a buffalo herd with transplanted animals from Yellowstone was begun in Utah back in the early 1940's. They were placed in the Henry Mountains, in exceedingly rugged terrain, and by 1950 a token hunt was held as a control on the herd. Since then a few permits have occasionally been available, by drawing, for residents.

Several Texas ranches periodically have allowed a buffalo hunt for

Cougar in Texas has come to electronic call; note loudspeaker, visible in bush.

surplus animals. Over past years, Colorado has had several small herds under state management. Up to a half-dozen permits have been offered some years, for control measures. Back in the late 1920's Montana bison were transplanted to Alaska. Expectations for broad expansion did not pan out. The range could not support more than a few hundred. Transplants from this herd in the Delta-Clearwater region were made to the Chitina area and a herd now called the Copper River herd developed. Hunts are staged some years, with very limited permits.

There are wood bison in certain localities in the Northwest Territories. So far, hunting for these on a limited basis has been open only for residents. The kill in a recent season was 88. Wood buffalo also are found in Alberta, in Wood Buffalo National Park and its fringes. Currently they are not hunted. (The herd was sharply reduced by disease some time ago, but hunting will probably be revived when the numbers have risen.)

Nowadays hunting timber wolves is frowned upon in many quarters.

However, wolves are abundant in some places where they may be legally hunted, and a substantial amount of hunting is done for them. As a rule, big-game hunters after other species in Canada and Alaska consider a chance to bag a wolf as a trophy extreme good fortune. Not many are killed, and usually as incidentals. There are wolves that may be hunted in Alaska, the Yukon, the Northwest Territories, Alberta, Manitoba, Ontario, Quebec and Newfoundland-Labrador.

A few hundred still exist in Minnesota. That state has been trying desperately to arrange management for the wolf. Under the plan, it would be placed on the game list. A specified number of animals would be taken annually for control, and a large inviolate preserve with no hunting would be set aside. But here again the ill-informed emotionalists stepped in, showing a live pet wolf on TV programs and at lectures, and killed the chance to have the bill made into law. As a result, instead of having a refuge and restricted hunting, Minnesota's wolves currently get no protection at all.

Animals such as those briefly covered in this chapter well illustrate our need to bend every effort toward careful and enlightened management of all wildlife. Everyone must come to realize that *no species is unimportant.* Every one of them that makes the "Game List" has an illimitably better chance for survival. For, as has been said many times, not a single animal in an endangered position on this continent has come to that point *because* it was considered game. Game management has made magnificent strides in this century. The abundance of such animals as elk and antelope stand as proof of the validity of the management principle. Even the very presence of various animals in short supply proves how tenaciously both the hunter and the game manager supported by him work to keep them present.

Changes in land use, and destruction of habitat, which continues with highways and growing cities and villages gobbling up thousands of acres daily, are the truly lethal enemies of wildlife. Thus, every hunter should give all-out support to the true conservationists—the game biologists and managers—and try to convince without undue emotion the non-hunters and the anti-hunters that all should join forces. Without the tremendous financial support sportsmen give to scientific management, there would soon be no wildlife even to argue about!

INDEX

PICTURE ACKNOWLEDGMENTS

Special acknowledgment is made to Erwin A. Bauer, Hal Swiggett and Charles Elliott, who not only contributed chapters to this book but supplied a generous number of fine photographs to illustrate those chapters. Mr. Bauer's pictures appear in Chapters 4 and 17, Mr. Swiggett's in Chapter 5, Mr. Elliott's in Chapters 14 and 16.

Elsewhere in the book, the majority of pictures are by the author. Supplementary photographs have been obtained from the following sources, credited in the order of appearance:

Page 23—Colorado Game, Fish & Parks Division

      46—Bureau of Sport Fisheries & Wildlife

    164—Perry Shankle, Jr.

    178—North Carolina Department of Conservation & Development

    206—Colorado Game, Fish & Parks Division

    219—New Mexico Department of Game & Fish

    220—Colorado Game, Fish & Parks Division

    221—Montana Chamber of Commerce

    223—New Mexico Department of Game & Fish

    228—Ontario Department of Tourism & Information

    240—Ontario Department of Tourism & Information

    242—Bureau of Sport Fisheries & Wildlife

    289—British Columbia Government, Department of Travel & Industry

    293—Bill Browning photo, Montana Chamber of Commerce

    297—Don Domenick photo, Colorado Game, Fish & Parks Division

    298—Don Domenick photo, Colorado Game, Fish & Parks Division

    299—David L. Spencer photo, Bureau of Sport Fisheries & Wildlife

    303—Bill Browning photo, Montana Chamber of Commerce

    306—Newfoundland Department of Resources

    318—Bureau of Sport Fisheries & Wildlife

    323—Tourist Branch, Manitoba Department of Tourism & Recreation

    354—New Mexico Department of Game & Fish

    356—New Mexico Department of Game & Fish

    367—South Dakota Department of Highways